# English Abbeys

# ENGLISH
# ABBEYS

HUGH BRAUN

FABER AND FABER LTD
3 Queen Square, London

*First published in 1971*
*by Faber and Faber Limited*
*3 Queen Square, London*
*Printed in Great Britain by*
*W & J Mackay & Co Ltd, Chatham*
*All rights reserved*

*ISBN 0 571 09612 3*

to the men of the abbeys
who gave of their best
for the greater glory of God
and for the honour of
their country

# Contents

# Notes on Plates

―――

13. THE WEST FRONT OF LANERCOST PRIORY. A charming Augustinian façade of the thirteenth century. Note the elaborately moulded west doorway. The nave has a north aisle only. *N.M.R.*        *facing page* 128

14. THE CLOISTER AT FURNESS ABBEY. A Cistercian cloister looking north-east towards the eastern processional doorway at the foot of the massive transepts. Three arches form the façade to the chapter house; adjoining them are smaller ones leading to the inner parlour and the slype. Above are the windows of the monks' dormitory. *N.M.R.*        129

15. BEAULIEU ABBEY FRATER. A Cistercian frater preserved at the Suppression and converted into a parish church. Note the reader's pulpit with its arcade giving light to the wall-stair by which it is reached. *N.M.R.*    144

16. EASBY ABBEY FRATER. The great hall of a Premonstratensian abbey rebuilt during the Gothic era above a vaulted undercroft. *N.M.R.*    145

17. RIEVAULX ABBEY. The splendid thirteenth-century choir and transept fill the foreground. Behind them rise the ruins of the great Cistercian house dominated by the immense frater. *Noel Habgood.*    160

18. FOUNTAINS ABBEY. Dr. J. K. St. Joseph's aerial view of this great Cistercian abbey displays the long frontispiece of the lay-brothers' house extending from the west front of the church. Behind it is the cloister with the remains of the aisled chapter house clearly visible beyond it. Dominating the claustral scene is the great hall of the frater. On the north extends the splendid church which the King himself suggested should be retained as a cathedral. Beyond the Chapel of the Nine Altars the foundations of the infirmary hall may be seen, and beside the church rises Abbot Huby's bell-tower. *Dom David Knowles and Dr. J. K. St. Joseph.*    161

19. THE CHAPTER HOUSE OF CLEEVE ABBEY. Looking out of a Cistercian chapter house across the cloister
towards the outer parlour. Note the typical west wall with
its doorway flanked by two-light windows. The vaulting supports the floor of the dormitory above. *N.M.R.*     176

20. THE CHAPTER HOUSE OF FURNESS ABBEY. The
aisled chapter house of a rich Cistercian abbey. Here the
'four-poster' plan has been extended to six and the whole
apartment raised in height. *Rev. Maurice Ridgway.*     177

21. BUILDWAS ABBEY CHURCH. A typical twelfth-century Cistercian nave with its pointed arches unmoulded
and carried by crude circular pillars. Note the simple
clearstory. *N.M.R.*     196

22. THE INFIRMARY HALL OF HAUGHMOND ABBEY.
A fine Augustinian hall of the Gothic era. It was converted to domestic use after the Suppression when the
small doorways leading into the kitchen offices were
inserted. *N.M.R.*     197

23. TINTERN ABBEY CHURCH FROM THE SOUTH.
The cloister here was on the north side next the River
Wye. The church was rebuilt late in the thirteenth century to a more compact plan. Note the loss in length in
the nave balanced by the gain to the transept. *N.M.R.*     204

24. TINTERN ABBEY LOOKING EAST. Still Cistercian
in its simplicity, the building has been illuminated by the
provision of huge areas of glass set in Gothic tracery.
Note the remains of the stone screen walls backing the
lay-brothers' stalls. *N.M.R.*     205

25. THE GREAT GATEHOUSE OF THORNTON ABBEY.
The magnificent Augustinian gatehouse was built after a
'licence to crenallate' had been granted in 1382. Above
the gate passages are splendid apartments for guests,
which once included the King himself, Henry VIII.
*N.M.R.*     228

# List of Line Drawings

# Preface

One of the attractions of the English countryside is the presence over it of the venerable buildings of other days. While some of these are still occupied, most of them present today strange spectacles of weathered stonework either softly clad in native verdure or rising starkly above tended sites. Memorials of another age, of days and customs which have passed away.

Probably the most dramatic of these strange ruins are the castles, relics of times when warfare was as endemic as football is today, when most towns were walled about and it was customary for a great lord to live in the shadow of tall stone towers. Even in these days it is not difficult to people these buildings with lords and ladies, mail-clad soldiers and shambling servants. It does not require much imagination to hear from afar the blare of trumpets, the swish of arrows, the distant thunder of a drawbridge coming down. Castles are in every man's blood from the time he builds them on the sands of the seashore.

But amongst the ruins of the past are others with a very different message, as peaceful as those of the castle are belligerent, and often presenting a strange appeal to the senses which at times may equal, though in a different fashion, that of the arrogant fortress. The castle offers the romance of high gallantry—the abbey that of peaceful meditation and the afternoons of yesterday.

These are the pictorial qualities of the abbeys, and as such their lonely ruins must always play an important part in composing the pageantry of the English countryside. But to the serious student the abbey ruins present a problem which an experience limited to modern times does little to help us appreciate. For while battles are with us today, monasticism as a concept has long vanished from the comprehension of men. Holy Church, once the basis of our philosophy and social behaviour, is now little more than a legend.

The idea that men could spend their whole lives in prayer and meditation seems today a fantasy . . . that such men, banding together in small communities seldom more than fifty strong, should devote a large proportion of the wealth of the nation and almost the whole of its building potential to raising structures entirely useless but simply of superlative beauty, when today we build entirely for utility and in utter scorn of appearance. Thus while we may admire the old abbeys for their romantic charm, some of us may interest ourselves in the nature of their architectural problems and how these were solved. But to understand the thoughts and motives of the men who raised them would mean striving to retrace our whole system of cerebration until we could reach the inexperienced unsophisticated mentality of the men of the Middle Ages.

To simplify the nature of the architectural problems involved, we can state at the outset that those of the abbey architects were of two quite different characters. First and foremost was the urge to create a building of superlative architecture in which to offer up prayers. This aspect of abbey architecture is an aesthetic one and will not be dealt with in this book which is an examination of the other problem, that of the accommodation of the community engaged in offering up this worship.

The beauty of the abbey churches continued to exercise an appeal even at the time of their violent suppression, so that many were allowed to project their transcendence for the enjoyment of future generations. Once permitted to survive, their maintenance seems to have been accepted as a charge upon the nation without any protest due to religious confusion. During the late eighteenth century, in particular, the expansion of culture, development of the sense of patriotism, and concern at the already noticeable effects of the industrial revolution, had the result of inspiring an interest in the finer architectural achievements of the Middle Ages.

It was at this time that the development of the Gothic novel and a revival of what was so quaintly imagined to be the *romance* of medievalism brought interest to bear on the aspect of the abbey church in ruin. At Roche in Yorkshire, Capability Brown flooded the whole abbey site so that the ruins of the church should stand reflected in the waters. From this time on, the ruins of English abbeys became established as what would today be called a tourist attraction.

The nineteenth century brought with it the development of an interest in English Gothic architecture, and the abbey churches really came into their own.

During the last quarter of the century the interest of the amateur archaeological excavator was turning more and more towards the exploration of abbey sites and the fascinating occupation of preparing scale plans of the foundations unearthed. It was probably these activities which disclosed the hitherto ignored fact that abbeys were not just large churches but that these formed only a part of extensive and elaborate complexes of buildings connected with the accommodation of the monastic community.

Such distinguished antiquaries as W. St. John Hope and his friend and successor Harold Brakspear devoted their whole lives to the excavation, privately financed, of once powerful and now vanished abbeys. In doing so they disclosed an exciting amount of material of unexpected extent and offering fascinating problems for research.

The present writer has spent many hours entranced by the beautifully drawn and chronologically coloured plans of Hope and Brakspear, assisted by the far too humble pocket book on monastic houses compiled by Professor A. Hamilton Thompson and published in 1913 by the Cambridge University Press. This little book had to serve him in his own researches until the appearance in 1961 of Mr G. H. Cook's excellent book, packed with information, entitled *English Monasteries*.

Nowadays of course our vanished abbeys are being excavated by gangs of students helped by building contractors all supervised by learned professors and subsidized by public money. It is all very much a business, far removed from the pleasurable occupation which such activities formed for the amateur antiquary of a century ago.

During the past four hundred years the ruins of our abbeys,

deprived of their protecting roofs, have been suffering severely not only at the hand of the stone-robber but also from the assaults of the elements. It is therefore fortunate that a government department is now concerning itself with the preservation of a number of them, cleaning them up, pointing disintegrating stonework, and even excavating foundations of missing buildings in order to try to complete the picture of some great monastic house of other days.

It must be confessed that many of the ruins thus preserved and tidied up have lost much of their aesthetic charm and while of greater interest than before to the student may well seem rather less attractive to the average visitor. Maybe the Ministry of Works will be able to devise some means of restoring to the ruins something of the patina of age—even the softness of verdure—to their carefully pointed snags of masonry.

As dwellers in one of the world's most beautiful countries it is remarkable what little care we have for our woodland, and how we sweep away centuries-old trees to free some site and never think of replacing them. In this fashion we destroy that embowerment which in a countryside such as ours is an essential factor in all planning (and this notwithstanding that in these days the transplanting and replanting of mature trees is a comparatively easy and inexpensive operation).

Of the number of visitors to an abbey site today, probably less than one-tenth are students of monasticism and its architecture. The remainder are lured to the ancient place partly by that subtle romance which haunts all ruins, but for the most part by some pictorial aspect, dramatic or enchanting, of the setting encompassing them. The writer would be among the first to accept and approve the majority view and indeed deplores the clinical appearance which far too many of our ancient sites present today.

The old abbeys certainly have not lost their appeal to the senses of most of us. No one could entirely escape a feeling of awe at the sight of the great crag of masonry looming over Malmesbury which is all that is left to remind us of the black monks who for so long ruled over the Wessex countryside. And not even the most devoted architectural scholar could fail to be charmed by the Cistercian beauty haunting the Vale of Rievaulx. Even small children can enjoy themselves scampering about the ancient apartments where once the white-clad lay-brothers of Fountains shuffled like ghosts beneath their gloomy vaults. But the writer hopes that this book may make some converts among the less sophisticated visitors to the study of the particular significance of the various remains they are inspecting.

Even the most ardent students of the relics of the Middle Ages must find that the great appeal of the abbeys lies in their great churches, whether they are nowadays of cathedral rank, such as mighty Gloucester, or merely large parish churches such as those of Selby in Yorkshire or Sherborne in Dorset. But except for possibly only one of these, Christchurch Priory in Hampshire, where the monastic choir seems today just as it was when the monks closed its doors for the last time, these buildings have for the most part been secularized in Victorian days and their choirs converted into open chancels freely visible to worshippers in the nave.

But the great abbey churches still share with our cathedrals the retention of furniture and fittings long vanished from their brethren despoiled at the Suppression. Here may be seen screen-work, stallwork even, which dates from the monastic occupation. Here and there are chantry chapels founded by some medieval abbot buried, perhaps, beneath his chapter house of which the site has long been forgotten. Above all there are the sepulchres of great men of the Middle Ages who played their part in English history and won the right to an abbey burial.

In these great churches we can still receive a strong impression of the splendour and power of Holy Church, even though the apartment peculiar to the monks who built and worshipped in it—the monastic choir—has long vanished away. In particular we can admire to the full the sombre Byzantine interiors of the twelfth century and the soaring Gothic of the thirteenth—the architecture of transcendency . . . arcades, ranges of traceried windows, vaulted ceilings lifting high above our heads.

Those churches which have survived complete extinction have lost their high vaults and the tracery has fallen from once-glorious windows. But many a ruined abbey can provide the student of ancient buildings with a clearer vision of the results of Gothic inspiration than could ever be received from a great church in use today.

The most dramatic feature of the interior of a great Gothic church is its arcades. In our cathedrals and those of our abbey churches still in use one's view of the arcades is foreshortened, horizontally and vertically, so that although one can absorb a superb vision of grace and in particular appreciate that soaring quality which is the soul of Gothic, it is never possible to view each bay, and the range of these, with the eye of the architect who designed the feature. But in the ruin of an abbey church such as Whitby or above all Rievaulx it is possible to see the Gothic wonder exposed to view as on a drawing board. It is then possible to appreciate what went into the design of these wonderful features which, after all, were only provided to support a roof and were themselves quite absorbed within the dim interior beneath it.

There is a recognizable difference between the appeal of a great church in use today and a lonely ruin from the Middle Ages. The former is after all an anachronism. For not only are the monastic choirs gone for ever but those of the bishops have followed them into retirement, opened up so as to achieve the 'unbroken vista' which enables the worshipper in the nave to view the whole length of the great church. Such buildings are just over-large parish churches.

The beauty of a great Gothic church is something which lives on into eternity. But the spirit which created it has long passed from our life . . . we gaze upon it, shorn of its ancient setting and lacking its lost devotees as we enter it and walk around it for a while. Then we leave it and forget it instantly as we emerge into our world of computers and space travel.

The deserted abbey is as it should be . . . a ruin.

Belonging to an age-long past, relic of a way of life and thought long abandoned, it seems proper that it should stand as a memorial. No modern vulgarisms—and even pews are such—affront it, nor does the grime of an industrial age mar its fine-wrought stonework. And standing in its primitive beauty it may perhaps recall to us not only the devotion which inspired its creation but also the endless search for loveliness which enthralled our unsophisticated ancestors and which we now disdain so profoundly while concentrating upon the practical and economical in architecture.

Although its great church is the most impressive feature of an abbey it is only one of the considerable number of buildings making up a monastic house. The church was of course the *raison d'être* of the whole project, and was intended to represent a religious building of transcendental architecture. But its existence alone was not enough, for its accepted purpose was to provide a setting in which prayers might be offered in as nearly as possible unbroken continuity and, in intention, to perpetuity.

This meant the provision of accommodation for a staff of monks dedicated to the maintenance of worship within the great church. They had to be provided with living quarters, including an apartment for communal meals, cooking facilities and ample storage for provisions. A conference room from which to administer the community was regarded as essential. A monk, once accepted into a monastery, had to remain there until he died; thus provision had to be made for the accommodation of the aged and infirm. Travellers, and in some cases pilgrims to a shrine, had to be accommodated and fed; in some cases persons of importance had to be given hospitality. All these buildings had to be maintained by a workshop staff of craftsmen.

Thus we see clustered about the abbey churches we know so well an elaborate complex of buildings of all sizes and varying degrees of architectural excellence, from great hall and chapter house down to smithy and store-sheds.

It was this complicated group of buildings, gathered together in the shadow of a great church, that made up the monastic house. And investigation of the nature and siting of these can add a little to the interest of a visit to an abbey site. And when one wanders round the remains of such a perfect example as Fountains Abbey in Yorkshire, the main buildings of which are roofless but otherwise largely intact, one begins to appreciate just how extensive, and how important, these great houses of past days really were. One can understand why it was that the abbeys could recruit occupants for these splendid establishments, for in rejecting family life the medieval monk had transferred to a style of comfort which if austere was still vastly better than that of the peasantry about him and he would be living in buildings far finer than could be found outside the homes of the nobility.

The aim of this book will be to try to describe and explain the purpose of these buildings and the parts they played in the life of each of the principal monastic Orders. For each Order differed from the others, some to a minor degree and others, such as the Cluniacs and the Cistercians, having quite different outlooks.

The first chapter of the book will endeavour to give a picture of the men who lived in the abbeys and their manner of life and in what fashion they were administered, the second chapter some characteristics of the various Orders in which they were professed.

The third chapter will try to investigate the nature of the very early abbey churches in this country which have today all but vanished without trace, while the fourth will deal with the great churches of the eleventh and twelfth centuries, the greatest buildings of their age. These churches will not be discussed as examples of architectural excellence, for that would be an aesthetic study outside the scope of this analysis of the planning problems of the monastic houses and in what manner they were solved.

At the heart of the great church lay the monastic choir, an apartment of great interest and as it were the workshop of the community in which they gathered several times each day to perform their statutory worship. This and its developments into the glorious Gothic presbytery will be discussed in Chapter 5.

Chapter 6 will deal with the large house in which the monks lived, usually attached to the south transept of the church.

The great hall or refectory of the monks is considered in Chapter 7. As in all medieval domestic architecture, this was the nucleus of the house and its treatment in monastic hands plays an important part in the development of this finest of English domestic apartments.

The eighth chapter describes the western range of buildings which closed the cloister and which as well as the abbey's storerooms contained apartments such as the abbots' lodgings and guest rooms.

The development of the cloister, heart of the abbey buildings, is discussed in Chapter 9.

Architecturally the finest apartment after the church was the assembly hall of 'chapter house' of the community, always situated on the east side of the cloister adjoining the church. Chapter 10 describes this building and the apartments adjoining it.

The eleventh chapter deals with the little cloister which often adjoins its larger neighbour and contains the infirmary buildings housing sick and infirm monks, and in the Cistercian houses lodgings for the abbot.

The private houses of the abbots and priors, some of which are still used as residences, are discussed in Chapter 12.

Attached to the cloister on its west side was the great court of the abbey round which was gathered a host of buildings connected with the operation of the abbey, feeding and clothing the community, offering hospitality to travellers, and workshops from which to maintain the extensive group of structures forming the monastery, all examined in Chapter 13.

The foregoing chapters will have dealt with the rich and powerful abbeys following the Benedictine Rule. But early in the twelfth century a new Order, the Cistercian, entered the country and began to found houses 'far from habitation'. These rural abbeys aimed at a more austere life, eschewed wealth, and supported themselves by husbandry. Their abbeys were set out on a standard plan before being occupied by a team of colonists from a mother abbey; this plan will be discussed in Chapter 14.

One cannot but be aware that in addition to the great abbeys there were a great number of small monastic houses called priories, many of them colonies of some Continental abbey. During the thirteenth century numbers of friaries were founded by the new Orders of friars. These less important, but equally interesting, monastic houses will be investigated in Chapter 15.

Chapter 16 describes the disaster which in 1539 overcame all the monastic houses, large and small, when monastic life in England was brought to an end and the great houses with their glorious churches were largely levelled with the ground.

Some churches, however, were saved either wholly or in part, while considerable portions of their subsidiary buildings were converted to secular use. Examples of surviving monastic architecture will be examined in Chapter 17.

It is perhaps unfair to the builders of these great establishments not to call attention to the magnitude of their efforts and the effect these must have had upon the architecture of medieval England. Chapter 18 will therefore review this position.

This book is not intended solely for armchair study. Its compiler hopes that through reading it persons interested in our ancient buildings may be encouraged to explore on their own initiative some abbey site and endeavour to discover for themselves the whereabouts of its various buildings and what part each played in the functioning of the abbey when it was busily occupied by the monks and their servants so many years ago. Chapter 19 has been designed to assist the prospective explorer of abbeys.

Conjectural chronology is always an interesting occupation for the abbey visitor, so a special chapter, No. 20, has been added giving what it is hoped will be useful information on some ways of dating old stonework and architectural features. The subject is of course a wide one and could be discussed in a complete book. The chapter concerned can do little more than give some general hints.

Antiquarian exploration can be an unrewarding occupation unless one can succeed in absorbing some kind of impression of the living background to the dead stones of archaeology. When one is analysing the *aesthetic* aspect of great architecture one is apt to find oneself inspired only by what might be termed the metaphysical background common to all aesthetic achievement. But the abbeys were live buildings planned for and once accommodating a large and active community; thus they must be considered as *practical* building problems.

The difficulty which we encounter today when so engaged is due to the need for understanding what these problems were. The way of life represented by the medieval abbey is something which has vanished from memory and can be no longer equated with any contemporary establishment. It was a way of life which had probably been losing much of its purpose several decades before being forcibly terminated in 1539.

It is thus virtually impossible to achieve an insight into the life within a medieval abbey. The last survival of a similar kind of existence might have recently been found, in a very liberalized form, at the older colleges of Oxford and Cambridge, the chapels of which convey to a very limited extent the form of the monastic choir.

All one can do is to study the monastic Rule and try to imagine it converted into terms of daily life and in what fashion this may be illustrated by the buildings in which this was lived.

Even to attempt this survey needs a specialist authority on monasticism. Nowadays the writer on monastic subjects has the very great advantage of access to the writings of Dom David Knowles, who has devoted a lifetime to research into English monastic history, producing voluminous literature containing everything the purely tradesman historian could desire. The present writer confesses with gratitude that everything in the present book which is clearly outside the scope of architectural research has been extracted from Dom David's writings and is the product of his work.

His breath-taking series of photographs, entitled *Monastic Sites from the Air*, obtained with the assistance of his collaborator Dr. J. K. St. Joseph, is a contribution to archaeology of which any country in the world could be proud.

# I

# The Men of the Abbeys

Before investigating the monastic remains of this country we should find out something about the people who used the abbeys and what problems they presented, in doing so, to the medieval builder. For in architecture it is the problem which appears first, and the method of its solution; only thereafter can we go on to examine any special developments deriving from what begins as the solution of a practical problem.

The task entrusted to the abbey builders was to perfect a system of monastic architecture which could be used to erect firstly buildings of the highest quality available in which to worship God in accordance with the practice of the Christian religion in its Roman form. And then to provide buildings of varying quality to provide all that was necessary to accommodate a community isolated from the world and requiring to be self-supporting in respect of food and lodging.

The life of the monk was a highly specialized existence. Western monasticism, which derived from that practised by the 'Orthodox' monks of Asia Minor and Syria, was instituted in the form we are considering in the first half of the sixth century at Monte Cassino as the Benedictine Order.

St. Benedict's plan was to establish a 'family' of men living a life of meditation upon the Christian philosophy and offering up perpetual prayer to the Triune Deity. His community was to eschew charity and be self-supporting; its members were to engage in manual work or some kind of craft.

The organization of such a body of men at that time would have presented a considerable problem, as the manners and customs of the day were primitive and the principle of marching in step unknown. Thus St. Benedict devised for his community a strict Rule, based on such virtues as discipline, routine and regularity. A daily programme was introduced in which it has been calculated that four hours were spent in prayer, four in meditation and six in manual exercise or craftsmanship.

The Benedictine Rule formed the basis of all subsequent western monastic Orders.

At the beginning of the eighth century the Anglo-Saxon Benedictines were represented at Monte Cassino while their abbeys of 'black monks' were being founded in this country. Their timber churches, however, and the humble buildings in which the monks lived, were doomed to be destroyed by the Danish invaders, so that by the next century the reign of Alfred the Great found Anglo-Saxon monasticism virtually extinguished except for marshy Glastonbury in Somerset and sea-girt Lindisfarne off the Northumbrian coast.

One may wonder how it was that in view of the constant sacking and burning of the Anglo-Saxon abbeys they managed to keep going at all. The answer lies in the use of timber construction which is a very speedy system of building. (In cyclone regions such as North Queensland, where all buildings are of timber construction, the devastation resulting from cyclonic assault is very swiftly reinstated.)

Certainly the timber abbeys of the Anglo-Saxons continued through the first half of the tenth century, sufficiently numerous for the King, Edgar the Peaceable, to comment on their worm-eaten condition, which suggests that they had been left in peace long enough to attain that state. Their renaissance under his counsellor St. Dunstan is said to have been due to the King's narrow escape from a stag while hunting by Cheddar Gorge, as a result of which St. Dunstan was appointed to the abbacy of Glastonbury. Thereupon the whole of the Anglo-Saxon Benedictine abbeys were reformed and very probably largely rebuilt, possibly in stone.

By the year 1000 there were two important abbeys at Winchester, and others at Abingdon in Berkshire, Ramsey in Huntingdon-shire, Ely in Cambridgeshire and Peterborough in Northampton-shire. Their churches would have been too small to survive the great rebuilding boom following the Conquest, but their architecture was such that they were regarded as the most beautiful churches in western Europe.

By the middle of the eleventh century Continental influence had become so strong that the Norman abbots placed over the old Anglo-Saxon houses had no difficulty in replacing the existing churches with huge buildings which were the greatest churches of their age. Nevertheless the Anglo-Saxon tradition was sufficiently well established for the wealth of carved ornament which we incorrectly call today 'Norman' to survive and even develop to embellish the fine stone buildings which were rising.

In these days of great business concerns it seems to us surprising to learn that at the time of the Conquest one-sixth of the wealth of the country was in the possession of the Benedictine Order. And scanty though the traces of this once so powerful organization may appear today its relics are still imposing enough to impress even the modern tourist.

Royal Westminster, founded by Edward the Confessor just prior to the Conquest, is of course world-famous and is surprisingly complete, its principal loss being its great refectory hall. The abbey church of St. Albans in Hertfordshire, which rivalled Westminster in claiming the premiership of English abbeys and triumphed, is now a cathedral. St. Edmundsbury in Suffolk, in its day the greatest church in Christendom, is represented by a vast mass of masonry, the core of its west front, within which has been constructed a complete dwelling house; the abbey wall, enclosing the great church as well as two parish churches and pierced by two fine gatehouses, presents the most impressive medieval spectacle in England.

Towering above embattled Malmesbury in Wiltshire is the great fragment of a Benedictine nave, now a parish church, while across the Somerset border the lovely abbey church of Bath represents the swan-song of the Benedictine architect.

In Anglo-Saxon days there was a powerful Benedictine colony

in the Fenland still remembered by the glorious churches of Ely in Cambridgeshire and Peterborough in Northamptonshire, both of them now cathedrals. But the almost equally powerful Fenland abbeys of Thorney and Ramsey have little of interest to show us today, while lonely Crowland can still impress us with the spectacle of what must have been one of the most beautiful of Benedictine abbey churches represented by a towering fragment rising out of the fen.

Perhaps the most striking illustration of the Benedictine hegemony over a whole rich area of England may be seen by the valley of the Severn, lorded over by the mighty abbey of Gloucester, today a cathedral church. Close by is the great church of Tewkesbury, while in Worcestershire stands the lovely choir of Pershore Abbey attached to a graceful tower. The writer has always tried to pass through Pershore on the hour so that he can pause in the crossing of the church and hear the thunder of the tenor high above, pealing out its tremendous requiem for the monks of old who raised this loveliest of buildings. With its dramatic hills rising as a backcloth we may see the priory church of Great Malvern and its humbler but daintier neighbour that of Little Malvern. Along the tributary Avon once stood the rich abbey of Evesham, still represented by a stately tower which must have been well known to Shakespeare. Nearby, deep-buried in the foothills of the Cotswolds, was the famous abbey of Winchcombe, of which not a stone remains.

Lying athwart the heart-land of Wessex stretched the manors of the four great abbeys of Romsey in Hampshire, Wilton and Amesbury in Wiltshire, and Shaftesbury in Dorset. Romsey remains as a stupendous church, considered by many to be the finest example of its style, Shaftesbury is represented by a few poor foundations. Even the sites of Wilton and Amesbury have been lost.

Nothing resembling the monastic houses has ever existed in any other era of history. During the Middle Ages they combined to administer great areas of the country, a power in the land equalling that of the secular nobility, placidly sharing government with them and in alliance invincible.

Head of each house was the abbot, elected by the community but his appointment confirmed by the Crown. The reason for this becomes obvious when one considers that by election to the abbacy the erstwhile anonymous monk became a personage playing an important role in the political life of the country. During the thirteenth century three-quarters of the ecclesiastical element in Parliament consisted of abbots, a fact to ponder on as one strolls today across lines of low mounds which may be the sole memorial of the abbot's realm. Twenty-five of the abbots of the greatest monasteries were allowed to wear the episcopal mitre and were accounted barons of the realm, high promotion for the monk musing uncomfortably upon his straw mattress in the long dormitory.

Houses which were founded as offshoots of a great abbey were usually called priories and had a prior as head of the house. The houses of Augustinian canons were priories but twenty-five such as Cirencester and Waltham were afterwards elevated to the abbatial dignity. All the Cistercian houses, which were founded as colonies of twelve emigrant monks from a parent abbey with a new abbot as head, were thus from the beginning abbeys.

The Cluniac houses, no matter how rich and powerful, remained as priories subject to the Abbot of Cluny in Burgundy.

Second in command to the abbot was the prior; in a priory the sub-prior. It was these 'warrant officers' who administered the house during the very frequent absences of its head on business or political journeys.

A number of special appointments existed within the abbey to assist with its efficient administration. Chief of these was the cellarer, the 'quartermaster' who was responsible for the provisioning of the community. Attached to him were the granger who was responsible for the supplies of grain to the bakehouse, the fraterer who saw to the appointments of the refectory, and the sacrist who supervised the maintenance of the abbey buildings. Cooking was in the care of the kitchener but the actual cooking was done by lay-servants of which the abbey had a number, probably about equal in strength to the community itself.

The chamberlain was responsible for the monks' clothing and

had under him tailors, laundresses, and a barber. The precentor organized the church services. The almoner not only dispensed alms to indigent persons who called at the great court of the abbey but also journeyed about the neighbourhood seeking out those in need or help. In the abbey itself the infirmarer was in charge of a large department which cared for the aged monks and those temporarily sick.

The guest-master was an individual upon whose shoulders a great deal of responsibility rested, especially in the event of a visit by an important traveller demanding hospitality for himself and his suite. All travelling being in those days performed on horses, the abbey smithy came under the control of the guest-master. But except for the occasional appearance of some important personage at the abbot's table in the refectory such excursions would not have affected the daily round of the cloister monk.

The daily programme in the abbey routine seems to have been designed so as to make sure that no one would enter a monastery unless he intended to devote himself to the life of a religious.

Although his day really began with the first monastic office of Prime at six o'clock he would have to leave his mattress in the dormitory at about two in the morning. He slept in his clothes and dressed by putting on his night shoes, in which he would shuffle down the night stairs—if his abbey was fortunate enough to possess these, for else he would have to make his way through the cloister—into the dim vastness of the great church to engage in four hours of prayers leading on to the office of Prime. And not until he had been in the choir for some five hours would he be able to leave the church to exercise his stiff legs in the cloister, or, should he choose, to occupy his mind with reading.

About eight o'clock the monks changed into their day shoes and washed themselves at the 'laver' by the refectory door before taking a quick breakfast and returning to the choir for the office of Terce. This was followed by the gathering of the whole community in the chapter house for the daily conference which might take anything up to an hour to get through. Released from chapter the monks set to work, manually or at some craft such as writing, until dinner in the refectory at about midday.

After the meal came the third office of Sext, then work again until None at about two o'clock in the afternoon. Supper came at about four o'clock and at five they gathered once more in the church for Vespers after which they changed into their night shoes. By about seven o'clock, after a further visit to the church for Compline, they were settling down for the night in their bleak dormitory.

The above is but a very approximate description of the daily life of the monk. Its main features, it will be seen, were the attendances in the choir for the monastic offices, the daily session in the chapter house, periods of meditation, study and manual work, and intervals for meagre meals.

While the ordinary monk lived a life of seclusion amongst his brethren, the monastic life, while denying its followers all enjoyment of the pleasures of the outside world, did not release the community as a whole from social duties towards their fellow men.

The principal social service enjoyed by St. Benedict upon his monks was that of hospitality. The abbeys all carried out this charge to the best of their ability and sometimes at considerable expense and inconvenience. They were the hotels of the period, sheltering the traveller for at least two nights, and more if he were a person of importance.

The housing and feeding of travellers and their animals, and the care and shoeing of the latter, must have taken up much of the time of the brother guest-master. One can imagine a discussion between this official and a sacrist engaged on urgent repairs as to how long each might have the services of the blacksmith.

Most abbeys had some sort of accommodation for travellers in a part of the western range of the claustral buildings, or in guest houses provided in the great court of the abbey which adjoined this. When the abbots took to building private houses with great halls and private chambers similar to those of the lay nobility they could accommodate persons of rank within these, possibly on occasion giving the house up to the King or a great lord on a journey, and resuming for a space the abbot's bed, which always remained available for him in the monks' house across the cloister.

The abbeys had to make provision for sick and aged persons,

1. Pershore

2. Tewkesbury

not only of their own community but for old people forced upon the abbey by the King or a powerful noble who wanted to relieve himself of the responsibility for them. Another practice affecting the abbey infirmary was that of buying 'corrodies', contributions made by lay-folk to the abbey in order to assure themselves of accommodation and care in their old age.

Another service of less certain value to the public was that of sanctuary, offered to all criminals except those accused of high treason. Only some twenty abbeys possessed the right of sanctuary; this was as well for the privilege was very liable to abuse. Westminster Abbey, as one might well imagine, was at one period infested with wanted criminals. On the other hand sanctuary may have offered to the criminal the respite of a cooling-off period during which his alleged offence could have been reviewed while his actual whereabouts presented no problem.

Housing as they did so many individuals with a taste for meditation and study, it would indeed have been surprising had the abbeys failed to become seats of learning. By the closing decades of the Anglo-Saxon era such abbeys as Winchester, St. Augustine's at Canterbury, and Malmesbury were not only translating the Classical writers but were compiling national and ecclesiastical histories of which the Anglo-Saxon Chronicle is the most impressive.

The scriptorium of the abbey was usually the sunny north alley of the cloister. Before the days of the printing press most books were written and illustrated in cubicles contrived in these strange studios huddled between the buttresses in the lee of the windbreak provided by the walls of the great abbey churches.

Centres of book production were St. Albans Abbey and the cathedral priory of Durham.

The foundation of the colleges at Oxford and Cambridge, however, by attracting persons less interested in prayer and more in study and writing, considerably reduced the output from the monastic cloisters from the thirteenth century onwards.

Whether the monks as individuals played much part in education must be doubted in view of the fact that their enclosed profession excluded them from the world and the world from them.

The Orders of canons regular, however, whose pastoral duties carried them about the countryside, may well have enabled them to perform tutorial tasks also.

But whether enclosed monks or peripatetic canon walking or jogging about the countryside on a pony, the men of the abbeys were undoutbedly an important factor in English medieval society. Nor do the remains of the great buildings they raised form the sum total of their contribution.

# 2

# The Monastic Orders

References were made in the previous chapter to monastic Orders other than the Benedictine. This was, however, the basic Order in western monasticism upon which all others were founded. Its monks wore: over shirt and underclothes, a cassock of black, white, or russet, over which was thrown the black cloak having a hood attached to it which was the garment peculiar to the monk and in the case of those of the Benedictine Order gave them the popular title of 'black monks'.

There were, however, a number of other Orders in medieval England, each varying slightly in their interpretation of the Rule as laid down by St. Benedict, which they varied to suit differences in the composition and aim of each breakaway Order. These differences affect the planning and architectural treatment of their abbeys. The individualism of the various Orders as reflected in their architecture is a subject which has not yet been objectively examined and is worth a study.

The original concept of monasticism as illustrated by the Benedictine Rule had been one of austerity in all things. At the beginning of the tenth century, however, the monks of the Burgundian abbey of Cluny began to wonder whether austerity was in reality the correct approach towards the act of worship. They felt that their tribute should be of the highest quality in all things, in particular with regard to the ritual employed.

From elaborate ritual to a fine setting in which to worship was but a short step. Thus the Cluniac Order began to develop monastic architecture to a degree not yet attempted by the Benedictines.

Cluny quickly found adherents and the Order prospered. Priories were founded all over western Europe, all owing allegiance to the Abbot of Cluny, who became a kind of second Pope. The great church of Cluny was enlarged until it far excelled both in size and architectural splendour the church of St. Peter in Rome itself. It was pulled down only at the beginning of the last century as an offence to revolutionary susceptibilities.

William the Conqueror favoured the Cluniacs and founded the priory of Lewes in Sussex which became the head house of the Order in England.

The English Cluniac churches were impressive and of the highest architectural merit; in them the ceremonial setting of the worship was matched by a more elaborate ritual than could be found in the Benedictine churches. The popularity of the Cluniac Order had become an indication of the fashion in which monasticism was spreading and had become a power in western Europe, supported by rapidly accumulating wealth and represented by huge building complexes far surpassing in size and architectural splendour anything else in existence.

The Cluniacs continued to found their priories all over England, rivalling all but the greatest of the Benedictine abbeys, and each owing allegiance through the channels of a colonial system to the Abbot of Cluny. The Cluniac houses were not encouraged to engage in outside activities such as education or social services of any description. This, added to their foreign allegiance, made them unpopular with the English people as a whole and in 1376 Parliament demanded that its English communities should thenceforth be restricted to Englishmen.

In view of the opulent nature of the Cluniac achievements it is unfortunate that geological conditions have conspired to deprive us of a view of the mother house in England, the priory of Lewes in Sussex, a county so desperately short of building stone that within hours of the surrender in 1539 and the handing over of the place to Thomas Cromwell the demolition squads were tearing it down with such energy as to leave only a few snags of walling remaining as memorials of one of the greatest of English monastic houses. The priory of Thetford in stone-less Norfolk was similarly despoiled of all its architectural stonework. Nearby, however, a fine Cluniac west front remains in the less needy village of Castle Acre.

It should be appreciated that monks were not in Holy Orders but were laymen who had taken the monastic habit and were living in a community under a Rule. The priests who staffed a cathedral church, called the canons of the cathedral, lived in a kind of community represented by the cathedral close, but were not recognized as such, since they were not under the discipline of a Rule. The result was the foundation of the Augustinian Order of canons *regular* as opposed to the *secular* canons of the cathedral.

The Augustinian canons lived in priories in much the same fashion as those of the Benedictines, but were not strictly enclosed, as they had to go about their work in the parishes with the rest of the priests of the countryside.

The Augustinians acquired wealth, possibly for the reason that being priests they were better able to perform those prayers for departed souls known as 'chantries' for which payments were made towards the finances of the Church by persons desiring these perpetual memorials.

But the great advantage the Orders of canons had over the Orders of monks was that the former, being priests, were educated men with more sophisticated ideas capable of being expressed in the chapter house to the benefit of the community. It is very noticeable when studying monastic planning that the Augustinians had no intention of being bound by Benedictine conventions and were often trying out new ideas for improving the working of their houses.

The Augustinian churches were very fine, but they concentrated upon the choir and presbytery and did not waste money in excessively extravagant naves. They had only one really vast church, that of Waltham Abbey in Essex, memorial to King Harold, though the surviving church at Christchurch Priory in Hampshire is a very large and notable building. The naves of both these churches are large. Waltham Abbey once had yet another nave eastwards of the existing one, with the crossing and presbytery beyond this.

For the most part, however, the ordinary Augustinian naves tended to be nominal features forming one side of the cloister and having no aisle to the south so as to increase the protection given by the mass of the church to the cloister itself. Often, however, there was an aisle on the side of the nave away from the cloister.

The Augustinians, with their intelligent chapters, must have played an important part in the political life of the country. Yet few of their priories became abbeys and only three, Cirencester in Gloucestershire, Thornton in Lincolnshire, and of course mighty Waltham, achieved the mitre as compared with twenty-three of the Benedictine abbeys.

The Augustinian churches did well at the Suppression, three of them, Bristol, Oxford, and Carlisle, becoming cathedrals of the New Foundation; this compares very favourably with the Benedictine contribution of Gloucester, Peterborough, and Chester, though for a time the church of Westminster Abbey held cathedral rank.

There are indications that Augustinian foresight in making the local people welcome in their naves may have contributed to the survival of so many of their churches. Christchurch is of course the most notable, but Cartmell in Lancashire and Brinkburn in Northumberland are also notable survivals. Surviving naves are numerous—Dunstable in Bedfordshire, Lanercost in Cumberland, Worksop in Nottinghamshire, and of course Waltham being fine examples.

At Hexham in Yorkshire the choir and transepts of a splendid Augustinian church remain.

Most of these remains are of early date and some of them, such as Waltham and Dunstable, represent Augustinian work of the massive twelfth-century type. But what they could do when the Gothic arrived may be seen in the parish church of Little Dunmow in Essex which is the south aisle of the presbytery of a great Augustinian priory. Only a single arcade is left, but this remains a lovely example of thirteenth-century Gothic, and may well serve as an indication of what has been lost when the Augustinian choirs were torn down.

In the Cluniac Order we see the Benedictine concept of poverty being set aside in favour of opulent display. This apart, there were Benedictines who felt that without this retrograde movement the monastic idea was abandoning its original idea and sliding away from the basic idea of austerity and poverty. The inevitable reforming campaign was the result, another Burgundian abbey, that of Cîteaux, being the source of the reaction towards a closer adherence to the Benedictine Rule. The result was the foundation of the Cistercian Order, one which became of great importance, especially in this country.

The Cistercians, the 'white monks', publicly abjured all the normal sources of feudal wealth such as revenues from land and tithes from parish churches. Determined to be self-denying, they rejected good food and warm clothing. Their abbeys were to be founded 'away from habitations'. Their lands were to be exploited solely by themselves. As this would interfere with the religious duties laid down by St. Benedict's Rule, however, they would have found it necessary to engage persons to work their lands. Instead they admitted into their abbeys numbers of lay-brothers who were not professed monks but had the privilege of a sheltered life in a well-administered community in exchange for their services in the fields.

Dom David Knowles has suggested that the comparison between the Cistercian abbey and the Benedictine might be as between an Argentine cattle ranch and a great land-owning institution such as Trinity College in Cambridge.

Cistercian abbeys were all founded by the system of colonization. The efficiency of their organization is illustrated by the fact that the buildings of each new abbey were first completed and only then occupied by the draft of an abbot and twelve monks posted to it from the mother house.

Throughout the twelfth century the white monks of Cîteaux covered the countryside with their houses and flourished despite inconveniences due to their lack of the same security achieved by their rivals the long-established Benedictines. During the thirteenth century, however, they began to have second thoughts concerning their position in the land, eventually deciding to accept the same sources of income previously rejected. Thereafter their churches became buildings of superlative beauty in an architectural style still honoured today by all those who love beautiful buildings.

The feature which they retained, however, and which still distinguished their Order from all others, was the complement of lay-brothers who although an important part of the community did not join the monks in their choir but used the nave of the church.

The mother house of the Cistercians in England, Waverley Abbey in Surrey founded in 1128, has suffered from the depredations of stone-hungry builders in post-Suppression days, and is today rather sadly represented on the site by a few poor fragments. Indeed, although one might have expected that the sites of the Cistercian abbeys, set 'far from habitations', might have saved them from the assaults of the stone-robbers, they have been just as badly robbed as those of the urban Benedictines. In many places they have been virtually obliterated, but as most of their sites are unencumbered by later building these have yielded interesting results to the archaeologist with a spade.

Few of the original abbey churches have been suffered to remain, notable exceptions being Buildwas Abbey in Shropshire and the great ruin of Fountains Abbey in Yorkshire. On the other hand some of the later buildings, such as the churches at Rievaulx in Yorkshire, Netley in Hampshire, and Tintern in Monmouthshire, are yet standing to a degree of completeness which enables us to form a good picture of Cistercian architecture.

It is unfortunate that none of the great churches of the Cistercians, all of them buried deep in the English countryside, has been suffered to remain in use, though the early nave of Margam abbey church in Glamorganshire and the wholly enchanting Gothic presbytery of Abbey Dore in Herefordshire are still in use as parish churches.

Lesser Orders which espoused the same reforming aims as the Cistercians were the Tironians and the Savigniacs; these Orders, however, eventually merged with the Cistercians. The great abbey of Furness in Lancashire, of which there are considerable remains, was originally Savignac.

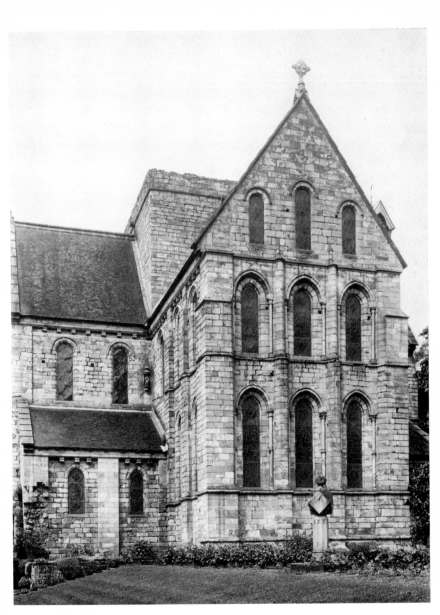

3. Brinkburn

4. Kirkstall

The obvious appeal of the Cistercian Order encouraged the canons regular to institute their version of it to set beside the Augustinian Order of black canons. The Premonstratensians or white canons flourished in the English countryside and built many fine abbeys copying the Augustinian plan of a nave with an aisle on one side only. Several of these churches remain in part, in particular Bayham in Sussex, Leiston in Suffolk, Eggleston in Yorkshire, Coverham in Yorkshire and Halesowen in Worcestershire. Easby Abbey in Yorkshire can show some dramatic ruins but its church has been swept away.

The Premonstratensians also employed lay-brothers to work their farms but on a much smaller scale than the Cistercians. The Premonstratensian abbeys have no lay-brothers' houses attached to them; the western range is sometimes merely cellarage without even lodgings above, so it seems likely that the lay-brothers were accommodated outside the claustral complex.

It is interesting to attempt some comparison between the salient features of the monastic plan as utilized by each of the principal Orders. The Benedictines owned the rich abbeys and priories, the former mainly urban, the latter scattered about the countryside in the midst of groups of manors owned by a parent abbey. Their churches were large and their lay-outs extensive and complicated, as befits autonomous establishments acting on their own initiative.

This compares strikingly with the Cistercian houses, all abbeys and set out to a standard plan adaptable to houses all of much the same size with no small priories to consider.

The houses of the Augustinian canons, however, were all originally priories. They built fine churches but their domestic planning is found to be the reverse of standard, the architects displaying initiative by adopting devices from both Benedictine and Cistercian sources and adding tricks of their own.

The houses of the Premonstratensian canons stand in a class apart. Founded by a French aristocrat, St. Norbert, the white canons were enjoined by their founder to observe good manners. Thus to the intelligence of the Augustinians they seem to have added something of refinement in design which one may see in particular in the remarkable church at Bayham Abbey in Sussex (Plate 31) with its unique east end. Their frater at Easby Abbey in Yorkshire (Plate 16) is closely approaching the great halls of the Cistercians in architectural dignity.

Most of the Orders founded houses for women who lived much the same kind of life as the men and whose houses were planned along much the same lines. A number of the Benedictine nunneries achieved a state as magnificent as any of the Order, the Wessex abbey group of Amesbury, Shaftesbury, Wilton and Romsey—only the church of the last remains today—being especially notable during the Middle Ages as finishing schools for princesses and havens of retirement for the Queen Mother.

An Order peculiarly English which never left this country was that founded by St. Gilbert of Sempringham in Lincolnshire to make provision for double houses containing nuns on the one hand and on the other canons who would conduct the Mass for them.

The church was central with cloister and conventual buildings on either side. Sempringham itself and Watton in Yorkshire are the best known of the Gilbertine priories. These were both double houses, but there were some Gilbertine priories which remained wholly male and never had their complement of nuns.

The original concept of monasticism, as practised in many of the Byzantine monasteries of Syria and Egypt, had been one of men living entirely solitary in 'cells' isolated even from companions. One western Order, that of the Carthusians, adopted this plan to some degree in that each monk had his own cell instead of sharing a common dormitory, but worshipped with his brethren in a small but stately church and shared at mealtimes a common refectory, doubtless for convenience in the preparation of the food. The plan of a Carthusian abbey thus differed completely from those of any other English Order in the arrangement of the cloister; this will be discussed in detail in Chapter 9. The Carthusian churches were quite small, in no way comparing with the appearance of a monastic church as generally accepted.

The monasteries were establishments which formed no part of the ecclesiastical administration of the country, being founded as private ventures. They were indeed subject to periodic visitations from the bishop of the diocese in which an abbey might be situated, with the exception, however, of the five great abbeys of Westminster, St. Albans, St. Edmundsbury, Evesham, and St. Augustine at Canterbury.

Even before the Norman Conquest the English bishops were important personages. At that time, however, they lacked cathedral churches as we know them, their thrones being set as often as not in the chancel of some building little more imposing than a parish church, which happened to be the see of the bishop's diocese. A church needs maintenance; this could be carried out by parishioners but a bishop could not organize the construction and maintenance of a cathedral. Possibly by the eleventh century some arrangement had been devised and proper cathedrals erected at places such as Sherborne, Elmham and other sees now transferred elsewhere. When built, a cathedral had to be maintained; again there were no parishioners to do this. Eventually an organization was created by which each cathedral had a complement of priests called canons who maintained the services within it as in a monastery—indeed very probably the idea was copied from the Benedictines—so that the church had a permanent staff.

After 1075, when the cathedrals were transferred from the rural sites to within the perimeter of walled cities, large cathedral churches were built to offer some comparison with the churches of the Benedictine abbeys and advertise the dignity of the bishop. Each cathedral church had within it a choir similar to that of the abbey, in which the canons gathered at service time to maintain the daily prayers. This resulted in the formation of a community of a sort, but one acknowledging no Rule and therefore impossible to discipline, in mediaeval days a serious disadvantage to the bishop who was nominally the head of his community within his church.

The remedy was found to be to attach to the cathedral a monastic house with a prior to act as its head. These 'cathedral priories', the most notable of which was at Canterbury itself, played an important part in mediaeval monastic life and must have had a hand in assisting the bishops to raise their cathedral churches towards the architectural dignity they display today, providing the bishop with a church suited to his dignity and enabling him to perform his pastoral duties without having to concern himself with administrative problems.

It is important to note that the occupants of a cathedral priory were Benedictine monks and that the choir within the cathedral was a monastic one.

It should also be understood that the cathedral canons were canons *secular*, not to be confused with the *regular* canons of the Augustinian, Premonstratensian, and Gilbertine Orders.

The Orders of friars which entered this country during the thirteenth century and founded many friaries with their fine churches and planned their houses on rather different lines from those of the old Orders, will be discussed in Chapter 15.

# 3

# Early Churches

—————

The Benedictine Rule did not anticipate the erection of a church, certainly not an edifice of the scale associated with it nowadays. All that St. Benedict required was an 'oratory', that is to say a building reserved for worship in the form of prayer.

The early Celtic monasteries formed communities of men and women living in small huts gathered within the shelter of a compound and worshipping separately in two or more only slightly better huts which formed their oratories.

The foundation of similar monasteries in this country inaugurated the Benedictine settlement here. Architectural history, however, has demonstrated indisputably that the practice of worship requires for the dignity of the deity invoked the provision of a building of special quality. Thus the oratory had to become *ecclesia*—a church.

The form of the first monastic churches of any architectural pretensions to be erected in this country must necessarily be a matter for speculation, not only because of that interlude in monastic history during which their buildings were systematically destroyed in the course of pagan invasions, but also for the reason that subsequent antiquarian interest does not appear to have been sufficiently enthusiastic for any primitive shrine to have been preserved. Indeed that same spirit which had founded the church encouraged its custodians to be forever rebuilding it in more and more splendid form.

The effect upon architecture of the appearance of the Christian religion makes a fascinating study. The sudden development of

Christianity from a spiritual concept into a paramount social factor was due to the impulsive action of the Roman Emperor Constantine in declaring it as the State religion of his empire. It was perhaps the greatest event in architectural history.

By that simple announcement he also declared obsolete the whole panoply of Corinthian spectacle which glorified the world of his day. For when he drove away into the shadows that Olympian pantheon which had inspired the achievements of the Hellenistic architects, mighty Baalbek and its fellows almost on an instant became ghost-temples doomed to neglect and gradual decay.

What was to take the place of all this glory?

Christian churches were now wanted. But what was a Christian church?... nobody had ever seen one.

Churches were wanted immediately. There was no time to build anything so urgently needed. The Empire is without a God ... there is no time to devise anything of monumental scale or dignity. Only basic requirements can be considered!

The change in the practice of religion was revolutionary. The pagan temple had been a house for the god represented in the form of a great statue, the worshippers gathering beyond the altar set against his portal in the open air.

The new religion required covered space for communal participation in a Sacrament. Congregations would be on an Imperial scale.

Thus the first churches were simply large covered areas with their widely spanned roofs supported across rows of colonnades—often using second-hand columns salvaged from destroyed temples to save time in turning these. To disguise their undistinguished appearance they were given the title of *basilica*—regal building—in token of their spiritual if not architectural dignity.

The type of building which has continued to be known by this designation remained the standard church-form in the regions coming immediately under the spiritual sway of Rome. The 'basilican' plan is characterized by a long axis, a wide nave span separated from lateral aisles by two rows of colonnades or, later, arcades supported upon columns. An apse terminates the vista;

this feature had been introduced into buildings to give dignity—
in a temple behind the statue, or in a court of law behind the
justices.

Externally the basilica had no distinguishing features.

This was a disadvantage which contemporary architects were
forced to remedy.

Hellenistic monumental architecture had relied for its appeal
upon ramparts of towering columns surrounding a massive cliff-
like block of masonry.

The last great temple of Imperial Rome had been the Pantheon,
a rotunda surmounted by architecture's latest discovery—the
dome. It was too monumental in conception and construction to
be quickly repeated, and its circular plan was ill suited for communal worship upon an axis, so the architects of the first churches
ignored its message; but three small and dainty chapels on a circular plan and having a dome surrounded by aisles were built by
the Emperor at Jerusalem and Bethlehem.

The thrusting dome was too insistent a feature to be neglected
by the architects of Constantine's new capital at ancient Byzantium, so that when sufficient time had elapsed to enable proper
consideration to be given to church design it was agreed that the
dome should be the crowning feature of each.

Thus the standard form of the Byzantine church was established
as a centralized structure surrounding a dome. This was carried
upon four massive piers of masonry connected by four tall arches,
and these features led into four short but lofty projections like
the arms of a cruciform church, the whole central mass being
surrounded by a containing wall enclosing a square plan. (See
Fig. 1.)

Bypassing the basilicas of the Italian peninsula the tall cruciform churches reached out from Byzantium to cover western
Europe. Here, however, they had to abandon the dome for lack
of engineering skill and craftsmanship, and to replace it with a tall
timber roof of spire-like form. (See Fig. 2.) It is this ascending
element in Western Byzantine architecture which may have played
a large part in transforming the swelling contours of the original
church silhouette towards the soaring achievements of the Gothic.

Tower and spire were constructions eminently suited to timber-building, the basic system employed in western Europe during the second half of the first millennium.

We are so used to recalling our own great abbey churches as buldings of excessive length that it is necessary to remember that this type of church is almost entirely limited to England. The Continental type is more closely allied to the Byzantine ideal, lifted vertically to end in a lofty steeple but with its lateral arms,

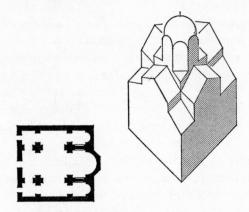

Fig. 1    *Typical Byzantine church*
One of the most common types of early
Byzantine church. The central dome is carried
upon four piers spanned by tall arches which
lead into four short 'wings', the whole enclosed
within a square

the western included, restrained in length so as to enhance rather than detract from the aspiring silhouette.

This concept remained the basis of European church architecture and its insistence upon height led eventually to the complete absorption of the central feature within a building raised to an inconceivable height—hence the towering churches of Beauvais, Soissons, Le Mans, and many other great French creations. Indeed, height was the element in architecture which the Gothic was expressly designed to illustrate.

Upon analysis it would appear that the vast sprawling churches which covered England as the eleventh century was turning towards the twelfth—the largest buildings in the world of their day—must be regarded as aberrant architecture. Obsessed with length they failed to obey the first requirement of monumental architecture which is an emphasis upon the aspiring element of height.

Internally these great churches may instil a sense of awe by reason of the remoteness of their terminal feature—a vista to be blocked up in any case once the monastic choir has been introduced into the building—but externally what little impression of height one might have received is distracted by the sensation of amazement at the building's horizontal panorama.

Let us examine what might be considered as architecturally the most perfect of England's post-Conquest abbey churches, that of Romsey in Hampshire. In its nave, four original bays remain. The remaining three are said to have been rebuilt in the Gothic style. There are certainly indications that the nave did not end originally with the westernmost of the four original bays, but that is not to say that the nave was originally seven bays long. The rebuilding of a church normally began at the east end to provide a more splendid presbytery. On the other hand it is quite conceivable that a short nave might have been lengthened.

Visual evidence suggests that the nave was originally five bays in length of which the choir occupied four and the westernmost, which was a kind of narthex, had an inner porch—possibly with a slender bell-tower above it—at the west end of the north aisle. (See Fig. 13a.)

Even had the nave of the twelfth-century Romsey Abbey been only seven bays long this would have been far less than the general average of eleven—at St. Edmundsbury fifteen—exhibited by a contemporary Benedictine nave.

When one remembers that the nave of the original Byzantine church was very short indeed it seems not inconceivable that the nuns of Romsey were content with a nave just long enough to hold their choir. And with a nave of five bays' length one sees a very different picture of a Benedictine abbey church from that displayed by the long buildings of the great abbeys.

If one imagines the tower of Romsey Abbey—which by the way

contains bells which it is worth travelling far to hear—crowned by a soaring timber steeple, flanked by the two existing tall two-bay transepts, to the east a presbytery only three bays in length, and the nave reduced to no more than five bays, one can form an idea of the Western Byzantine church as it may have been conceived by the architects of the eleventh century. A building of such compactness surmounted by a tall central steeple would have been a structure meriting the designation of a noble pile.

Surround such a structure with buildings of which none—other than those of the monastery itself—was more than a single storey in height, and one can still better appreciate the immense dignity of such a church. We can still see something of the effect today displayed by some early Continental churches.

The steeples of these English abbey churches have all vanished long ago. We have descriptions of them indicating their enormous size, their height, and above all their great elaboration. Illustrations of them still exist indicating such features as their rising in decreasing stages and the rows of windows surrounding their bases as with the Byzantine domes. Before the days of lead roofing every church tower had to be covered with a steep timber roof covered with shingles; it is of interest to note that throughout the Middle Ages a church tower is always called a steeple to differentiate it from the military variety and to call attention to its most impressive feature. The actual spire itself is called a broach, that is to say, a spit.

The Bayeux Tapestry shows the church towers but creates a Byzantine atmosphere by indicating what appear to be domes but are probably the heavy lead 'cops' closing the apex of the steeple.

The foregoing is intended to be a discussion upon what may have been the aim of the church-builders of the end of the first millennium. Let us see what remains of the buildings themselves.

An important ninth-century Continental church is that of Germigny-des-Prés near Orleans erected about the year 910. Its plan is pure Byzantine, its central tower carried upon four piers surrounding a crossing from which led the four short arms of equal length.

After his irruption from sanctuary on the marsh-girt mound of

Athelney near Glastonbury and his subsequent thrashing of the
Danish army at Ethandune in 878, King Alfred founded an abbey
on the site which had given him refuge. A brief contemporary
description of this church tells of its foundation upon four pillars
set deep in the earth. On a marshy site any stonework would have
had to be deep-set, while timber posts would have had to be
founded upon heavy sleepers and not set into the ground to rot.

We seem to have here a church on the normal Byzantine plan.
A royal foundation, it would probably have been the last word in
contemporary design. Indeed we are told that it was the first
building of its kind to be seen in this country. It would appear
likely that we can proceed to derive future abbey churches from
this prototype. (See Fig. 2b.)

The accommodation would probably have been arranged with
the monks' choir in the western arm of the cross facing across the
tower-space towards the altar in the eastern arm (see Fig. 13a)
exactly the same arrangement as we find in the great abbey church
of the twelfth century.

Thus by the end of the ninth century the general picture seems
fairly well established. But there is still a wide gap to fill, between
the end of the sixth century when St. Augustine brought the Rule
of St. Benedict into this country and the day of the stone building
at Athelney. This is the gap of the Dark Ages in England.

Again we have clues. The churches were of wood—they were
as a result always being fired by the Danish armies. Thus antiquaries seeking information concerning their probable appearance
need to investigate contemporary timber-building techniques. As
the period was one of Byzantine domination in architectural style
the form of these churches is likely to have been centralized and
not 'Romanesque' basilican.

The normal span of an early church in this country is about
fourteen feet. This is the span of the timber churches remaining
in Essex. These are square on plan with their tall roofs carried
upon four posts mounted on massive sleepers. The fine church
of Blackmore, however, has two intermediate posts along the
flanks in the style of the Byzantine 'duplex bay' developed from
the galleried churches of antiquity. The overall span of the

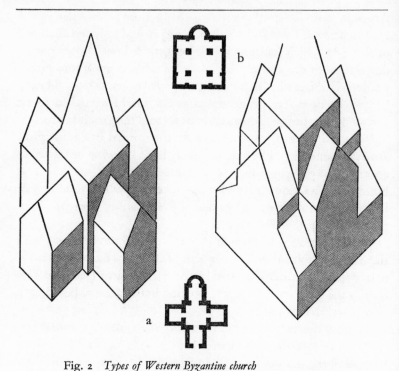

Fig. 2    *Types of Western Byzantine church*
The central feature is a tower. In (a) its four
walls are pierced by small arches leading to the
small 'wings'; from this type the English parish
church is developed. (b) Shows the sophisticated
Byzantine plan with four piers; this is the basic
form of the abbey church. The towers are
capped by a timber spire or 'broach' in place of
the dome which invariably completed the
Eastern Byzantine church

surrounding timber walling is about thirty-two feet which is the
length of two poles.

Searching for the remains of stone walling we find these at St.
Martin's church at Canterbury set twenty-four feet apart, a very
wide span for walls barely two feet thick. The foundations of
sleeper walls fourteen feet apart, however, indicate that they are
only screen walls and that the roof was carried upon a posted interior similar to that at Blackmore. As it seems unlikely that such

thin walling could have been carried up to form the steep-sided
gables required by early roofing materials we may be virtually
certain that the 'aisles' at St. Martin's church were carried round
its ends, as at Blackmore.

The chancel at St. Martin's continues the lines of the sleeper
walls and with a span of fourteen feet its walls could probably have
been relied upon to carry a roof if they were kept down in height.

A certain amount of material is available to enable us to attempt
to discover the probable form of the English abbey church during
the four centuries following the foundation of the church of the
abbey of St. Augustine at Canterbury about the year 605 and prior
to its replacement by a great building of the Benedictine renaissance.

St. Augustine himself would undoubtedly have subscribed to
the 'basilican' school which called for a long church with a pronounced axis. A church at Bradwell in Essex, believed to have been
actually founded by him, shows a nave fifty feet long and just over
twenty feet in span, suitable proportions for a 'Roman' church. Its
walls are two and a half feet thick and well built of Roman brick
pillaged from the ruins of the nearby *castrum*, and, although they
are twenty-four feet in height, could have been satisfactorily
roofed even at the beginning of the seventh century with the
advice of persons equipped with a knowledge of Rome.

But at St. Augustine's Abbey at Canterbury the foundations of
an ancient abbey church—of what period is not at all certain—
have been excavated and bear no resemblance to the church at
Bradwell. Its wall are one foot nine inches in thickness and their
span—similar to that of a mediaeval cathedral—is twenty-eight
feet. The weight of timber required for such a span could hardly
be safely carried by such walling. It is of interest to note that the
much thicker walls of a large parish church of the fifteenth century
stand about eighteen feet apart. The inference from the remains at
St. Augustine's compared with that from others of a series of early
Kentish churches is that the walls were the screen walls of aisles
and that the actual inner supporting structures, almost certainly of
timber, have disappeared.

The group of churches—again of unknown date—to which the

abbey church belongs are the churches of St. Martin and St. Pancras at Canterbury, a church at Rochester which may have been the original cathedral, and the church of Reculver—all in Kent. The walls enclose areas varying in width from thirty-eight to forty-two feet and their spans vary from twenty-four feet to twenty-eight feet, possibly suggesting variations in the length of

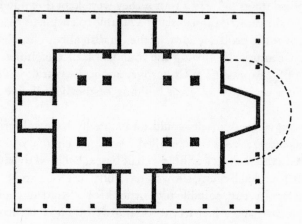

Fig. 3   *Conjectural plan of Anglo-Saxon timber church*
The outline of the plan is based on existing
sites in Kent. The central structure is based on
the timber architecture of Essex

the local pole. The proportions in every case represent a width of two to a length of three—a far cry from anything remotely 'basilican'.

The clue to the probable appearance of such a church would lie in the presumed form taken by the central feature of the church around which those walls the foundations of which we see would have been set as screens, these very probably originally of timber also.

The timber churches of Essex are believed to date from the eleventh or twelfth century which would account for their survival so long after their predecessors had been converted into bonfires by the Danes.

One of these churches, that of West Hanningfield, which has lost its surrounding 'aisles', has its turriform central structure surrounded by four short arms making it resemble a timber copy of a Byzantine cruciform church. If this could be set within the foundations of a Kentish-type church it would indeed produce a perfectly recognizable attempt at a common type of Byzantine church with, of course, a tall western type steeple taking the place of a dome. (See Figs. 3 and 4.)

It is to be hoped that in future the excavators of ancient abbey sites will look for vestiges of sleeper foundations indicating the site of an early timber church. These appear to have been set a pole's length—sixteen feet—apart measuring centre to centre. Allowing for the size of the timber used, which is about two feet square, this gives a span of fourteen feet. The overall width of the church seems to have been about two poles—thirty-two feet— giving an internal width of twenty-eight feet, or more above the foundations if the walls be of timber screens.

The only timber screens remaining are at the Essex church of Greensted. They are formed from the offcuts left from squaring logs, set into heads and sills just as one sees in the country today.

It is to be hoped that some day we may be able to interpret fully the fascinating illustrations bequeathed to us in the Bayeux Tapestry. It is clear that the timber walls of churches were water-proofed with oak shingles hung with their lower edges rounded so as to throw the water away from the joints of the course below, in the manner of eighteenth-century tile-hanging, giving a curious fish-scale appearance.

One feature of the Dark Age timber churches has not survived into stone architecture. The Byzantine church usually had a long western portico called a 'narthex' passing across the west front. From contemporary accounts we know that our early churches had these porticos carried along the sides as well; we find the remains of their foundations at St. Augustine's Abbey and at the church of Reculver. The ancient 'stave-churches' of Norway have these encompassing porticos, possibly using them to protect the timber walling from driving rain; it seems not improbable that they were so employed in this country.

These porticos must have been interesting appendages to the early timber church and have added to its general pyramidal

appearance. Their leeward alleys might have been used for religious instruction; they may even have been the form first taken
by the cloister in this country. Certainly they were used for the
burial of churchmen, being sometimes built up with solid walls to
form mortuary chapels for important prelates.

A mysterious building stands within its lonely moat near South
Elmham in Suffolk. In an absolutely stone-less region it is clumsily
constructed of flints. In plan it has a square nave on the eastern
side of which was clearly an altar flanked by a pair of doorways
leading into a presbytery or choir having as its eastern termination
a large apse.

Elmham was the seat of an Anglo-Saxon bishopric, moved from
Dunwich nearby and eventually to its present site at Norwich.
The ruin of South Elmham, planned like an abbey church with
nave and choir, may perhaps be the original cathedral church
designed in imitation of the church of a Benedictine abbey.

Although its walls are four feet in thickness—flint is an awkward
material to retain firmly in a wall if set in the weak lime mortar of
early medieval days—the church's width of twenty-six feet makes
it unlikely that it could have been roofed in a single span. One is
therefore again tempted to suspect the loss of a timber inner
structure probably burnt by a Danish army sweeping through this
very exposed region.

The eastern portion of the church at South Elmham has approximately the same dimensions—thirty-eight feet by twenty-six—as
the series of Kentish churches discussed above. Can we again
imagine a posted interior culminating in a tower like that at
Blackmore but possibly more elaborately fashioned?

We are then left with the problem of what happened over the
square nave. Was there another steepled roof here also, as in the
long stone churches of the eleventh century? A comparison with
early German cathedrals suggests that the timber-builders of
Anglo-Saxon England might have been quite willing to roof a
cathedral with two steeples.

The Byzantine church ended in an apse. The absence of this
terminal feature would have been inconceivable. But a circular
building cannot be properly constructed in wood owing to the

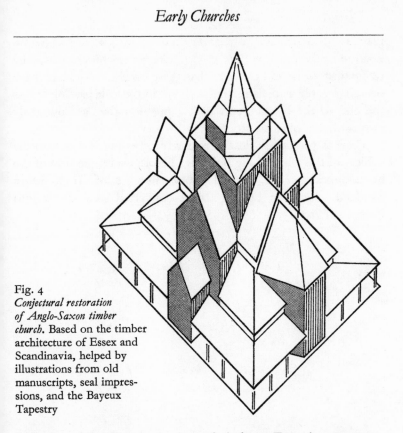

Fig. 4
*Conjectural restoration
of Anglo-Saxon timber
church.* Based on the timber
architecture of Essex and
Scandinavia, helped by
illustrations from old
manuscripts, seal impres-
sions, and the Bayeux
Tapestry

difficulty of bending its horizontal timbers. Even in masonry a circular wall-face is troublesome to construct; for this reason the Byzantine apse was usually semi-hexagonal externally.

This form was easily converted into timber and thus was widely used in Anglo-Saxon England as well as much later in some of the great churches such as that of Bayham Abbey in Sussex. The English polygonal apses are of course the same inside as out.

It seems very likely that the apse of the early timber church was of this form. We have to explain, however, the wide apses of the Kentish churches and that at South Elmham. May these perhaps have been of the nature of ambulatories—a surprisingly early device in the great churches of the Continent—passing round a lofty timber apse forming part of the central structure?

Another feature which complicates an analysis of the Kentish plans is the arrangement of triple arches which seem to bear no relation to the cross-section of a timber-posted church. It may be of interest to note, however, that these arches would not have been in a gable wall, as at Bradwell, but in the aisle passing across the end of the building; in such a position they are not truly chancel arches but aisle arcades.

There is yet a great deal of research to be undertaken into the subject of these intriguing buildings before we can be sure of the exact appearance of the tall abbey churches of Anglo-Saxon England which the Danish armies converted so joyously into beacons of victory.

# 4

# The Greatest Buildings of their Era

King Edgar the Peaceable, who reigned over England during the third quarter of the tenth century, is reported as complaining that all the monasteries in his realm were 'nothing but worm-eaten and rotten timber and boards'. This suggests that Anglo-Saxon mason-craft had made little progress during the half century and more since the erection of Alfred the Great's abbey church at Athelney. It also indicates that the King at least recognized that the proper material in which to construct an abbey was stone.

We know that these timber churches were very elaborately ornamented and regarded as the most lavishly decorated churches in Western Europe, which may well account for the wealth of carved ornament handed down from the woodcarvers to the stone-carvers who embellished the great churches which were soon to appear in this country.

But that the craft of the mason was developing there can be no doubt. It is true that only just before the Norman Conquest, when Edward the Confessor was building his great new abbey at West-minster, he had to import Continental masons to do the work. Or was he just being over-cautious about employing local men? For this is the miracle . . . that only ten years after the Battle of Hastings the English were raising the greatest buildings of their era.

It is scarcely conceivable that the Continent was denuded of its masons—for building on a vast scale was simultaneously pro-ceeding there as well—in order to execute a vast building pro-gramme. Moreover the architectural style of the buildings is either clearly Anglo-Saxon, as in the nave of Waltham Abbey in

Essex, or if more formally Byzantinesque as at Blyth Priory in Nottinghamshire begun in 1087, is primitive to a degree, clearly the product of the vernacular.

The most striking fact of all is the enormous size of these buildings, for the abbey churches of St. Albans Abbey and Winchester Cathedral are the longest churches in the world.

Consider again the miracle this represents. For the craft of masonry is a very skilled one, requiring not only the cutting of stone but its fashioning into the most complicated shapes known to solid geometry and indeed far beyond this—stones required for joining the ribs of vaulting systems for example. This is not something quickly learnt from masons imported from the Continent as instructors. Anglo-Saxon masoncraft must have been developing for some time waiting for the funds and encouragement to employ it. One of the most interesting aspects of the situation is the manner in which the woodcarving motifs were transferred without any difficulty to the embellishment of masonry.

The church plans of the close of the millennium were undergoing a change. For notwithstanding the aesthetic superiority of the Byzantine church with its high-towered nucleus, the adherence of western Europe to the Church at Rome rather than at Constantinople made it inevitable that the long axial 'basilican' plan would eventually become standard for the Western Church. It was moreover better suited to worship towards an alignment—facing Jerusalem—and could be extended longitudinally where the centralized plan could not.

If one examines the available evidence of the architectural development of Romsey abbey church one finds that the apsidal work at the east end of the tenth century was removed and the new church built round it on such a plan that the new crossing, transepts and presbytery could serve as a new east end to the older church until such time as the choir could be bodily transferred into it while the earlier building was being pulled down altogether.

The choir was then brought back into the four easternmost bays of the new nave, one more bay having been provided to serve as a narthex or retro-choir—probably a reconstruction of a feature of the earlier church—necessary in order to achieve access to the

5 . Llanthony

6. Llanthony

choir door. At Romsey Abbey, a nuns' house, the nave of this very beautiful church remained five bays in length. But as we well know, the Benedictine builders of the eleventh century were seldom content with naves of this purely practical extent.

By the end of the tenth century the nave of the great Benedictine church in England was developing an attenuation which was in the end to exceed anything on the Continent. The reason for this is not clear but a suggestion is that it was to provide an area for those processional displays favoured by the Church and for which the English climate demanded protection from the weather.

An important factor to remember when one is trying to work out the history of the development of a church is that any longitudinal enlargement almost invariably had to take place in an easterly direction, for the reason that the west front of a church was generally the western boundary of its property, the area immediately before it—the 'parvis' (Paradise)—being a space customarily dedicated to the public. Even if the church had wanted to expand in that direction there might well be at hand a commercial area of market place having in it stalls or even shops.

At Waltham Abbey in Essex, the huge eleventh-century church with a long nave and transepts had everything east of the central tower pulled down and a complete new church with a new nave, crossing and transepts, and presbytery built on to the old nave.

Where extension to a turriform church was needed this was just left as it was and the new church added on its eastern side. The complete church retained the turriform west end—what is known in Germany as a 'west work'—and had a long nave with a new cruciform feature added at its eastern end with the new choir accommodated west of the crossing in the eastern bays of the nave and a new 'lantern tower' in which were windows to light the crossing darkened by the deeper limbs surrounding it. (See Fig. 5.)

The original turriform structure may often become accepted as an interesting form of western feature and retained as such, as may be seen in a number of great churches in Germany. It may be remarked in parenthesis that Continental contacts across the North Sea existed along with those across the Channel. The early tower could be retained to carry the bells—the new lantern tower being

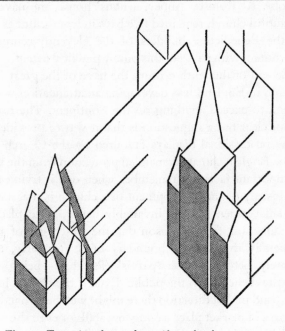

**Fig. 5**  *Extension of an early turriform church*
The long new 'basilican' nave built on eastwards of the early church which remains as a
'west work' carrying the bells until it is replaced
by a proper bell-tower still provided with
lateral wings to form a transeptal west front.
A timber church is shown. A stone 'four-
poster' (see Fig. 2b) might be retained for some
time as a western bell-tower

too flimsy for this purpose—and the wings flanking it to north and
south could, with it, provide a wide frontispiece of unprecedented
dignity to the great church. The arrangement perfected to form
a noble façade may be seen at Ely Cathedral—originally an abbey
church—in Cambridgeshire; the foundations of the cathedral at
Old Sarum in Wiltshire show that it had a western bell-tower
flanked by short transepts or wings. The Scottish abbey of Kelso
in Roxburghshire retains a fine frontispiece with a central tower.
This arrangement, clearly standard to the Rhenish great churches,
may well have been the Anglo-Saxon form of west front in use

with the large churches prior to the adoption of the twin-towered west front which gave the builders an opportunity for lighting the nave with a large west window. One may probably ascribe to the earlier arrangement the origin of the bell-tower at the west end of the English parish church.

The series of magnificent Benedictine abbey churches rising throughout the countryside at the opening of the twelfth century probably raised the ire of the reforming Cistercians, whose churches lacked any architectural treatment other than what was structurally necessary and were moreover built to order, to a standardized plan, by the abbot of the house which was sending out the colony that was to worship in it when completed and would thereafter wash his hands of it.

The long cumbersome nave could not be dispensed with as it was used by the lay-brothers as their choir. It was normally nine bays long, lined with rather crudely designed circular pillars carrying arcades of pointed arches. There was a simple clearstory above the arcade with no gallery over the aisles as in the Benedictine churches. The transepts projected two bays from the crossing and had each an eastern aisle. The presbytery projected two bays also and had no apse, possibly intentionally rejecting what was at the time an inevitable Benedictine eastern termination. (See Fig. 22.)

Ultimately, however, the Cistercians had to abandon their puritanical notions and accumulate incomes like any other Order. By the thirteenth century they were not only rebuilding their east ends—and sometimes the whole church—on a magnificent scale but in doing so were making up for past errors by creating architecture of superlative beauty to grace this country for centuries to come.

The important foundations which introduced the Augustinian Order into this country modelled their churches upon those of the Benedictine but on a smaller scale. With the expansion of the Order across the countryside, however, the churches of the twelfth-century priories became very much less imposing and tended towards the Cistercian plan but with shorter naves— having no lay-brothers to accommodate—often with only an aisle on the side farthest from the cloister. The churches of the White Canons, the Premonstratensians, were similar to the later Augustinian examples. Both Orders, however, joined in the thirteenth-century building boom and expanded their eastern arms to conform to contemporary fashion.

The canons' churches were often provided with eastern aisles to the transepts in accordance with the style introduced by the Cistercians. (See Fig. 11a and Plates 3 and 4.) The community being composed entirely of priests needed space for altars at which they could perform their daily duties; only Premonstratensian Bayham in Sussex, however, went to the extreme length of adding an eastern transept.

The churches of the Carthusians, being small and aisle-less, most nearly approached the original ideal of an oratory.

The churches of the Orders of friars which entered this country during the thirteenth century had a peculiarity in that their naves and choirs were built quite separately with a central tower which not only divided the two but actually formed a gatehouse through which the cloister was entered. These churches will be examined in Chapter 15.

The foregoing descriptions of the great abbey churches of the eleventh and twelfth centuries have explained how from the centralized church of Byzantine days were developed the immensely long buildings which in their day were the largest buildings in the world. (See Fig. 6.)

Winchester Cathedral and the abbey churches of St. Albans, St. Edmundsbury, and Waltham, were all about five hundred feet in length.

But this curious prolongation of the nave of the church only served to weaken the effect of what was in reality the most important portion of the building, its presbytery containing the high altar. This remained nothing more than the old Byzantine cruciform church with its arms doubled in length stuck on to the end of the interminable nave.

Soon after the Norman Conquest, however, French influence introduced the longer choir of four bays with an apse at the end, the whole of which was surrounded by an aisle, a device which was re-introduced later by the awakening Cistercians. The real lesson of all these adventures, however, lay in the realization that something must be done to balance the excessively long nave; hence the replacement of the old two-bay presbytery with one of four bays. This became standard for most churches other than those of the Cistercians before the twelfth century was out, the White Monks following soon after.

The four-bay presbytery had the effect of improving the balance of the lateral view of the great church but was in itself an admission

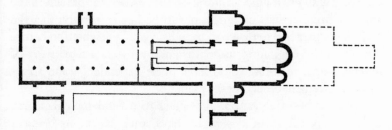

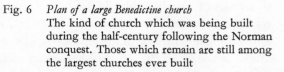

Fig. 6    *Plan of a large Benedictine church*
The kind of church which was being built during the half-century following the Norman conquest. Those which remain are still among the largest churches ever built

of the foolishness of building long naves. The Continental builders had never fallen into this error and as a result had filled the thirteenth century with towering edifices far outshining in magnificence anything this country could produce.

It was not until after the middle of the thirteenth century that the abbey builders of this country began to return to the idea of the church as a compact edifice surrounding a central feature. Cistercian Tintern (Plate 23) is a perfect example of the finalized form of the English great church which became the fashion for parish churches also, as seen in such splendid buildings as those of Patrington in Yorkshire and Ilminster in Somerset, both centres of late-medieval masonic activity.

At Tintern the transepts have each three bays, one longer than at Romsey Abbey, the presbytery four—now the standard length and a bay longer than at Romsey—and the nave six bays, half as long again as the presbytery but still well in balance with it. The central feature has fallen, but the church must have composed well about it.

The last great abbey church built in this country, at Bath Abbey in Somerset, has much the same proportions as at Tintern. Its central tower, as befits the region which erected it, is a very magnificent creation, rising to a great height, but prevented by its late date from comparing with some of its predecessors in Somerset.

While a discussion of the elevational aspect of the monastic churches really belongs to a book on the aesthetic approach to the study of architectural design, it has to be borne in mind that the church planner had perforce to have his visual presentation before him from the beginning, notwithstanding the fact that many of its elevational features would have to be dependent upon structural requirements affecting the plan.

Thus medieval elevations depended to a fundamental degree upon the principle of design by bays, each elevation being a repetition of a series of bays individually designed but placed end to end as required to achieve the whole; this of course explains why Gothic architecture remained primitive and could not survive the sophisticated approach of the trained Renaissance architect.

The medieval system of design began and ended with the bay. Each had to be considered both as regards its plan on the ground and how this became affected as the structure rose. For the bay is a unit of *building*, not an elevational unit; its elevational presentation is an aesthetic exercise which follows the acceptance of its structural suitability.

Basically, the purpose of walls is to carry a roof. Thus the support of the roof is the primary problem the builder has to solve.

A feature of Byzantine church design—and the Byzantines, heirs of Imperial Rome, were skilled engineers—was the introduction of upper floors or galleries, rendered possible in permanent architectural language by the use of stone vaulting. The small square angles of the building beyond the arms of the main cruciform structure were often so treated, a device which was not only useful in providing abutment to the crossing piers but also enabled the aisle walling to be raised to the same height as the rest of the building thus producing not only a square plan but a cubical presentation of sturdy appearance to support the central dome.

The two-storeyed aisle was carried through into Benedictine church design with, however, the main walls raised above the aisle roofs to form clearstories for lighting the nave which in an aisled structure was rather far away from the aisle windows. Behind the clearstory windows ran galleries set in the wall for cleaning access, these were the 'triforia' which presented to the interior of the church attractive arcades of triple openings.

Owing to a misinterpretation by a Victorian antiquary of an account of a twelfth-century fire at Canterbury Cathedral, this designation has now been transferred to the galleries above the aisles. The Georgians, who were interested in antiquarian research, called them 'nunneries' under the impression that the intention had been to reserve them for women. Eighteenth-century tickets for Coronation ceremonies were marked 'nunneries'; Beckford set them high up round the octagon at Fonthill.

Another suspicious architectural term as 'clearstory', which in the twelfth century was called triforium. William of Worcester, who made a tour of English abbey churches about the year 1480, when painted glass must have been widely used in them, called them—rather delightfully—over-histories'. Is it possible that the main windows in the aisles were called 'the histories'?—if so what delightful displays they must have been, However, 'clearstory' has been so determinedly established by the Gothic revivalists as to have even found its way into railway carriages!

It is pleasant to think of the interest shown by William of Worcester in his tours of what must to him have been a far more ordinary series of buildings than they appear to us today. He paced out his churches and gives us their dimensions. His pace works out at nineteen-and-a-half inches long, which we might have dismissed as a monkish shuffle did we not find that, at the Suppression, a foreman in charge of church demolition had a pace of only an inch longer. This is of course two-thirds of the standard military pace of today and seems to indicate a far more leisurely method of progress during the Middle Ages than would suit us today— possibly due to ill-fitting footwear.

The reconstruction of plans is a fascinating exercise. But the architectural archaeologist, though he may be untrained in the science of building construction, should endeavour to relate the plans he is preparing with structural problems they may be indicating at some point above the ground.

Systems of vaulting are a case in point. The construction of vaulting is very much simplified if the bay over which it is to be thrown be made square so that the curvature of both of the opposed transverse arches forming the vault shall have the same radius. Thus the eleventh-century aisle is usually set out as a series of square bays with each arch of the main arcade equal to the width of the aisle.

The unit employed in setting out was the pole, literally a pole and intended to be sixteen feet long. As there was, however, no national standard of length each building cut its own and in doing so varied its interpretation of the linear foot. The Tower of London and Lincoln Cathedral seem to have used a pole of eighteen feet.

The pole was used for setting out the church upon a grid four poles wide, the main span occupying two of these and the transept projecting one bay outside the aisle wall making an overall width of six poles.

While the aesthetic presentation of medieval architecture is beyond the scope of this book it is necessary to introduce the main features of the architectural development of elevational architecture during the Middle Ages.

Broadly speaking, the elevational architecture of the eleventh and twelfth centuries—nothing of adequate significance remains of earlier date—was a derivation from the Byzantine style of architecture originating in Constantinople and spreading throughout Europe until it reached its western shores.

In England it settled down to a style of stability and adherence to ordinance. The arrangement of the arch orders and the piers carrying them was sensible and orderly, the gallery front was designed as a series of simple arches, and the clearstory with its cleaning passage and triforium arcade of arched triplets completed a basic ordinance for the bay elevation. This fine style, which might be called 'Anglian', is seen in Saxon Winchester, Peter-borough Cathedral, and such abbeys as Binham and Blyth.

But Roman authority was bound in the end to insist upon the expulsion of all traces of Byzantinism and enforce the adoption of a style which was to be 'Romanesque' and based upon the reintroduction of the Classical column. The Continent accepted this necessity as early as the eleventh century and began to employ Corinthianesque pillars in its churches, the arches they carried being balanced in an uncomfortable fashion upon their capitals. This enforced introduction of a motif alien to natural development deprived the Continent of ever creating a homogenous Gothic style such as was to become the glory of this country.

Towards the end of the eleventh century we find grotesque imitations of the Classical column appearing in such churches as Durham Cathedral and Waltham Abbey. They have Byzantinesque capitals and are scored with Anglo-Saxon axe-work. At Gloucester and Tewkesbury (Plate 2) they appear without these, to set a fashion of circular pillars which, however, becomes standard in parish churches throughout the West of England and ousts the heavy piers of the Anglian style. The Cistercians adopted the style unequivocally, adding the Gothic pointed arch. (Plate 21.)

A system of ordinance derived from the Byzantine construction was the use of massive piers for the crossing and each alternate support in the main arcade but with lighter pillars set alternately between them. This is the 'duplex' bay system which, after it became the practice to cover the main span with a high vault, enabled this to be set out in a series of great bays each of which incorporated two bays of the main arcade. The vaulting shafts of the high vault were carried right down to the floor beside the main piers of this, the intermediate supports, having less to do, being kept lighter in design.

The duplex bay can be seen echoed in elevational architecture by the choir arcade of Romsey Abbey and retained into the thirteenth century in the charming choir of Boxgrove Priory in Sussex (Plate 7), where the great bays are actually retained with notable architectural effect.

The great churches of twelfth-century England, notably primitive in their internal ordinance, were even less distinguished architecturally in their external presentation with their comparatively low walling, small windows, and in particular for the lack of those buttress compositions which played such a large part in the elevations of late-medieval architecture.

It seems difficult to believe that the builders of the greatest churches in the world of their day—unlike their distant mentors, the Byzantine engineers—had no knowledge whatsoever of the stresses invoked by arcuated construction other than that such strains existed. Knowing that insufficient abutment would let an arch down, they had not the least idea how the amount of the opposition should be calculated. Nor had they any conception of the principal of counterpoise and how to hold the abutment down by placing a heavy load upon it.

The weak point of the great churches was the crossing with its four tall arches carrying a light lantern which was simply a resumption of the clearstory over the ridges of the four roofs impinging upon the tower walls. Each of the four tall piers had side pressure from the much lower arcades set against it and striving to bow it—the resulting distortion can be seen dramatically illustrated in Salisbury Cathedral. A large number of crossings collapsed under these combined pressures. But one of the guiding inspirations of the medieval builder was faith that his work would not let him down, so he seems in some cases to have tempted fate by raising a lantern tower by a storey to provide a belfry, as at Tewkesbury, St. Albans, and Norwich Cathedral. This in fact turned out to be the correct move, for the top-loading which resulted from this additional weight saved the crossing arches below from collapse.

The lantern towers continued to collapse right through the thirteenth century, one of the results of these disasters being the creation of the glorious octagon of Ely.

The success which attended the raising of lanterns to form belfries inaugurated the era of soaring central towers raised simply for the joy of creating a structure of superlative beauty visible from afar. What is so extraordinary is that their builders had no idea when they started work on a tower founded upon four isolated piers whether they would ever be able to complete it. The constructional problems involved in building towers such as those of Lincoln Cathedral would have been fantastic. Imagine the scaffolding alone, and the problems attending upon the raising of such masses of material—timber, stone, mortar—to such a great height above the ground. And over all the problem of the crushing strength of the four crossing piers. Did the builders ever wonder whether the next stone hauled up would be the last as the whole structure slid into ruin?

How many of these glorious creations toppled like factory chimneys in a cloud of mortar-dust during the years following 1539! From the beginning of tower-building in this country, all were covered with tall steeples, some of them of great complexity, the forerunners of the 'whispering spires' which would have contributed so dramatically to the architectural splendour of medieval England.

It is noticeable that the abbey church of the twelfth century does not appear to have been provided with a *campanile* in which to hang its bells. What was the arrangement at, say, Norwich Cathedral before its lantern tower was raised to form a belfry? Some churches undoubtedly retained timber belfries belonging to an earlier church. It is noticeable that the twelfth-century Cistercians, prohibiting stone bell-towers, permitted the erection of timber bell-towers provided these were not elaborately constructed, which points not only to the survival of the timber tower at such a late date but also to the fact that these could be of such elaborate appearance as to offend against Cistercian susceptibilities.

The position adopted by the bell-tower is marked for all time by the magnificent structure at Ely. As has been suggested, the great church of the eleventh century may sometimes have been added to the east side of an earlier timber church, probably a tall structure carrying its bells within the timbered interior of its central feature. Such a structure might well have been retained, after the rebuilding of the church in stone, to serve as a bell-tower until such time as a stone one could be erected. This is what apparently happened at Blackmore where the tower was never replaced.

Until the building of the splendid tower at Fountains Abbey shortly before the Suppression, the Cistercians seem to have had no stone bell-towers. They were however allowed timber towers so presumably erected them. The only fragment remaining of a Cistercian lantern is at Kirkstall Abbey in Yorkshire (Plate 4) and this was clearly raised at a very late date to provide a belfry. It may have replaced a timber tower and this may in fact have been the Cistercian method of providing themselves with belfries by hanging the bells in a timber steeple above the crossing.

But the standard site for a bell-tower was at the west end of the church. Winchester Cathedral had a western tower, pulled down in order to enable the nave to be properly lit by a large west window. This was probably the reason for the doubling of western towers which provides most of the English cathedrals with their west fronts. Double west towers are seldom found at abbeys, but the two medium-sized priories of Kirkham in Yorkshire and Llanthony in Monmouthshire (Plate 6) both had twin-towered west fronts—a typical example of Augustinian enterprise.

Other Augustinian churches which had twin west towers are those of Worksop and Thurgarton in Nottinghamshire.

The Benedictine abbey of Elstow near Bedford has a detached bell-tower sited to the north of the nave in the same position as that of Chichester Cathedral and the destroyed one at Salisbury.

The bell-tower of the medieval parish church was frequently built beside the nave where it sometimes served as a porch-tower. The Augustinian priory of Stavordale in Somerset had a tower attached to the south side of its nave opposite the cloister, while the Premonstratensian abbey of Bradsole in Kent has a large tower forming the central feature of a chapel set in the angle between the nave and the north transept and today representing the most prominent feature of the ruins.

Towards the end of the monastic era there seems to have been a move towards the building of western bell-towers at the ends of abbey churches. The windows of the nave were now very much larger and the necessity for a west window no longer existed. Moreover every parish church had a western bell-tower, many of them being exceedingly fine features. Lilleshall Abbey in Shrop-

shire, Bolton Priory in Yorkshire, and Furness Abbey in Lancashire began large western towers but were checked by the Suppression. A huge tower was erected over the two westernmost
bays of the nave of Malmesbury Abbey in Wiltshire but it fell
down, an example of the risks run by the medieval builder with his
reliance upon the triumph of faith over ignorance.

The west towers completed at Wymondham Abbey in Norfolk
and Christchurch Priory in Hampshire are of contemporary
parish-church design but very large in scale. They almost give an
impression of having been erected in order to give the nave of the
monastic building the appearance of a parish church.

All these towers were erected at a period when the Suppression
must have seemed on the horizon. The early Cistercians would
have been shocked to have seen the beautiful north tower of
Fountains Abbey (Plate 27), just completed in time, as was the
even more splendid bell-tower of Evesham Abbey as a swan-song
to one of the greatest of English Benedictine abbeys.

These later towers would all have been covered with flat lead
roofs and surrounded by battlemented and pinnacled parapets
presenting a very different appearance from the earlier towers with
their tall timber steeples. But steeple and tower fell together when
one of the piers which had carried them for so long was mined and
sprung after 1539.

Beneath the towers which remain today from medieval England
we see the abbeys as large churches—perhaps as cathedrals but as
likely as not just parish churches to which they have been converted. But the soul of each great church has been destroyed—
consigned to oblivion when the heart of each, the monastic choir
to accommodate which these splendid churches were so laboriously
built, was torn away and thrown on a bonfire.

# 5

# The Monastic Choir

The Rule of St. Benedict envisaged its adherents as offering up their prayers in a humble class of structure described as an oratory. But it soon became apparent that the monks had to be established in a proper church which could accommodate them in a more dignified state. The need was for some setting in which they could be seen as a choir.

The churches with which St. Benedict would have been familiar were the basilicas of Rome, long structures each terminating in an apse before which rose a rectangular platform called a *bema* upon which a choir led the responses. Derived from a similar platform found in the contemporary synagogue the *bema* would probably represent what would have been at that time understood as an architectural 'choir'.

The problem was how to fit this into the type of church which under the aegis of Byzantine architects was being erected throughout Europe.

The ordinary small churches were basically square apartments surrounded by four projecting bays of no great depth. To the east was the altar in its apse. One might suppose that the place for the choir would have been in the western bay facing this and extending into the central area or crossing if necessary.

The question constantly poses itself as to whether the early Byzantine abbey church, whether of the Eastern or Western type, ever in fact had a nave. There was no reason for it to have provided one. The abbey church belonged to the monks; the laity had their parish church.

It seems not unlikely that the centralized type of church was entirely occupied by the monks who had their choir—presumably, but far from certainly, provided with seating in what was to become the Western fashion—in the western arm of the cross. (Fig. 13a.)

However far back we go, however, we seem to find the monastic choir invariably approached from its western end; if this tradition goes back to the centralized church it makes it certain that the west end of the church must have formed a kind of internal narthex to the choir. The conjectural plan of Romsey abbey church (Fig. 13b) suggests this, as does the plan of South Elmham where the actual choir screen would have been part of the internal timber-work east of the twin-doored 'rood screen'.

Is not the abbey nave as we know it simply the result of tacking on an unnecessary western appendage to a centralized Byzantinesque church in order to convert it into a Roman 'basilica'? Were the laity really welcomed in the nave of the abbey church and was it originally intended to provide a nave altar and facilities for worship to people who already had their own parish churches?

As the square Byzantine plan began to develop an east–west axis more in line with 'basilican' practice, the western bay might be increased in projection so as to begin to appear as a true nave independent of the crossing and thus providing more space for the choir of the monks.

If we accept the normal position of the eleventh-century monastic choir as representing development along traditional lines, it would seem probable that the explanation suggested above is the reason for its being sited immediately west of the crossing.

For this is the position of the monks' choir in the long nave of the eleventh-century abbey church (Figs. 6, 12 and 13c), the rest of the building to the west being assigned to the laity, the nave having been gratuitously lengthened for the purpose and perhaps to provide an area for processional display.

The division between the monastic part of the church and that given over to the laity was rigidly indicated by a stone screen, the rood screen, which formed the reredos for the nave altar. Pass doors on either side of this enabled processions to enter the choir from the nave.

Monastic rood screens remain in a number of churches through having been retained at the Suppression when the monks' part of the church was destroyed leaving the public nave untouched. They may be seen at Malmesbury Abbey, at St. Albans Cathedral, and in a ruined state at the Fenland abbey of Crowland.

East of the rood screen was the choir-screen proper, the *pulpitum*, the western limit of the monks' choir and containing its entrance doorway. The space between the two screens was known as the retro-choir and was the predecessor of the college ante-chapel. It is said to have been used by sick monks unable to sit or stand through the long choir services. The duplication of screens was, however, unavoidable in order that the choir door should have some protection and the nave altar a reredos. The retro-choir would also have served as a useful acoustic barrier between nave and choir.

The choir was designed as a completely enclosed apartment set in the midst of the great building about it. (Fig. 12.) It was a long room, having at one end the high altar and at the other end the seats of the monks set facing each other and across the western screen on either side of the entrance doorway.

In an aisled building, as was usual in the great abbeys but not necessarily so in the case of the smaller houses, the sides of the choir were enclosed by screens, filling the openings between the pillars of the arcade.

Eastward of the choir stalls was the presbytery, an open area separating them from the high altar set beyond the altar step—of which, by the way, the medieval church had but one. It was this space which was usually sited beneath the most striking architectural feature of the church's interior, the high-arched crossing supporting the lantern of windows far overhead. Where the side-screens of the choir passed this area lateral doorways led into the transepts with their side-chapels.

The loss of these monastic choirs has left us no chance of being able to appreciate the perfection of their architectural setting beneath the soaring caverns mounting upwards towards a corona of light.

It is tempting to think of the high dome as the symbolic element

7. Boxgrove

8. Dore

in Byzantine church design. Externally it seems to be pointing to the heavens—in its steepled western form the illusion is even more insistent. Internally both achieve the same effect of a high vault surrounded with light, attracting heaven-wards the prayers of the worshippers gathered below.

Certainly until the end of the eleventh century the monastic choir was never far removed from the crossing. Down-draughts

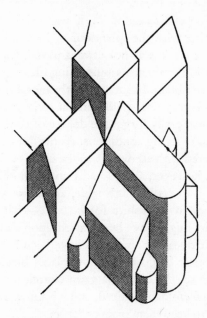

Fig. 7
*Early Benedictine east end*
The eastern arm of the church ends in a tall apse. Small apses are added at the ends of the aisles and in the eastern walls of the transepts

notwithstanding, some choirs were actually sited immediately beneath it. An impressive choir still discoverable today is that of the Bishops of St. Davids.

The seating arrangements of the choir were very different from what we find in the great churches—Christchurch Priory in Hampshire is a notable exception—since they have been fitted out as Victorian chancels with seatings for surpliced choirboys.

There was originally just the one row of seats passing down the sides of the choir and along its western screen on either side of the choir door. Today there may be three rows of seats leaving little more than a passage down the centre. The old choirs, lacking this clutter, would have been seen as splendid apartments having the dignity of a great council chamber. One can today recover something of the effect by visiting the modern abbey of Quarr in the Isle of Wight.

The western stalls from which the lateral seating could be supervised would have been occupied by the abbot, the prior, and other senior officers of the community such as the precentor, sacrist or cellarer.

The choir seating itself was originally simple benching contrasting with the splendour of its architectural setting. The floor of the choir was not always paved, for paving stones are found only in certain areas and paving tiles were very difficult and expensive to obtain. In such cases the monks had to make do with straw.

When gazing spellbound at some magnificent medieval church one can easily forget the degree of civilization it may represent in terms of living conditions. As the floor of the nobleman's hall was covered with straw so was the choir of the church. The lord in his hall, however, always had some kind of boarded or paved dais on which to set his high table, and there are indications—at Byland Abbey in Yorkshire for instance—that the seating in the abbey choirs might have been raised upon similar platforms. The abbey choir does not appear to have been heated by a hearth as in the domestic hall, but in some places braziers may have been used. Even so, the cold of a great church on a winter night must have been formidable indeed, and it is known that the monks often used furs to keep them from collapse.

During the fourteenth century the seats became proper wooden stalls each having lateral protection and, no doubt still more appreciated, projecting canopies to preserve their occupants from the draughts sweeping down from the windows of the lantern. It was in the design of these canopies that the woodcarvers were able to extend themselves until they rivalled in their pinnacled ebullience the chantries and tomb-canopies lining the presbytery away to the east. All these furnishings played their part in keeping the choir as tightly enclosed as possible, the only gaps being the choir doorway to the west and the two upper doors at the crossing leading to the transepts.

The presbytery was the focus of the architectural effort within the church. Set in the lateral arches the chantry chapels and the canopied tombs of the great men of the medieval world added to the hall-like character of the enclosed choir and led the way towards the high altar.

At the extreme end of the choir was the reredos, the splendid sculptured back-cloth to the high altar. Those of St. Albans, Southwark, and Winchester remain to give us some idea of the

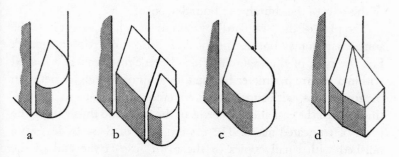

Fig. 8   *Types of apse*
(a) shows the apse in its simplest form, (b) the same added to a chancel, (c) the two combined under the same roof to give an apsidal end to an eastern arm. (d) shows the polygonal form probably derived from timber-built Anglo-Saxon apses

magnificence of these great tableaux even though their niches are today empty of their ancient statuary.

Beside the high altar on its south side was a group of stone seats carried up above the heads of the niches with elaborate canopies and finials all in sculptured stonework. These are the sedilia, permanent seating for the priests engaged in the celebration of the Mass.

Among the most beautiful of the remaining sedilia are those in the ruins of the presbytery of Furness Abbey in Lancashire. Gloucester also has a fine group of four; Tewkesbury and Selby also retain them. Like all monastic furniture they are of fourteenth- or fifteenth-century date.

It will be remembered that the great Benedictine churches of the eleventh and twelfth century were really little more than early Byzantine churches on the end of a long 'basilican' nave and that their eastern arms were only some two bays long and often aisle-less, with just the terminal apse to provide some sense of dignity. Such a plan was perfectly adequate for the accommodation of the monks' choir and the presbytery beyond leading up to the high altar, but it must have looked very cramped aesthetically and above all allowed no space for procession behind the altar. Development of this part of the church was bound to ensue.

The plan of the 'standard' Byzantine church is often given the somewhat clumsy but not unapt designation of 'cross-in-square'. For the plan of the main structure is cruciform but is enclosed within a square perimeter by the filling-up of the angles between the four limbs, with square areas covered with lean-to roofs abut-ting against the east and west arms of the cross and thus having the form of truncated aisles. The eastern ends of these 'aisles' were finished with small copies of the main apse at the end of the chancel. (Fig. 7.)

Thus the Byzantine east end almost invariably displayed ex-ternally a group of three apses, a main one flanked by a pair of smaller copies. This became the standard eastern termination for the Benedictine abbey church of the beginning of the second millennium.

The difference between this and the 'cross-in-square' proto-type, however, lay in the fact that the arms of the cross now projected beyond the original square outline, so that the chancel, transepts, and nave began to develop the dimension of length. The small square aisles followed suit, beginning to adopt their normal medieval position as flankers to the long axis of the building.

While the western arm became extended to a considerable length, however, the monastic choir remained in what was prob-ably its original site immediately west of the crossing, now at the east end of a long nave. (Fig. 13c.)

We have arrived at a stage where the presbytery of the abbey church projected two bays from the crossing and had a square gabled end carrying three apses. The next stage was a Continental development which appeared in this country only in a few of the more important abbeys.

The monks seem to have set great store upon processional activities. The site of the high altar at the east end of the church formed an obstruction to a possible processional route behind it. The solution was to carry the main apse on pillars connecting the arcades of the side aisles and bring these round to meet each other

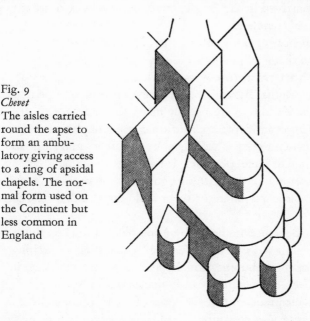

Fig. 9
*Chevet*
The aisles carried round the apse to form an ambu-latory giving access to a ring of apsidal chapels. The nor-mal form used on the Continent but less common in England

behind the altar. This is the French termination known as the *chevet*; it was eventually developed by the construction of a ring of apses projecting from the semicircular aisle (Fig. 9) until it attained the fine form seen in the thirteenth-century rebuilding at Westminster Abbey.

The *chevet* appears in this country round about the year 1100 in various forms: at the end of a two-bay presbytery or one extended to four bays as at Norwich Cathedral. At Tewkesbury in Glou-cestershire (Plate 2) it surrounds a semi-hexagonal apse; at Canter-bury Cathedral the apse is itself two bays in length with its sides canted towards each other, making four bays in all with the apse.

St. Augustine's Abbey at Canterbury had a normal French-type *chevet* with a four-bay presbytery and three small apses projecting from the aisle.

The apse, one of the most interesting of architectural features, enjoys a great antiquity. Structurally a horizontal arch, it probably originates from early attempts to build a revetment façade to an earthen mound so that an access tunnel, entered through a doorway contrived in the façade, could be provided in order to reach the burial chamber.

Stonehenge, the tomb of the Sun, is a great moundless apse and the rising silhouette of the five great trilithons recalls that of an earthen mound. (See Appendix.)

The original Byzantine apses, never intended to be regarded as external features, were usually made semi-hexagonal on the outside. This type of apse appears in a number of places in this country in parish churches as well as abbey churches and cathedrals such as Lichfield. Here, however, it is always the same inside and out, so it seems likely that the English apse is derived from Anglo-Saxon carpentry attempts to provide their timber churches with apses.

The Benedictines began by using plenty of apses. But it should be remembered that those features which look so exciting on the plans of their churches which have been excavated may in reality have been comparatively insignificant and in no way comparable with their predecessors, the apses of the Byzantine churches. The main apse was certainly tall and impressive, but those attached to the low aisles would have been no higher than these. (Fig. 7.) Quite often the apses at the ends of aisles do not show at all externally, as at Romsey Abbey.

It may have been a combination of the Celtic influence which never adopted the Byzantine apse but was content with a gable, or it may have been the timber-building tradition of the Anglo-Saxons which was to blame, but the fact remains that the apse never became popular in this country and our ecclesiastical architecture relies upon no opulent Continental *chevet* for its effect. There was just one period when it seemed as though it might return, as a result of King John's belated attempt to placate the

Cistercians he had been ill-using and at the same time encourage them in their new acceptance of the need for fine architecture, by founding Beaulieu Abbey in Hampshire. Its magnificent church—begun about 1221 and now utterly vanished—had a presbytery of three bays and was surrounded by double aisles which met around

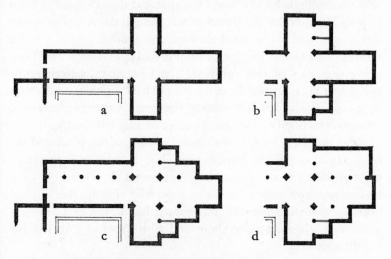

Fig. 10    *Development of canons' churches*
The great Augustinian churches followed the Benedictine plan. But the more normal plan was a simple cross of four long arms, none of them aisled (a). Eastern aisles to the transepts, universal with Cistercian churches, were often included in the canons' plans (b). An aisle was added to the nave on the side opposite the cloister, and short aisles on both sides of the eastern arm (c). The last addition might be a large lady chapel flanking the presbytery (d)

its apse to form a processional ambulatory with ten chapels in the outermost aisle. During the thirteenth century the Cistercians repeated the *chevet* in its full Continental elaboration at Croxden Abbey in Staffordshire and Hayles Abbey in Gloucestershire both of which had five projecting chapels; a century later the Cistercian *chevet* at Vale Royal Abbey in Cheshire was built with seven of these. These adventures seem all the more remarkable when one remembers that the Cistercian Order had been founded with the express purpose of discouraging architectural extravagances.

The only examples remaining of the *chevet* in this country are to be seen at the Benedictine abbeys of Westminster and Tewkesbury, and at Norwich Cathedral.

These were undoubtedly Continental intrusions into English architecture. The Celtic gable-end remained the accepted termination for an English church and the apse was discontinued as soon as possible, even by the Benedictines, though the semi-hexagonal form continued to be used through the Gothic period for the termination of the presbytery, Pershore Abbey and Bayham Abbey being examples of this survival. The Cistercians, entering this country in 1128, refused from the start to have anything to do with it, a rejection which was among the first of their architectural reforms which led to the development of English Gothic.

After the great burst of monastic building which produced the huge churches of the Benedictine abbeys and the Augustinian priories, many monasteries were built round churches built on a less extravagant scale. This was especially true of the canons' houses, Augustinian and Premonstratensian, whose first churches were often aisle-less throughout and with naves of a reasonable length. (See Fig. 10a.)

These second-rank churches, however, generally had long transepts with altars along the east walls, often in Cistercian-type transept aisles. (See Plates 4 and 32.) Sometimes the innermost chapels projected eastwards for an extra bay so as to form short aisles to the presbytery but not extending to its east wall. (See Figs. 10c and 11b.) This was a device borrowed from the Benedictines but the canons dispensed with the fussy little apses and contented themselves with plain east walls in what was becoming the standard English termination.

The early Cistercian churches were also built with aisle-less naves. These were soon, however, to be replaced by large structures capable of accommodating the large numbers of lay-brothers required by the Cistercian organization.

The first Cistercian presbyteries had been humble projections, clearing the crossing by two bays and having no aisles, though perhaps a pair of flanking chapels lacking any connection with the presbytery (See Figs. 22 and 24.) The Benedictines sited chapels in the transepts, each in its small apse; the Cistercians built an eastern aisle and set their chapels in this, a much tidier arrangement.

During the early part of the thirteenth century they almost invariably decided to develop their presbyteries on a scale commensurate with the nave, extending it by a bay or two and flanking it with proper aisles to the full length of the arm.

Viewed from the inside the French *chevet* was an uncomfortable-looking feature owing to the difficulty of making an arcade turn

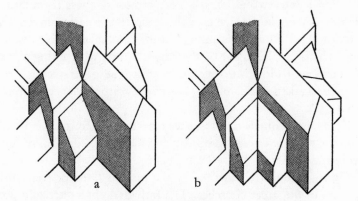

Fig. 11   *East ends of canons' churches*
Eastern aisles to transepts were common to most monastic churches (a). Short aisles to the eastern arm are also often found (b)

in so small a radius as fifteen feet or so. It certainly meant crowding the pillars together in an unattractive fashion and caused the arches above them to be absurdly stilted.

The few English *chevets* were designed much more sensibly around the semi-hexagonal 'Anglo-Saxon timber' apse so that three normal arches performed the same task as the five distorted ones trying to turn the apse of the French *chevet*. The remains of the *chevet* at Tewkesbury Abbey (Plate 2) illustrate the English plan.

But the Cistercians had their own ideas, based apparently upon the Anglo-Saxon timber churches. Having carried their aisles to the east wall they supported this on three arches and just turned the aisle across beyond them (Fig. 23a), a neat if unspectacular solution which could have been seen at the great church of Byland in Yorkshire. The eastern aisle was filled with five chapels in a row, the ambulatory being achieved by simply setting the high altar one bay in front of the eastern arches.

At Abbey Dore in Herefordshire (Plate 8) the Cistercians developed the eastern aisle in a more sophisticated fashion by constructing a narrow building passing across the east front of the church (see Fig. 23b) having a row of four slender pillars along it dividing it into two aisles, the westernmost of these forming the ambulatory while the five chapels occupied the easternmost. The interior effect is quite charming, but the external effect is now lost through the replacement of the original roof with a single low-pitched lean-to looking very un-Gothic. The gables at each end have been taken down making the whole feature appear meaningless.

This interesting device was later repeated at Hereford Cathedral with the gable ends carried out beyond the aisle walls so as to form projecting transepts.

During the thirteenth century the eastern transept frequently appears in the great churches. The cathedral choirs actually produced a second crossing (see Fig. 14) and some abbey churches, such as Waltham, did the same. But the low wings flanking the extreme east end of the church were more to the monastic taste as they enabled the provision of a long row of eastern chapels. (See Fig. 30.) Malmesbury Abbey had these lateral wings and at Pershore they may be seen flanking a semi-hexagonal apse. It is interesting to note the similarity between the plan of the monastic east end and that of the Late Gothic parish church. The purposes, however, are probably not the same.

The monastic eastern transept reached its culmination in the Chapel of the Nine Altars at Cistercian Fountains (Plate 27) where, as at Durham Cathedral, it was raised to the full height of the church.

This was a strangely insular retort to the Continental *chevet* and helps as much as anything to explain the simple approach made by the early Gothic architects to their problems. But it was too primitive in its effect to be able to compare with the magnificent

Continental coronas, and was abandoned for a typically English solution.

It was appreciated that all the presbyteries needed was length enough for the ambulatory and its chapels. The wider bays—twenty feet or so—which were being used made it possible to fit both ambulatory and chapels into a single-bay addition to the presbytery. So the final acceptance of the uncomplicated east gable was finally accepted, the eastern aisle abandoned and the east gable carried forward to the east wall with the aisles flanking it to the end (Plate 17), forming an eastern termination which, if not so elaborate as the Continental form, maintained a sense of dignity which prevented its appearing austere.

It will be remembered that the central tower of the pre-medieval church had been provided simply to serve as a 'lantern tower' continuing the clearstory over the junction of the four arms of the cross. Enterprising attempts to raise the central feature, as at St. Albans or Tewkesbury, to provide a belfry having met with success both in crowning the building with a splendid central tower and having at the same time reduced the lateral pressure on the piers supporting it, the central bell-tower had by the end of the twelfth century become a standard feature. Thus the rebuilding of the eastern arm was usually combined with the replacement of the whole central crossing and transepts, the crossing piers themselves being designed as stately groupings of richly-moulded pillars (Plate 9) very different from the crude Byzantine piers of the twelfth century.

The thirteenth-century movement aimed at the provision of completely new east ends in place of simple chancels spread to the parish churches and many an old twelfth-century nave was thus splendidly augmented, special attention being given to the pillars and arches of the crossing.

A desire for the development of the presbytery, the eastern end of the monks' choir, is understandable if only in order to enhance the charm of this important part of the church. But another factor was the necessity of providing space for the interment of the great men of the country who were rightly regarded as worthy of permanent memorials. (See Fig. 12.) And where the shrine of some

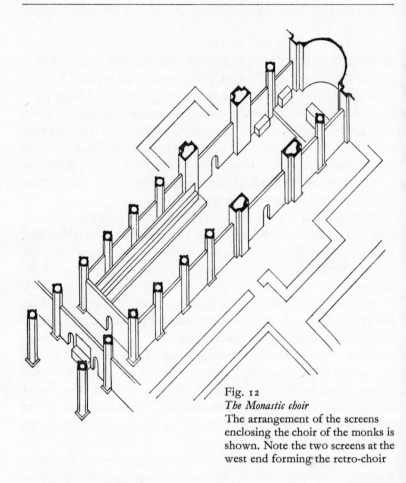

Fig. 12
*The Monastic choir*
The arrangement of the screens
enclosing the choir of the monks is
shown. Note the two screens at the
west end forming the retro-choir

local saint existed, as at Westminster or St. Albans, a chapel was
required for it behind the high altar; this would still further
extend the eastern arm of the church.

Monastic ritual seems to have called for plenty of exercise in the
form of processions, the church in particular being explored at
least once a week during a perambulation of every one of its
altars. This made it desirable to plan a route which would enable
the procession to proceed smoothly round the building without
having to retrace its steps.

The original plans had envisaged the high altar set against the east wall, awkwardly situated to include in a processional route. The French and Cistercian systems for providing an ambulatory behind the altar have been discussed above. The final decision, however, was to provide two bays of the church east of the high altar to produce a processional way with a row of chapels along its eastern side, against the east wall.

In this fashion were the monks' choirs improved, and the eastern arms of the great churches extended until they at least began to balance the long naves and often, in the case of the smaller abbeys, began to assert the greater dignity of the presbytery.

The tragedy of the abbeys is that it was these lovely Gothic presbyteries which became the principal targets for the destroyers of 1539, possibly for the reason that they not only indicated the most sacred part of the monastery but also because they could be appreciated as works of art too lovely to be preserved without threatening the permanence of the Suppression.

So they all came down, many to be represented today only by tracings on the ground as at Thornton in Lincolnshire, Kirkham in Yorkshire, and Whalley in Lancashire, razed with what seems to have been a deliberate intention to leave no trace of something of beauty which national policy dictated must henceforth be forgotten.

It does not appear to have been in the minds of the builders of these long presbyteries—at Augustinian Kirkham eight bays in length—to transfer the monastic choir into the eastern arm. Long before these tremendous architectural excursions took place this project had been considered.

One of the greatest abbeys in Europe was that of Cluny in Burgundy, seat of an Abbot who ruled as a kind of second Pope over an immensely rich and powerful monastic Order. His deputy in this country was the Prior of Lewes in Sussex, who during the twelfth century enlarged his priory church in a truly spectacular fashion by pulling down its eastern arm and building in its place a complete new church with nave, crossing, transepts, and presbytery ending in a French-type *chevet*. He thus provided for his choir a complete church. Its four-bay nave contained the stalls of

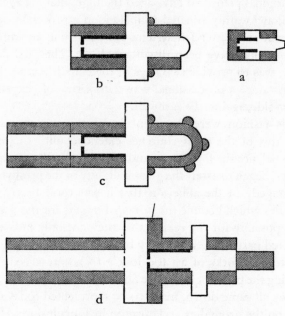

Fig. 13    *Positions of choir*
(a) shows the conjectural position of the
choir in an Anglo-Saxon timber church.
(b) shows a simple church providing no
nave for the laity but only a retro-choir
acting as a lobby before the choir door
(see Romsey). (c) shows the fully-
developed great church of the twelfth
century and (d) the final stage after the
choir had been moved entirely into an
enlarged and elaborated eastern arm

the monks. Eastwards of this was the new crossing with transepts,
and finally a French-type *chevet* with five radiating chapels.

Later in the century the Augustinian abbey of Waltham in
Essex constructed a similar addition, this time with a new nave
eight bays long with the choir accommodated in its eastern half,
transepts four bays long with eastern aisles, and an eastern arm
five bays in length. Of this huge church only the original nave, a
most impressive example of early architecture, remains today.

The unpopularity of Cluniac Lewes may have contributed to the determination with which its great church was razed in 1539, but it seems a pity that Waltham, with its tomb of King Harold, was so thoroughly destroyed by Englishmen. But Glastonbury, burial place of Arthur himself, was contemptuously handed over to the wreckers.

At Salisbury in 1220 was begun a cathedral church which must be taken as indicating the current trend of thought among some of the planners of great churches. Here the eastern arm was built as a complete church with the bishop's choir in its 'nave' and east of this another set of transepts opposite the choir doors; finally there are a presbytery, ambulatory and eastern chapels. (Figs. 13 and 14.)

The bishop's church was thus set completely east of the great crossing which with its transepts was given over to the laity. This was an obvious development and its principle was adopted, as will be seen in Chapter 15, when the friars began to build churches in this country.

The eastern transept, introduced so long ago at Lewes Priory, did not find its way into many of the abbey churches of this country, but a notable example may be seen in the impressive ruins of the Premonstratensian abbey of Bayham in Sussex (Plate 31) a church which was clearly in its day a notable contribution to the architecture of this country by its distinguished Order.

Introduced for aesthetic reasons in order that the monks' choir should not be deprived of the spacious effect of a crossing, the eastern transept also had a practical use in that its eastern wall could be used for chapels. A variation upon this device is the remarkable transept at Fountains Abbey (Plate 27) which is set right across the east end of the presbytery and has in it nine altars.

As the Cistercian churches were all dedicated to Our Lady they had no need to concern themselves with the provision of lady chapels. Other Orders, not so fortunate, had to choose between one of two sites for this. They could upset the balance of the presbytery by enlarging an aisle, as at Thetford or Castle Acre, both of them Cluniac priories. (See also Fig. 10d.) Or they could project it eastwards from the main ambulatory (see Figs. 14 and 30), reducing its chapels by two and setting the lady chapel between the remaining pair. The Benedictine lady chapel can be

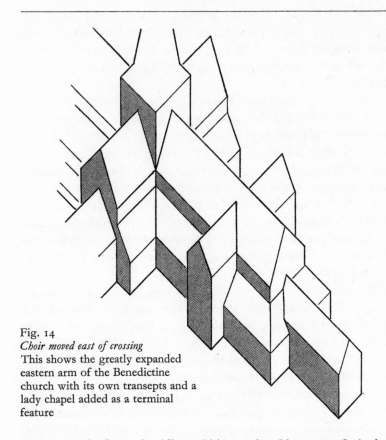

Fig. 14
*Choir moved east of crossing*
This shows the greatly expanded
eastern arm of the Benedictine
church with its own transepts and a
lady chapel added as a terminal
feature

seen to good effect at St. Albans Abbey and at Gloucester Cathedral
in which it extends not from an eastern aisle but a tall east wall
containing a window of tremendous illumination.

The thirteenth century was a period during which the chancels
of parish churches were being lengthened. Smaller priories
lacking the funds to pull down and rebuild their presbyteries with
aisles and ambulatory were often content to build a longer eastern
arm without aisles. The interesting ruined church of Finchale
Priory in Durham with its long transepts as well as presbytery
suggest the form of the contemporary parish church. By the fourteenth century even the more important priories such as that at
Bolton in Yorkshire (Plate 32) were concentrating upon erecting

aisle-less presbyteries lit by very large traceried windows in the completely developed style of the High Gothic.

The most essential aspect of the monastic house was its privacy. The services in the splendid choirs were entirely limited to the professed monks and novices, the public being rigidly restricted to the nave. In order for them to obtain even a glimpse of the community and its ritual they would have to wait there for an occasional emergence—on Sunday, for example—of a procession round the nave. For the monks themselves such a procession may well have been a pleasant change from the tedium of huddling in their choir for hours on end.

The procession left the choir on the side farthest from the cloister. It then passed to the transept with its chapels and thence all round the east end of the church to the opposite transept. Where the nave aisle joined this was the doorway, called the eastern processional doorway, leading into the east walk of the cloister. Through this the procession passed to visit the chapter house and various other claustral apartments to be included in the inspection.

Reaching the west walk of the cloister they passed the outer parlour and re-entered the nave of the church by its western processional doorway. They would then treat the laity gathered in the church to a view of the community mustered in their turn for inspection. The procession finally came to a halt before the nave altar before dividing to pass through the doors in the rood screen to the retro-choir and the main choir doorway.

Were their shades to return today they would find no rood-screen, no *pulpitum*, no dignified Gothic apartment to receive them . . . only a jumble of Victorian choir seats crowding them in as they disappeared into the halation of a great east window.

# 6

# The Monks' House

St. Benedict's Rule enjoined his monks to live together in a common house. But he was living in a country where such things were possible, a land which had become the heir to great building traditions and had experienced architecture in many advanced forms. The provision of such a structure as a common house would have been utterly beyond the capabilities of a group of Celtic monks struggling to survive the Dark Ages. Their monastery would have been a collection of huts erected out of the same materials and in the same fasion as any other hut. The indication that they lived in a community would probably have been the presence round their settlement of a ring fence or hedge of stones. Excavation has shown that there were indeed a number of such sites scattered about the country, each consisting of a number of primitive huts.

Even when we arrive at the period of the Danish invasions, reading in the Chronicle that monastery after monastery was burnt we know nothing of what these were like architecturally though we can form some vague impression of the timber churches from existing examples of later date. The actual dwellings, however, have not yet been investigated to find out whether there existed anything in the nature of a common house. One can say with probability that it was unlikely that a monastic house of the primitive Anglo-Saxon period resembled the timber hall of the secular landowner. Of one thing only can we be certain: that it was of a single storey.

To be able to appreciate the spectacular development in

domestic architecture accompanying the monastic colonization of England at the beginning of the second millennium one has to consider the state of this in England at the time. Stone houses were non-existent. A stately home was represented by a timber hall closely resembling a barn and probably in an equal state of confusion. Ordinary houses were hovels of poles and thatch.

In addition to bringing with them a sophisticated building technique employing the craft of masonry, the monks introduced a new mode of life, that of living on an upper floor or *piano nobile*. Hitherto no one in this country had ever lived above ground level. The monks scorned to live anywhere else!

The Romans had built multi-storey houses. The Byzantines had followed their example as did also the Arabs whom the Crusaders encountered in the course of the Crusades. In fact the world which centred round the Mediterranean and its limbs was living on an upper floor.

Two-storeyed private houses of stone appeared in this country at the close of the twelfth century and seem to have been called 'King John's Houses' for this reason. But the monastic house appeared in this country a century and a half earlier. The arrangement of the two types is identical, the only difference being in length. They both have two storeys of which the upper is the living-room, and both are entered up a stair to a doorway on the first floor.

The important feature of each is that architectural innovation —the upper floor. The feature which is called in mediaeval Latin *solarium*. The feature which is not, and never has been, a 'solar'!

When will students of medieval matters abandon the use of this word to describe the great chamber of a mediaeval house? There is no such word. The word 'soller' was used during the Middle Ages to describe first a timber floor and later any kind of upper floor such as that supported upon stone vaulting. What we now call a 'rood loft' in a parish church was in its own day called 'the soller above the screen'. True this was Latinized as *solarium* but this does not give it a solar origin and it certainly never was intended to represent a sun room—in this country of all places!

At the time when the word was introduced—it seems possible that it has the same root as the French *solive* meaning a floor joist—an upper floor was not only a novelty but in its own right a notable feature—a *piano nobile*. A soller was not a room but a stage. The preposition employed with it was 'on'—*on* the soller, never *in*.

And soller is still used today to indicate the timber stages in a mine-shaft.

The Classical Romans lived in single-storey houses which spread their accommodation over a wide area. The Byzantines set their living accommodation on an upper floor away from the noise and other annoyances of the terrestrial world.

Probably the earlier two-storey houses had timber upper floors. But in the monastic house it would seem that timber might not have been considered a suitable material for this purpose, being too impermanent, or perhaps even too unarchitectural. To take matters still further, medieval manners combined with the straw which took the place of carpets might have rendered timber floors insanitary and liable to rot.

Thus all monastic upper floors were built up from below in the form of stone vaulting. Over narrow ground-floor rooms this would be a tunnel vault, but over wider spans would have been divided up into a series of bays for covering with cross-vaulting on the 'groined' principle. A normal rectangular ground-floor apartment would be divided lengthwise by a row of pillars passing down its centre so as to produce a series of small vaulting bays each as nearly as possible square on plan and thus with a side equal to half the width of the room. In this fashion every room in a monastery having an upper storey was planned so as to provide on its main floor a strong fireproof and rot-proof 'stone soller'.

By the last century of the first millennium, Western European architecture had reached a stage at which the upper storey had become an accepted element in domestic planning. Suspended floors could be of wooden planks. Some of these floors may still be in existence from medieval times. The writer believes he has found a medieval timber floor at Cleeve Abbey in Somerset; its planks are six inches thick and a foot and a half wide.

But the timber floor would probably have been regarded by

9. Rievaulx

10. Rievaulx

the twelfth-century abbey builders as a type of construction unworthy of architectural consideration.

Medieval architecture belongs to the class known as *arcuated* which is to say that openings were spanned by arches of stone. Arches are turned upon a temporary centering of timbers, withdrawn after the arch has been completed. If openings are kept equal in span the centering timbers can be used again and again, except in arcades in which each arch supports with its abutment those on either side of it.

A series of stone arches set end to end so as to produce a long tunnel creates what is known as a stone vault. Tunnel or 'barrel' vaults—as they are called today—can be made of any length. They could also be thrown over a considerable span as can be seen in the choir of Ewenny Priory church in Glamorganshire.

But while in theory an arch can be turned over any span, in practice the amount of timber centering required can become unwieldy and expensive. Moreover, the rise of a semicircular arch is in proportion to its span, so that if turned for the purpose of creating an upper storey it might take up too much of this before the floor level was reached. Thus it was the invariable plan for the ground floors of two-storeyed buildings to be divided up with the rows of pillars described above.

By this means it would have been possible to have turned a pair of barrel vaults running side by side down the room to carry the floor above. Alternatively it would have been equally possible to have continued each arch in the central arcade across the room from wall to wall.

What actually was done was to adopt both these systems. Thus in each vaulting bay of the building there was a transverse vault intersecting with a section of a longitudinal vault, the two meeting and the diagonals crossing each bay. This system of vaulting with the two opposing vaults meeting at diagonal lines called 'groins' is known today as a groined vault. By making each vaulting bay square on plan and the silhouettes of the opposing arches equal the complications of forming the vault could be greatly reduced. It is for this reason that we find the plans of two-storeyed buildings so dimensioned that each is capable of being divided up internally into a series of equal squares, with a pillar at each intersection of the grid.

Groined vaulting was devised to serve two purposes. As originally conceived by the Imperial Roman engineers it was intended to be used to form a combined roof and ceiling and a more decent architectural covering than a jumble of timbers. Developed by the Byzantine engineers and used for church roofing, the stone vault was eventually introduced into this country during the eleventh century.

Vaulting serves two purposes. In its supporting role it carries the 'stone soller' above the aisles at the same time providing them with a decent ceiling. It attains its apotheosis when it is thrown over the main span of a church, high in the architectural heaven above the church paving, its stonework and carving becoming ever more elaborate until, in the twilight of the age of the abbots, we see it reach aesthetic perfection at Gloucester or Sherborne.

In order to construct a vault over perhaps thirty foot of span it was necessary to devise a method of economizing in the timber centering all of which had to be lifted up to a great height and moved about as the vault grew. The system developed was to construct the groins of the vault as a series of light arches or 'ribs', thus dividing each bay into four triangular 'severies' which could subsequently be filled in with a masonry 'web', worked on movable centering carried between the ribs. This is the 'ribbed vaulting' which during the eleventh century came to be used everywhere in the monastic churches and below the upper floors of their houses.

Of the later development of the Gothic rib-patterns one must comment in another place, for this belongs to the aesthetic aspect of architecture.

The most common feature encountered in the two-storeyed domestic architecture of the abbeys is the vaulted undercroft, carrying the main floor over, and always having a row of pillars down its centre. At first these pillars were sturdy but during the twelfth century they became slimmer and developed properly moulded bases and caps of the standard Byzantine 'cubiform' type. But with the coming of ribbed vaulting towards the end of the century builders began to dispense with pillars and carry the ribs down the supporting masonry until it reached the floor.

This variation in ordinance was developed during the Gothic era with the intention of relieving architecture from the tyranny of having to indicate the springing line of an arch by introducing an 'impost'—survival of the 'abacus' capping the Classical column. The 'continuous impost' was far more suited to the sweeping lines of the Gothic and we see it during the thirteenth century accepted

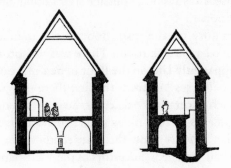

Fig. 15    *Section through monks' house and
rere-dorter*
The monks' dormitory is
shown raised above its vaulted
undercroft. At the same level
is the rere-dorter with its
passage giving access to a row
of seats set above a channel
through which was led the
great drain of the abbey

as appropriate for the nave arcade of the small Augustinian priory of Llanthony in Monmouthshire. (Plate 5.) By the fifteenth century it was being employed everywhere to facilitate the sweep of panelling round the soffits and jambs of arched openings.

Scattered about England are a number of small houses—most of them known as 'King John's Houses' which date from the end of the twelfth century. They are small in area, about twenty feet by thirty, and two storeys in height. The 'soller' may be a timber floor but is sometimes stone-vaulted, springing from two pillars below in the standard medieval fashion.

The entrance to each house is by a stair leading up to a doorway set near one end of one of the side walls. There is no doorway on the ground floor.

The houses of the monks are built in exactly the same fashion as these private houses save that they are rather wider in span— say thirty feet—and of course many times their length. (Fig. 15.) The monks' house at Furness Abbey in Lancashire (Plate 14) is fourteen bays long, approaching two hundred feet. The entrance to the monks' house is always by an outside stair leading up to a doorway on the first floor.

The dormitory on the main floor of the monks' house must have resembled a barrack room. There was no sort of heating but straw was apparently laid on the floor in lieu of a carpet. The beds were straw palliasses but from the first there may well have been box-beds, such as certainly existed in the guests' lodgings, a frame of wooden boards having ropes stretched across it in the manner of the Indian's *charpoy*. By the fourteenth century the monks certainly all had such beds, ancestors of the Victorian box-mattress. It was about this time that the dormitories began to lose their barrack-room atmosphere when they were divided up by boarded screens into individual cubicles.

In parenthesis it may here be remarked that in medieval domestic architecture the visible masonry features represent the structure only. An arcade, no matter how attractively it may be presented, is a supporting feature demanded by the span. Attached to its delightful pillars may be screens of boards, or hangings of coarse material, dividing the apartment up into individual rooms of which no trace of their plan remains.

The monks' house was set at right angles to the abbey church, either attached to, or at least continuing the line of, a transept. Usually it was on the south or sunny side of the church. The entrance to the monks' dormitory was up a wide stone stair passing up the western face of the long wall towards a door high up at the end farthest from the church.

The west wall of the transept being in alignment with the west wall of the monks' house, a route came into being connecting the eastern processional doorway of the church with the foot of the stair leading to the dormitory, which route became the east alley of the subsequent cloister. (Fig. 18.)

The stair referred to was normally the day-stair only. For as the monks' day began soon after midnight every attempt was made to provide easy and if possible undercover access between the dormitory and the church. Thus if practicable the monks' house and the church transept shared a common wall, for it was then possible to run a 'night-stair' up the inside of the transept wall, as may be seen at Hexham Priory in Northumberland, to a doorway high up in the church leading directly into the dormitory. At Beaulieu Abbey in Hampshire, the north transept is aisled on both sides but in the south transept the place of the western aisle is taken by a night-stair set in a very thick wall. While every attempt was made to get the monks into church under cover for the night offices there were various architectural problems which often made its provision impossible, doubtless to the sorrow of monks turned out of bed on a bitter winter night to make a shivering way into church for several hours of prayer.

The usual trouble was that presented by the intrusion of the community's assembly room, the chapter house, which for reasons of architectural dignity was always sited next to the church with its entrance on the important east cloister walk. In order to provide this important apartment with a splendid interior it had to be raised to a decent height and if possible vaulted in a single span, to avoid the insertion of pillared supports, which raised its ceiling higher than ever. It will be appreciated that once the top of the chapter house had risen above the floor of the dormitory it was no longer possible to join the latter with the church transept: the plan for a night-stair came to an end.

The monks' house then had to finish at a gable wall independent of that of the transept. To shorten the distance between the foot of the day-stair and the church door the stair was sometimes moved to the nearer end of the monks' house and run up its gable end to a doorway in this. Thus the day-stair would also have to serve as a night-stair as well.

One should note that this rearrangement of the dormitory plan by changing its entrance doorway end to end would have had a revolutionary effect upon subsequent planning. For social position in medieval days depended upon distance from the entrance doorway, the position of which indicated the 'lower' end of any large apartment. In the beginning the abbot's bed would have been at the upper end of the dormitory, and eventually his cubicle would be there also. This might develop into a separate lodging or even a private house, for in some abbeys, notably those of the Cistercians, the abbot's house always developed from his bed in the dormitory.

A word on nomenclature. The modern English word 'dormitory' is derived directly from the Latin but its Anglicized version as employed during the Middle Ages was 'dorter'. So during the remainder of these chapters this designation will be employed to indicate the upper storey of the monks' house.

The number of individuals accommodated within the precincts of an abbey varied greatly not only in accordance with the size of the foundation but also as its fortunes fluctuated during the four centuries or so of its existence. The minimum number of monks was supposed to be twelve, a large abbey like St. Albans might go up to a hundred, the average was probably somewhere about fifty. There were also lay-servants and craftsmen about equalling in number the monkish strength. The Cistercian abbeys housed enormous numbers, at Fountains the total strength of monks and lay-brothers could have been at a time between five and six hundred. After the Black Death the abbeys, like all other institutions, suffered the loss of from a third to a half of their strength; from the Cistercian abbeys the lay-brothers disappeared never to return.

It will be appreciated that a community of this size living closely packed within an enclosed institution presented a problem in sanitation. That as early as the end of the first millennium the civilization of western Europe was able to accept such a challenge is an indication of the practical, as well as the aesthetic, state of architecture at that time.

The normal system of sanitation was to project a latrine outwards from the face of an outer wall, fortunately from an upper storey as the living accommodation was there sited. Where the

walling was of some thickness, as in a castle, a shoot could be contrived like the flue of a chimney.

The abbey required something more efficient than a row of such
latrines, so an ingenious type of structure, attached to the monks'
house and called its rere-dorter, was designed. Two storeys high,
it consisted of a passage running beside which was a stone-lined
drain through which was led a stream of water. Above on the first
floor was the same passage; beside it, above the slot containing at
its base the drain, was provided a row of seats set over this and
generally separated by screens. (Fig. 15.) The whole contrivance
was an extraordinarily civilized conception. Some rere-dorters
were of considerable length, that at Canterbury cathedral priory
being over a hundred feet long and seating fifty-five.

Similar buildings had to be attached to the infirmary hall or
dorter, and to those portions of the monastery, including the
abbot's quarters, in which guests were lodged. The large houses of
the lay-brothers in the Cistercian abbeys had to have their own
rere-dorter.

The main rere-dorter was always attached directly to the dorter
and entered from this. Usually it was projected eastwards at right-
angles so as to keep it as far as possible away from the cloister,
but where the dorter was long and projected far to the south it was
set across the end which made it easier to connect with the drain-
age. At Thetford Priory this was the situation, also at another
Cluniac priory in Norfolk, that of Castle Acre, where a fine twelve-
seater still stands, as does another at Kirkham in Yorkshire.

At Muchelney Abbey in Somerset a ten-seater rere-dorter is used
todays as a granary.

At Furness Abbey in Lancashire which has an exceptionally
long dorter, the rere-dorter was set half-way along it, parallel
with it and connected to it by a bridge.

The Cistercians often sited their rere-dorter near the middle of
the east wall of the monks' house, projected it eastwards at right
angles in the usual manner and set the abbot's house across the end
of it so that he and his guests could use it as well as the monks.
This made three sides of a small court; if the infirmary hall was
sited on the north side of this, covered access had to be provided

between it and the rere-dorter for the more active patients. (See Fig. 20.)

Whenever possible the rere-dorter was shared between departments of the abbey. In Cistercian abbeys where the long house of the lay-brothers needed a large rere-dorter this was sometimes shared with the guest rooms usually found in this part of the site.

While abbeys were almost invariably founded for obvious reasons upon well-watered sites, a few occupied hill-tops. The great Wessex abbeys of Malmesbury and Shaftesbury are examples; one wonders whence came the water-supply for these busy establishments. At Worcester Cathedral Priory the great drain can be seen tumbling down the hillside through the rere-dorter; today it is dry, but where was the original source of its water?

It has been computed that Fountains Abbey (Plate 18) may have had at one time from five to six hundred monks and lay-brothers in addition to servants and visitors. For the Middle Ages this would represent the population of a small town. The sanitary blocks of such a settlement would need a good water-supply to keep them flushed. The principle of water-borne sewage was, however, fully understood by the monks, who led streams into large tunnels of which the principal, the great drain, formed one of the major factors when starting to lay out an abbey plan on a new site. For a convenient stream had to be at hand, and a route levelled for the great drain so that it would have an even fall and be able to accept branches from all the various rere-dorters as well as the scullery washing-places connected with the kitchens of which there might be several. (See Fig. 21.)

Whether any system of sewage disposal existed is not known, but it was realized that the stream should run from west to east so that the kitchen in its westward position should be able to receive the water when it was reasonably fresh and the main rere-dorter of the monks' house should be the last to use it.

It might be as well to mention here that the great drain of the medieval abbey, long dried out, is the origin of the 'underground passage' of spicy legend.

No one can examine the vast array of assorted structures making up a medieval abbey with its complement of several score of in-

11. Rievaulx

12. Netley

dividuals without beginning to appreciate that the setting-out of such an elaborate complex of buildings must have been for those days a formidable problem, unlike anything else to be met with in the medieval world. So many factors had to be taken into account.

Life in an abbey was intended to be a hard one. But it was not practicable to carry the austerity beyond reasonable limits. There was, it is true, complete enclosure within a cloister, originally an open-air court having none of its later protection from outer walling filled with glazed windows. The whole situation must at times have been unbearably cold and draughty, even to the hardy man of the Middle Ages.

Thus every effort was made to plan the abbey so that the lofty church could be on the north side of the cloister in order that its bulk might keep off the coldest winds and let in as much sunlight as possible. The sunny south side of a tall church could reflect into the cloister a certain amount of warmth.

But although the southern cloister was the optimum situation, all too often there were factors affecting this. The cloister had to be near a stream in order that its buildings might be supplied with water. A cloister garth sloping towards a church would be difficult to drain of storm-water. A stream which flowed from east to west would make matters difficult for the planners for the reasons stated above.

In towns there were far greater difficulties. The traditional parish entrance for a church in this country is from the south. Thus there were reasons why a monastery could not be added on that side. So a northern cloister is usually found in ancient towns such as Gloucester or Sherborne.

The great church had to be sited first. As the largest building a level site had to be found for it. The next largest building was the monks' house which gave the site its north–south level.

To form an impression of the barrack-like aspect of the monastic dorter one must go to Battle Abbey in Sussex where the shell of a huge dorter still remains. The monks' house can also be seen externally to its full advantage now that the church it once adjoined has been swept away.

The best preserved of the remaining dorters is that at Cleeve Abbey in Somerset, a late apartment dating from a period at which much of the austerity had gone from monastic life; it is a fine apartment still roofed.

The houses of the monks were so sited that for the most part they were caught up in a jumble of structures at the south-east angle of the cloister, and thus could never have been admired for their size or for the simple perfection of their architecture with the long range of small windows lighting their dorters, as at Forde Abbey in Dorset.

With the houses of the Cistercian lay-brothers, however, the situation was very different. These reached southwards from the west front of the church and with this often must have formed a fine architectural façade.

The lay-brothers' house at Fountains Abbey dates from the middle of the twelfth century and presents one of the first grand façades this country experienced. (Plate 18.) Despite its humble two-storeyed elevation we can see in it the germ of the frontispieces of the Baroque abbeys of New Spain. As it stands it presents one of the great architectural displays from medieval England.

After the flight of the lay-brothers from Cistercian abbeys following the Black Death, their old houses were divided up and converted into guest houses. As such they were sometimes taken over at the Suppression and saved from destruction to be used as residences. Cases in point are the remains of the lay-brothers' houses at Beaulieu Abbey in Hampshire and Whalley Abbey in Lancashire.

# 7

# The Great Hall

The house of the monks was a large two-storeyed structure raised upon a simple vaulted undercroft and approached by an external stair like any hay-loft. Its windows were small and unglazed. Apart from its impressive size it would have resembled nothing so much as an ordinary farm-building.

We turn now to buildings belonging to a different class architecturally, presented with elevational dignity and embellished with details of distinction.

Most noticeable of these would have been the windows, for those of the dorter remained small and undistinguished, giving only the minimum of light and, being glassless, purposely kept small so as to keep out wind and rain; the only concession to architectural development would have been to change the tops of their heads from round to pointed.

As we proceed towards an examination of the more important buildings we find that their windows, as befits semi-public architecture, become larger in area and glazed.

A tall wide window such as was beginning to appear during the twelfth century offered glazing problems as the pieces of glass were small and held together with slender pieces of lead, the whole offering very little resistance to wind-pressure. It was therefore necessary for the abbey smith to prepare bars of iron—*ferramenti*—forming a grid of stanchions and saddle-bars to which the glazing could be secured by iron wire.

The enlargement of small windows was often effected by coupling them in pairs, a development of the old Byzantine belfry *bifora* with its little central shaft. The closer together each couplet became the nearer the intervening stonework approached the device known as the mullion which was eventually to transform medieval fenestration. Tall windows such as those of the church could be similarly coupled, then quadrupled, until with the advent of the 'traceried' head enclosed within a wide arch the Gothic window became perfected.

The design of these traceried windows of the fourteenth and fifteenth centuries followed one or the other of two distinct systems. There was the 'curvilinear' in which the lines of the tracery were gathered together and divided again to form curving shapes in the window head. The other was the 'rectilinear' in which the lines of the tracery were kept almost vertical so as to create a form of panelling.

Interior decoration was introduced by the abbey architects. During the twelfth century this most commonly took the shape of wall-arcading, rows of colonettes set close together and semi-circular arches interlacing as they spanned every alternate pair, as can be seen in the remains of the chapter-house at Much Wenlock Priory in Shropshire and used as ornamentation for the west front of a church at the priory of Castle Acre in Norfolk.

Wall-arcading remained the most popular form of interior decoration throughout the thirteenth century, notably in the refectory at Basingwerk Abbey in Flintshire, where the arcades have risen from being mere dados to embrace the whole wall-surface, echoing the tall windows of the hall. Incidentally it is noticeable how charmingly these refectory arcades managed to incorporate the pulpit stair into the designs.

With the development of window tracery during the fourteenth century the lines of this began to appear on the wall-faces, and on the rear walls of rebuilt cloisters, as a form of stone-panelled wall decoration. Broadly speaking, the system of interior decoration employed in medieval days was to imitate the window arrangement on blank wall surfaces. The remains of the fine octagonal chapter house at Thornton Abbey in Lincolnshire show this system in its highest form.

During the twelfth century the long-established Anglo-Saxon

carpenter gave place to the new trade of masoncraft which extended itself in no uncertain fashion by erecting many scores of huge buildings. Thenceforth, however, after the thirteenth century when English Gothic architecture reached its most glorious form, the carpenters gradually worked their way back again into power. They had of course continued to construct the roofs of buildings, hitherto steeply pitched, elaborately timbered, and covered with shingles. But the introduction of lead covering had the dramatic result of lowering the roof-pitch in order that the lead should not slip off it, a factor which completely changed the silhouette of Gothic architecture.

During the fourteenth century the carpenters—now become joiners of a very high degree of skill—began to concentrate upon the undersides of the roofs of important buildings such as parish churches in order to compensate the parishioners for having no stone vaulting to hide their timbered roofs. The joiners were in fact beginning to create the timber *ceiling*.

The roof-pitch dropped still farther until it became virtually non-existent, its underside literally a ceiling and, in the hands of the new joinery trade, a very splendid one. The first-floor 'sollers', which, with improved social conditions, were replacing the old stone ones, added very greatly to the appearance of the parlour beneath.

The keynote to interior decoration was the panelling of joinery; even into the stonework the forms penetrated, to dispose of the curvilinear tracery of earlier days until it had disappeared. The effect of this upon the window tracery was to straighten it out to suit, so that the last phase of Gothic architecture is the rectilinear with its arches reduced in pitch to a minimum and panelling everywhere.

The fourteenth century saw the beginnings of an interest in furniture. The old 'brattice' of vertical boards set alternately, derived from Anglo-Saxon building and still encountered everywhere in the country, gave place to properly joinered screens which as time went on became magnificent works of art, ornamented with tracery following the style of the windows. The use of screenwork enabled partitioning to be introduced into domestic buildings, especially into the dorters for the provision of cubicles.

The fourteenth century was the era of the canopied stalls in the abbey choirs; the next century saw the appearance of permanent pewing in the parish churches.

The foregoing remarks should act as an introduction to the architecture of the medieval period into which we have been launched with the thirteenth-century presbyteries of the great churches but which we left for a spell in order to examine the somewhat primitive houses of the monks who served in them.

We now turn to the largest of the domestic buildings of the abbey—its great hall.

St. Benedict required the brethren to eat their meals in a common hall, an order which was hardly necessary as it would have been impossible to have catered for them in any other way. Even the Carthusians, who lived in separate cells, still had to gather in a refectory at meal times and be served from a central kitchen. One wonders how the early Celtic monasteries managed for food; they would surely have found a communal dining-hall and kitchen a great boon.

It was presumably not until St. Dunstan's reorganization of Anglo-Saxon monastic life during the second quarter of the tenth century that the community began to be properly administered and housed, and not until just before the Norman Conquest, a century later, that the Continental claustral arrangement reached this country and we find the refectory as we know it settling down in its place as the great hall of the monks. Its Latin designation, by the way, has been abbreviated in English to 'frater'.

The domestic hall was of course a building well known to the Anglo-Saxons and dated back towards their origins. The native hall, however, was a communal living-room, the headquarters of a clan or a family with its dependants, only exceptionally of a palatial nature. As a structure it was designed to provide an approximately square area roofed over and surrounding a central fire-hearth. As the span of the main roof would govern the width of the building and might force a large hall to assume an inconvenient length, recourse to planning in three spans—aisled construction—enabled it to adjust width to length and produce something more nearly square on plan.

The feudal hall of the twelfth century was of this type, often four bays in length and with its roof carried upon a light construction of timber posts and beams or stone pillars and arches as in the well-known example at Oakham Castle in Rutland.

Amongst the owners of these halls were the lords spiritual, the diocesan bishops, the halls of whose palaces imitated those of the castles.

But these sprawling aisled halls were in fact residential halls, barn-like structures capable of being used not just for meals but as dormitories for servants and visitors who could find a heap of straw in an aisle.

The feudal hall, the first example of which in this country was the palace hall at Westminster built by William II, continued in use throughout the thirteenth century during which several magnificent examples with graceful arcades carrying their wide roofs were built in royal and episcopal palaces. With the improvement of living-quarters by the provision of private chambers and lodgings, however, the aisled hall shrank in area while maintaining its element of height as an indication of social prestige. It then became the dining-hall proper, the 'banqueting hall' of the fourteenth to the sixteenth century, symbol of Tudor pomp and hospitality. These great halls were derived from the dining-halls of the abbeys.

The monastic frater, although it was eventually to share the same stately proportions of the banqueting hall, began its development in a different way. For it was always a dining-hall and never at any period served, as did the feudal hall, as a dormitory, since one already existed in the house of the monks and visitors were always accommodated outside the cloister.

It had its dais and its high table for the abbot, below whom the brethren sat at long 'refectory' tables set in two rows down the apartment. Thus excessive length was a social gain to its owner and in the absence of a feudal fire no one need have felt out in the cold, unless it was the novices in their places close to the draughts from the entrance doorway.

Above the abbot's seat was a rood, an example of which,

Fig. 16  *Benedictine cloister from south-east*

From the transept of the church the long house of the monks reaches southwards with the chapter house projecting from it eastwards and the rere-dorter attached to the south end. On the opposite side of the cloister from the church is the great hall of the frater with the kitchen at its farther end. The cellarer's range closes the cloister to the west

painted on the wall-plaster, can still be seen in the frater at Cleeve Abbey in Somerset.

Half-way down the frater was an important architectural feature, the pulpit from which readings took place at mealtimes. These pulpits were set in the wall and approached by a stair set in the thickness of the wall and often finished on the hall side with a charming arcade of light design. Fountains Abbey has an example; at another Cistercian abbey, Beaulieu in Hampshire (Plate 15), where the frater has been converted into the parish church, the pulpit is still in use. The pulpit in Berwick St. James church in Wiltshire may have been transferred thence from Mottisfont Abbey in Hampshire, the owners of the church, at the Suppression. The frater pulpits at Chester and Shrewsbury still remain.

Whatever may have been the intentions of the first abbey-planners with regard to the provision of a cloister, as we have since witnessed its development there can be no doubt at all that in any kind of planning complex as extensive as a medieval monastery the buildings would have been grouped round a courtyard. The enclosed court had long been known in the lands through which historical architecture had been spreading; the great courts, palace and mosque, of the Arab world must have been well known by repute throughout Mediterranean Europe.

The early monasteries of Byzantine Syria, some of them going back to the fifth century, all have some kind of court or cloister, some forming with the church a claustral complex and others with the church in the centre.

By attaching the monks' house to the transept of the church the eleventh-century English planners had composed an L-shaped structure forming two sides of what might well become a court. A third side to this could be easily completed by setting the monks' hall parallel to the church and facing it across what might be considered as a potential cloister. This was in fact done, the south- or on occasion, the north-side of the cloister becoming the standard site for the monks' frater. A large building, simply its bulk, combined with those of the great church and the monks' house, assisted in the protection of the cloister from the lash of the tempests. (See Figs. 16 and 17.)

The secular hall invariably had a screen at its lower end to deflect to some extent the draughts from the entrance doorway. It seems possible that the same protection was provided in the monastic fraters, but the destruction of these fine apartments for their roofing lead has left so few intact that no woodwork remains today. The kitchen was attached to this end of the hall, but unlike its feudal counterpart the frater had no service doorways to this and the pantry and larder, the monks acting as waiters and collecting everything from a service hatch.

The frater began as a ground-floor apartment just like any other medieval hall. But under the influence of the Augustinians who seem to have been more ready to introduce planning innovations than the monks, the frater came to be raised upon a vaulted undercroft and thus set upon the *piano nobile* with storage below, a system adopted in the halls of the medieval universities and eventually by the builders of the Tudor banqueting halls.

The raising of the frater floor made it necessary for this to be approached by a stair. This had to leave the cloister at a spot normally occupied by the frater entrance and climb beside the west gable of the hall to a landing and another doorway at the end of the frater. If the day-stair to the dorter were in its normal position next the east gable of the frater the two would balance, each continuing the line of a cloister alley. Sometimes, as at Easby Abbey in Yorkshire, the frater stair was an internal one emerging in what would in a secular hall have been the screens passage.

As the frater was a building of major importance and possibly on occasion visited by important persons, if only ecclesiastics such as the diocesan bishop, its entrance doorway was always utilized for a display of ornament. Outside the church doorways the most elaborate entrance was that of the chapter house, the frater doorway following it closely in elaboration. While the chapter house doorway in the east walk was nearly always flanked by a pair of windows, however, that to the frater near the end of the south walk stood unaccompanied.

Near it, however, was always a laver or washing-place for the monks. They ate their food with a knife and their fingers, in accordance with the best manners of the times. It was as well to scrub one's hands before a meal to get rid of the stains of toil and afterwards to clean them from grease.

It has been explained earlier how the abbey-planners took great care in the survey of its water-supply so that this entered the cloister at its south-west angle where it could supply the kitchen

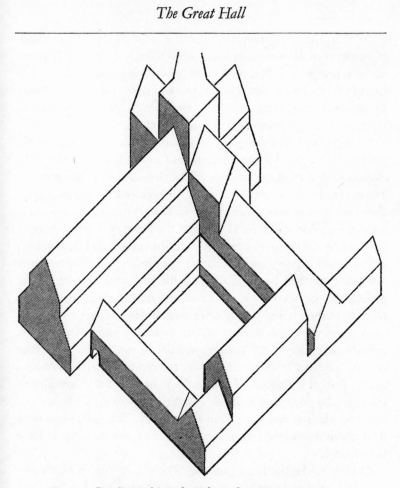

Fig. 17   *Benedictine cloister from the south-west*
In the foreground is the kitchen joining the cellarer's
range with the frater, beyond which is the monks'
house and their rere-dorter. The archway of the
outer parlour is seen in the cellarer's range near
where this joins the church

before passing eastwards to flush the rere-dorter. The kitchen was
at the lower, western, end of the frater, so that it was not far from
the laver which could obtain a supply of fresh water by means of
the lead piping which was well-known to medieval England.

The laver was always sited near the western end of the cloister walk—the southern—flanking the frater. It was generally a charming architectural feature—a long stone trough set in a wide niche under a low arch. Often there were towel-cupboards nearby. The laver in Gloucester cloisters—the most perfect cloisters remaining today—is a long structure, elaborately panelled in late Gothic style, projecting into the garth from the cloister.

Some abbeys had polygonal conduit houses set in the southwest angle of the cloister. The one at Canterbury Cathedral—the cloister here is on the north side of the church—is twelfth century. There are the remains of one at Much Wenlock Priory in Shropshire; another at Sherborne Abbey in Dorset has been salvaged at the Suppression and moved out into the town.

The importance of the great hall of the monks and its resultant architectural dignity meant that at the time of the Suppression most of them had been ceiled with the fine roofs current at the period and covered with the now ubiquitous lead sheets. This resulted in their being promptly unroofed. Since their proportions made them useless as private houses or farm buildings they were quickly demolished for their materials. Some of the Cistercian fraters, set deep in the countryside, remain today as tremendous ruins. But the fraters of the urban Benedictines, smothered amongst the crowding buildings of thriving towns, were occupying valuable land and were soon swept away. The exceptions were the cathedral priories' fraters, for which a use seems often to have been found.

Chester Cathedral is an example. The abbey church was saved to serve as the cathedral for the western portion of what had been the huge diocese of York. Of the original abbey church the north transept—as so often in towns the cloister is on the north—and part of the nave remain; the normal enlargement of the eastern arm took place during the thirteenth century, and in the next century the southern transept, which had been used by the townspeople as a parish church, was expanded to form an elaborate structure four bays in length making the abbey church something of a freak.

The cloisters, rebuilt during the fifteenth century, remain in use. The chapter house has been left but the monks' house has entirely disappeared. Opposite the church on the far side of the cloister, however, is the great hall of the abbey, preserved for use as a schoolroom. Its reader's pulpit is a notable architectural composition, a lucky survival amongst so many scores lost to us. To the west of the cloister is the great court of the abbey, now called Abbey Square, entered as usual by a gatehouse.

The most important survivals of the abbeys of the Benedictines may be found in connection with the traces of the cathedral priories whose monks once filled the stalls now occupied by prebendaries. One of the most notable of these is Worcester Cathedral, its stately tower rising in its splendour above the waters of Severn. Served originally by secular canons, the cathedral has been here since the tenth century, and was converted into a cathedral priory served by Benedictine monks after the Conquest.

The church provides an excellent example of thirteenth-century expansion of the eastern arm by creating a complete new church, with its own crossing and transepts, east of the central tower.

The cloister here is on the south, but its buildings are constricted by the fall of the ground towards the river. The chapter house adjoins the south transept and is a polygonal conversion from a circular original. This is as far as the conventional plan was able to go. The site presents about as awkward a problem as the abbey-planner might ever wish to encounter and illustrates the difficulty of adding a monastic house to a church already existing and adjoining a town; the church of Worcester is a very old foundation and had attracted a population well before the Conquest.

Where the abbey water-supply came from is not clear today, but the great drain, now dry, can be seen falling down the hill-slope from the west side of the cloister. Beside it, in diminishing stages, lay the monks' house, the rere-dorter and, sharing this, the great hall of the infirmary.

In its normal position along the south side of the cloister ranged the great hall of the monks, now the hall of the Cathedral School.

North-east of the cloister, in an unusual position dictated by the proximity of the river, was the great court of the priory entered by a splendid gatehouse which still exists.

The remaining Benedictine fraters are very few indeed. The

Cistercians in their isolated situations are better represented. As originally planned, the Cistercian fraters followed Benedictine practice. But as will be seen in Chapter 14, various considerations intervened which caused them to rebuild their fraters at right angles to the cloister alley setting it end-on to this.

Even in ruin, very magnificent are the fraters of the great Cistercian abbeys of Yorkshire. In every way superior to the contemporary castle and episcopal halls, their freedom from clinging aisles enabled them to light their interiors with ranges of very tall windows. With no internal arcades to impose a bay unit of normal length—sixteen to eighteen feet—they reduced their bays to twelve feet or so thus enabling their immensely high and narrow windows to stand more closely together; this produced a soaring effect more impressive than could be achieved by any church of the period with its plan, and consequently its elevation, controlled by its interior bay ordinance.

This is an aspect of Gothic architecture at its noblest which the destruction of these magnificent monastic halls of the late twelfth century has forbidden us ever to witness. But even as roofless shells they are inexpressibly stately. (Plate 16.) It may be that the great hall of Rievaulx Abbey (Plate 11) was the most perfect medieval domestic building this country has ever seen. The frater at Fountains (Plate 18), one hundred and ten feet in length, must have run it very close. What must these great halls have looked like before their roofs came down!

If only they had not replaced their original steeply pitched roofs with flatter ones covered with lead they might have been standing yet, as does the frater of Dover Priory, one of the few remaining intact outside the cathedral priories.

At the Cistercian abbey of Basingwerk in Flintshire, the church has entirely vanished save for the lower part of its west front. Part of the east claustral range remains in ruin, but the chief interest of the site lies in the ruins of its frater the walls of which rise to a considerable height. Although sited on the north–south alignment favoured by the Cistercians, it is set hard up against the day-stair to the dorter, instead of being in the centre of the south walk.

While the most dramatic of the ruined fraters are certainly

those of the Cistercian abbeys in Yorkshire, there is one great
Premonstratensian ruin which approaches close to them in desolate dignity—the great frater of Easby in the North Riding. (Plate
16.)

The canons regular seem to have planned their houses along
less conventional lines than those of the monkish Orders. The
Premonstratensians of Easby were no exception and a number of
unusual variations on the standard plan appear among its ruins.
The church has vanished but the stallwork of the choir has fortunately been preserved in the church at Richmond. The cloister lay

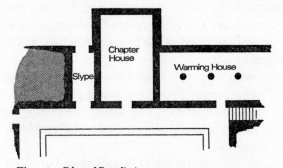

Fig. 18   *Plan of Benedictine east range*
The main thoroughfare of the cloister
joins the day-stair to the dormitory and
the church, passing on its way the
chapter house and the 'inner parlour' or
'slype' (compare Fig. 25 for Cistercian
variation)

to the south of the church, and on the opposite side of it was laid
out an interesting group of buildings connected with the great
hall of the infirmary to which a passage led out of the transept of
the church, a not unusual arrangement except that the infirmary
lay on the opposite side of the church instead of that occupied by
the claustral complex. Beside the infirmary hall were its various
adjuncts connected with the feeding of the patients and the lodgings for the infirmarer, and on the way to these buildings the
passage passed through what is believed to be the abbot's house.
Thus he and the infirmary were both connected directly with the
church.

The cloister itself was curiously laid out. The east walk gave access in the usual fashion to the chapter house or assembly hall of the canons (see Fig. 18), but on the normal site of their house we find the east range divided up into a set of lodgings, a conversion, apparently made during the fifteenth century, of what must have originally been the house of the canons.

The canons' dorter now appears in the western range where one would have expected their lay-brothers to have been housed, so it may be that after the collapse of the lay-brother system following the Black Death the canons took over the dorter and replaced their old quarters with the lodgings noted above, for what purpose one can only conjecture. The instruction of novices, who were often accommodated in this part of the Cistercian houses, is a possibility which suggests itself.

The long west range, its northern end next the church being given over to the canons, had its remaining portion converted into a guest hall and chamber over this. Below the canons' dorter was a 'warming house' where some heat could be provided, perhaps from a brazier.

The canons' rere-dorter lay alongside their dorter on its west side and attached to this was a remarkable structure. Exceptional for a medieval building in this country, it was three storeys in height, and seems to have been a block of guest chambers, a most extraordinary domestic type of structure to discover in an abbey. It is interesting to note that its floors were of timber, a change from the primitive 'stone soller' which during the Middle Ages had been the orthodox method of constructing an upper floor, seeming to denote an advance upon medieval manners, possibly under the influence of the cultured followers of St. Norbert.

In its normal position along the south side of the cloister stands the glory of Easby Abbey today, its great frater stately in its ruins and equalled only by a very few of its brethren remaining in this country. (Plate 16.) Built over vaulted cellarage, its kitchen adjoined it to the west in the usual fashion. Above the west end of the huge hall a timber 'loft' was constructed to serve as a flesh-frater or 'misericord'—surely an unhappy innovation for the

canons who had to sit below and sniff the savoury odours descending from the loft above as from a gourmet's paradise.

We have mourned the loss of the glorious churches of the age
of the abbots. But there may well have been other buildings which
have with equal fervour been swept away and which in their
fashion were an equal loss to the world of architecture. Chief of
these must surely be the great halls of the monks.

Amongst all this vanished splendour one humble frater remains to console us. It is at Cleeve in Somerset, at the skirts of
Exmoor. In a wild spot, one of its abbots used to augment his
income by holding wayfarers to ransom. The whole of the cloister
of this little Cistercian gem—its church has gone—was rebuilt
along more comfortable lines during the fifteenth century. The
little abbey has been preserved through having been used as farm
buildings and still keeps its roofs, none of them having ever known
lead. The charming frater with its West Country cradle roof intact
is overlooked by a huge rood painted on the plaster at its upper
end. How fortunate that this charming apartment never rose
beyond a roof covered with tiles.

Perhaps the most interesting survival of a frater is that at
Cistercian Beaulieu in Hampshire, preserved at the Suppression
in order that it might be used as a parish church. (Plate 15.) Today
the preachers of Beaulieu enjoy the privilege of occupying a magnificent Gothic wall-pulpit approached up an arcaded stair.

Waiting for a train at Ipswich railway station, a Victorian parson
noticed beside him a pile of obviously medieval timbers. Admiring
their elaborate mouldings he called a porter and learnt that they
had been taken down from the roof of a frater at a local friary. He
negotiated their purchase, assembled the roof, and built himself a
new church—that of Cholderton in Wiltshire—under it.

# 8

# The Cellarer's Range

The original intention of monasticism being to separate the monk from all contact with the world he had voluntarily abandoned, it was not enough for him to live in a communal residence. To preserve him from any possible temptation to escape he must be shut in behind a wall.

The great church, the frater opposite this, and the monks' house closing the gap to the east made up three sides of an enclosure from which access was available to all three of these buildings. All that was now needed was a barrier across between the west ends of the church and frater.

Some small abbeys such as Finchale in Durham were content with a wall closing the cloister to the west. Others built a range of buildings there but left them as single-storey structures suitable for accommodating unimportant stores such as straw or fuel.

The Benedictines soon found that the ground floor of a western building was of the greatest use as a range of storerooms for food-stuffs, cloth, and a number of substances required to meet the needs of an enclosed community. As the monk in charge of the abbey stores was known as the cellarer this building came to be called the cellarer's range.

With the cloister completely walled off from the world some access to it was required. The focus of interest to the public being the west front of the church, the entrance to the cloister was con-trived through the ground floor of the west range immediately where this joined the church. (See Fig. 17.)

A vaulted tunnel formed the entrance way. It was known as the outer parlour for within it took place any necessary contact with the outer world. Conversation between monks was not allowed in the church, dorter, frater or cloister, but was of course needed for extra-mural communications. The outer end of the parlour formed as it were the front door to the cloister and thus became a focus to any activities on the threshold before which stretched the great court of the abbey, the *curia*.

It was seldom that the western side of the claustral complex was left without an upper storey. Virtually the entrance of the abbey, it moreover immediately adjoined the west front of the church and would have looked like a dog-kennel attached to this finest façade in the abbey. Protection from the elements was moreover needed for the cloister beyond, and while the bulk of the church would have kept the tempest away from the sunny north walk where the monks worked at their book-production, the vital south-west angle would have been left very exposed.

As the upper storeys of monastic buildings were naturally reserved for accommodation, the upper storey of the cellarer's range was reserved for this purpose. With the very necessary liberation of the abbot from the communal dorter some kind of lodging had to be found for him. The west range was an obvious situation for him, as not only would he have been well placed for the reception of important guests but would have been strategically placed for the observance of what passed at the outer parlour generally. He would also have been quite close to the kitchen for his food.

In the cellarer's range of the priory of Ulverscroft in Lancashire, the upper storey shows signs of having been used by the prior and his guests.

By the end of the twelfth century it had become generally accepted that the abbot would need to be accommodated in a private house of his own in which he could meet persons on abbey affairs and entertain his guests. These abbots' houses more often than not developed out of the abbot's original lodging at the north, or church, end of the upper floor of the cellarer's range as may be seen at Castle Acre Priory in Norfolk.

In the same way his original guest rooms, at the southern end of the range would become detached to form separate apartments for guests. Subsequent provision of proper guest houses again might develop this part of the range, near the kitchen quarters. The abbot would of course be well situated for observing the activity in the *curia*.

The west side of the west range, facing as it did the great court of the abbey and having in it the only entrance to the cloister, became as it were an entrance front. With the abbot's house and the guest house beginning to play a part in its composition the architectural presentation of the building was beginning to develop far ahead of the bare west wall of early days. (See Fig. 21.)

Both the abbot's house and the guest house would tend to expand into wings set at right angles to the cellarer's range to add architectural interest to the elevation. The presence of the abbot's house would suggest a porch which in later monastic days would very likely be raised to form a tower porch similar to those on parish churches. Eventually these features developed still further into the complete abbot's tower as may be seen at Cerne Abbey in Dorset and the Premonstratensian abbey of Torre in Devon.

It will be seen later that the precinct wall of the abbey usually joined the claustral buildings beside the west front of the church, almost in line with its south wall and cutting it off from the entrance to the outer parlour. It was inside this wall that the abbey court was extended with its cluster of buildings of all descriptions: domestic, workshop, storage. The loss of these may be of small moment, but with them perished what must have been the most interesting domestic frontages in England, those of the cellarer's ranges. When one considers the great skill of the monastic architects and what they might well have made of the elevations of a group of domestic apartments and their frontage—just the kind of elevation which would have appealed to the medieval designer— it seems most unfortunate that the western sides of the abbey claustral buildings suffered more drastically, probably because of their accessibility to spoilers from the public area fronting the church, than the rest of the complex of structures making up the domestic buildings of the monastery.

It was that same accessibility, however, which resulted in the preservation of a number of the abbots' houses from the wreck for

13. Lanercost

14. Furness

occupation as farmhouses. While those of the Cistercian abbots, sited east of the cloister in the back-blocks of the abbey premises, have almost entirely vanished, those set in the standard position in the cellarer's range have often survived to this day. Another reason for the neglect of the Cistercian houses may have been that the infirmary and the graveyard of the monks were thereabouts.

One might have supposed that the cellarer's range with its group of semi-public domestic apartments might have appeared to the lay grantees of the abbey as suitable for conversion to a mansion, yet few of them seem to have been willing to accept the challenge and take advantage of the opportunity of developing the west front of the range into a fine domestic façade. The time was perhaps just a little too early. Some of course may have been converted to be subsequently lost through fire, bankruptcy or the hazards of the Civil War during which so many great houses were deliberately fired by their owners to prevent their falling into the enemy's hands.

The battlefield of Hastings presents a strange spectacle today. One reaches it through an enormous turreted gatehouse opening out of the market square of the town which grew up at the gate of the huge abbey built as a memorial to the fallen.

The great abbey church of Battle is levelled with the ground. Its high altar occupies the highest part of the site, the spot where King Harold made his last stand and where he died. Of the claustral buildings one huge ruin remains, the roofless shell of the monks' dorter. Chapter house, frater, all are gone. But the western range, which contained the house of the mitred Abbot of Battle, has survived the general destruction. His house had been rebuilt during the thirteenth century on an unusually elaborate plan and was consequently preserved to form a mansion which is now a girls' school. Beside this lie the remains of a large Tudor house intended by the lay grantee to provide a residence for the Princess Elizabeth, but never completed.

One of the most attractive of our monastic memorials is the church of Lanercost in Cumberland, belonging to an Augustinian priory founded in the second half of the twelfth century and thus

illustrating a more refined style than we find in the earlier foundations. The nave and north aisle remain to provide an excellent
example of the smaller conventual church of the period; it is,
moreover, built in a clear style which though perhaps a trifle
austere for the Augustinians forms a perfect example of the basic
architecture of its period. The west front with its three tall lancets
(Plate 13) is a composition not easily forgotten.

There is something exceedingly impressive about the great
lancet windows of the early Gothic, groups of which still frame
the clouds above the English abbeys. (Plates 11, 17 and 28.) At
sites like Dale Abbey in Derbyshire, Guisborough in Yorkshire,
Walsingham in Norfolk, towering gable ends which once held
elaborate traceried windows look incredibly forlorn now that
the tracery has fallen and gaping spaces are left appealing to the
sky. (See also Plates 4, 23, 27, and 32.)

But Valle Crucis in ruin is enriched by its stately lancets, and
there is a tremendous dignity about the haunted ruin of Frithelstock Priory in Devon with the three towering lancets at the end
of its vast empty nave.

The nave at Lanercost should not be missed by the amateur of
medieval church architecture. East of it one finds the inevitable
ruin of presbytery and transept, both aisled, and central lantern
tower. Below the three large windows in the gable of the south
transept the trace of the dorter roof can be seen, but the whole of
the monks' house has been swept away. East of it once stood a very
large rectangular chapter house, suggesting in its plan a lofty
building of the type seen in the chapter house of the cathedral
priory at Canterbury, obviously a very late addition. The frater has
gone from its position on the south side of the cloister but its
vaulted undercroft remains.

The western claustral range contained over the usual cellarage
an upper floor comprising lodgings, the southern end providing
for the Prior of Lanercost quarters far less commodious than those
of the Abbot of Battle.

At the Suppression the new owner remodelled the whole of the
first floor to form a long hall, adding a square chamber block to
its southern end which, balancing the west front of the church,

provided the finishing touch to a dignified front to his new house.

Newstead Priory in Nottinghamshire, another Augustinian house, provides one of the very few known examples where the whole of the claustral complex was preserved and during the nineteenth century converted into a mansion.

The church was razed at the Suppression except for the southern transept; until recently a billiard room occupied its ground floor with bedrooms over it. The chapter house served for a time as the domestic chapel. The whole array of vaulted undercrofts was retained with the apartments over them, the frater becoming the drawing-room.

The west front of the church survived and today looks rather mournful with its great window bare of tracery. Southwards of it reaches the cellarer's range remodelled with a new front; a fine frontispiece concealing the buried mysteries of a curiously transformed medieval monastery.

Turning from the black monks and the black canons to the white monks we find the cellarer's range of the Cistercian abbey performing quite a different function, for a second house was built along the west side of their cloister to accommodate the large number of lay-brothers who performed most of the manual work connected with the farming activities of these rural communities. The outer parlour remained in the usual place next the church, and sometimes the cellarage too remained as in the standard monastic plan.

But the whole of the upper floor of the west range was given up to be the living-quarters of the lay-brothers. Generally their dorter was at the northern end next the church, the end nearer the kitchen being their frater. Sometimes, however, they were housed entirely in the southern end with their frater beneath their dorter.

As this takes up all the accommodation of the west range one finds no abbot's lodging here. It is possible, however, that the northern end of the upper floor may occasionally have been used as lodgings for guests.

In 1349, however, there occurred an event which completely changed the Cistercian economy, for the Black Death massacred the lay-brothers and they disappeared from the Cistercian abbeys.

Thenceforth the house of the lay-brothers was abandoned and converted into lodgings for the prior and accommodation for guests. The abbot, as will be seen later, had long been housed east of the cloister.

St. Benedict's requirement that his monks should dine together in a common dining-hall meant the provision of a kitchen, a structure which became an essential adjunct to the monastic frater. It is unfortunate that all too few of these interesting buildings have survived to disclose to us their practical functions. The best known, the remarkable structure at Glastonbury, appears to be unique. Dating from the fifteenth century, it is a square building like any other monastic kitchen but its great hearths are set across the angles and the arches spanning them support a pyramidal stone roof in the masonry of which the flues are contrived. All four of these are gathered together to discharge into an elaborate central turret which is clearly a copy in stone of the louvered turret framed into the roof timbers of a contemporary feudal hall, and provided for the purpose of extracting the smoke rising from a central hearth. The whole building is a remarkable example of the ingenuity and skill of the medieval mason and is justly famous.

But this Glastonbury kitchen was part of an exceedingly rich abbey which was, moreover, in all probability the centre of a notable school of masons able to exercise their skill on an inexhaustible supply of excellent freestone. It was as it happens not the kitchen of the monks which we see today but a special building serving the abbot's house. A great concourse of pilgrims passed through Glastonbury in the old days, many regarding it as the most sacred spot in England. It is indeed fortunate that someone had the vision to preserve this unique structure from the utter desolation which has overwhelmed almost every other building of this famous abbey, leaving only two lines of scattered fragments, debris from a vast church, probably architecturally supreme, and the resting-place of a King of Britain who sleeps but to return.

The kitchen would have been designed to cook the flesh of animals in the form, no doubt, of whole carcasses. Meat was not part of the monastic diet, and the ordinary kitchen attached to the frater, though designed for cooking on a very large scale, had no need for the cavernous hearths and elaborate paraphernalia associated with roasting.

There were two parts of a monastic house which required meat meals. One of these was the infirmary department, for sick monks, many of them probably suffering from malnutrition, had to have their powers of resistance built up by attendance at the flesh-frater or 'misericord'. And as bleeding formed not only an important part of medical prescription but was a weekly operation believed to dispose of evil humours, the blood had afterwards to be restored by a temporary diet of meat. So attached to each infirmary hall was its special kitchen and flesh-frater.

The abbot of a medieval establishment could not be permitted to entertain his guests to a vegetarian diet, so the hall of his house, and any guests being entertained in the abbey *hospitium*, would have to be supplied from a kitchen separate from that serving the monks. It was this requirement which accounts for the remarkable building which is Glastonbury's so notable contribution to medieval architecture.

An interesting monastic kitchen remains in another Somerset abbey, that at Muchelney. Its great fireplace is designed on a very simple scheme which is met with in other monastic establishments such as the grange at Tisbury in Wiltshire and the warming house at Tintern Abbey in Monmouthshire. It simply consists of a pair of very wide arches spanning the kitchen from side to side with the hearth below; above this a pair of smaller arches help to carry the flue-turret over.

The planners of medieval monasteries, realizing that to share rere-dorters between dorter and infirmary or guests' lodgings would save plumbing, also discovered that by sharing kitchens between frater, abbot, and patients they would save cooks. And as these were probably in those days not of the highest skill, sharing the meat-kitchen, especially, might represent a wise provision. This suggested the placing of the abbot's house near the infirmary, as in the case of Cistercian abbeys, or near the guest hall, as in all other houses in which the abbot and the infirmary were separated by the width of the cloister.

At the Augustinian priory of Haughmond in Shropshire a kitchen was shared between the frater and the infirmary hall but was divided into two halves each with its large fireplace, the flues being gathered into chimneys which can still be seen.

In the standard monastic plan the monks' kitchen is at the lower or western end of the frater where it was also conveniently situated in relation to the cellarage in the west range where the foodstuffs were stored and the great court whence they were collected from granary and garden. The kitchen at the priory of Castle Acre in Norfolk is here situated and would also appear to have served the abbot's house which is conveniently close.

This kitchen, which had been razed to its foundations, had its roof carried upon four massive stone piers suggesting the existence of a central turret as seen at Glastonbury. The question is whether there was a central hearth—surely most inconvenient for cooking upon—or whether there existed, as at Glastonbury, a hearth in each angle of the square, with the four flues gathered over and collected in the centre. In default of another discovery of a more perfect 'four-poster' kitchen we shall probably never know.

The siting of the kitchen where the frater and the cellarer's range met each other must have added considerably to the attractions of the abbey façade, especially where, as was the Cistercian arrangement, no great court with its clutter of buildings concealed this from view.

One can easily imagine the belated traveller approaching from the west the long panorama of the abbey lit by the sunset, his interest hovering between the elaborate façade of the abbey church and, away to his right hand, the high flues of the abbey kitchen smoking cheerfully and suggesting the possibility of hot food soon to be enjoyed.

# 9

# The Cloister

Plans, especially if they be elaborately drawn, are fascinating things to study. But when examining the plans of individual buildings it is well to remember that it is not just areas of accommodation or communication at which one is looking. For each individual building has to be covered with a roof and the plan of each may be governed by that roof. Its walls have to carry its timbers without either letting the timber spread and slip or collapsing themselves under their pressure.

Planning enables you to get the accommodation that you want. But in the end all planning is governed by structural possibilities of which the principal problem is set by the roof.

Early-medieval roofs were open constructions of timber rafters set in pair or 'couples' across the building and tied together near the apex by short horizontal timbers called 'collars'. They were steeply pitched and covered with short lengths of oak boarding called shingles and set in much the same fashion as clay tiles are today. The shingles, however, would have been about a foot and a half or two feet in length. In a dry summer they warped and split and the roofs leaked upon the occupants of the apartments below. During the fourteenth century vital parts of the roofs began to be ceiled in with boarding known as wainscot which followed a curved form along the underside of the roof timbers and resembled the tilt of a waggon or wain.

Derbyshire and the Somerset Mendips produced a large proportion of Europe's lead, greatly in demand for covering roofs. With the general introduction of lead roofing in this country, the fourteenth century saw the pitch of roofs lowered as there was now no need for a steep pitch to cope with an inefficient covering. Moreover lead on a steep pitch slipped and 'crept'. The reduction of roof pitch brought with it the depression of the curvature of arches and in this way transformed Gothic architecture.

As roof pitch sank more and more under the influence of the plumbers it was realized that it could in fact be virtually flat.

The really important structural discovery resulting from this fact was that roofs no longer exerted that overturning pressure upon walling which had been the curse of the Gothic builders throughout the centuries and which they were only just beginning to find out how to check with buttresses.

But the aesthetic discovery lay in the fact that a roof was now a ceiling as well, and that there was no longer any need to worry about the untidy appearance of the medieval jumble of roof timbers and whether one could cover this with a high vault. For the carpenters, now joiners, could do wonderful things to the underside of a late-medieval roof.

In East Anglia, where lead was not so easily procurable, the carpenters kept to the steeply pitched roofs and worked up the elaborate timber 'trusses' spanning the building into elaborate forms of which the most spectacular was the 'hammer-beam'.

But generally speaking it had become accepted that what had been roofing timbers were now ceiling timbers as well. Embellishment of the underside of the panelling formed from the system of roof timbering produced some magnificent ceilings with which to close the Gothic era. Lofty halls such as monastic fraters and more intimate apartments such as first-floor chambers benefited from the dignity conferred upon them by such fine pieces of decorative carpentry.

The old 'stone soller' was now not so necessary, and timber floors took its place, thereby freeing the ground storey from the obstructive pillars and providing for the new privy parlours an elaborate ceiling.

At a period when money for the elaborate vaulted ceilings of the thirteenth century was no longer so freely available, the abbey builders could accept with gratitude the new system of covering buildings and look back with relief at the old stone vaulting which had been for so long regarded as the only really architectural ceiling.

For although the structural function of a stone vault was to support a stone floor to an upper storey, its aesthetic significance lay in the fact that it provided a waterproof and fireproof ceiling of superlative dignity.

The development of the ribbed vault from the barrel vault and through the rib-less 'groined' vault has been explained in Chapter 6. An improvement upon the primitive 'quadripartite' system of a pair of diagonal ribs was offered by inserting ribs along the ridges of the vault, thus halving the areas of 'web' left to be vaulted. Then came wall-ribs and extra sets of ribs between diagonal ribs and ridges. The idea was to concentrate on getting in as many ribs as possible thus reducing the areas of the webs. The devoted approach to their task which characterized the Gothic craftsmen made it necessary for them to convert every problem solved into an excuse for creating something of beauty, so still more short lengths of rib were introduced to make a stellar vaulting system. As one reads this one might spare a thought for the incredible problems in solid geometry offered by the carving of a stone where several elaborately moulded ribs met each other, and the necessity for covering the meeting-place with an area given up to the carver for converting into a lovely 'boss' such as may be seen in our cloisters and, still more impressive, up in the high vault where their detail could not be seen. These stellar systems are technically known as 'lierne' vaults from the name of the short lengths of ribs of which they are composed. (See Plate 2.)

Such was the persistent devotion of the masons, born of their long centuries of working at the architecture which was to have no equal, that they were able to build up the whole system of stones on the ground and set it up in a completely pre-fabricated bay of carved panelling. This had been gradually developing into a series of fans spreading from each point of support; hence the fan-like effect giving its name of 'fan vault' to the final form of the medieval stone ceiling which came to an end when the abbey lodges closed down for ever in 1539.

Fan vaulting, once no doubt spanning over many a tall church now levelled with the turf, but still to be enjoyed at the abbey churches of Gloucester, Sherborne, and Bath, must have been a very costly form of ceiling to raise above a high building. However, it was often used—as can be seen from a number of pathetic remains of its passing in the ruins of our abbeys—over the walks of cloisters which were rebuilt after the middle of the fifteenth century to improve the comfort of the strolling monks.

For the cloister was the real home of the monk, not the bleak dorter, nor the frater with its constant strange noises of clatter and mastication. The cloister was his retreat, his study, and at the same time his promenade where, it will be remembered, chat was forbidden.

The cloister has formed a part of monastic life since quite early days. At the monastic settlement now known as Um es Surab a few miles to the south of the Byzantine cathedral city of Bosra in Syria is a monastery founded in 489 which is typical of a number in that region. Its church is a simple aisle-less building vaulted in the local manner with slabs of black basalt. The cloister is to the north, for in that region, now part of the Syrian desert, the desire is for shade. The contemporary houses in the locality are two-storeyed, with loggias on the ground floor and balconies to the living-room over. The cloister at Um es Surab is similarly two-storeyed, divided up into small rooms which were presumably the cells of the monks on the upper storey and storerooms below. Above all rises a slender bell-tower typical of the monasteries in the region. The balconies in this cloister might have been used for sitting in the shade, the lower loggias would form the cloister promenade.

That was the fifth century in Orthodox Syria. The earliest cloister known in this country is that discovered at St. Augustine's Abbey at Canterbury which is believed to date from the tenth. Only its foundations remain, but they seem to bear a close resemblance to the cloister as we know it. The cloister was to the north of the abbey church, the foundations of which also remain.

The cloister court represents the enclosure symbolic of the monastic life. Around it, however, the covered alleys seem to perform two functions, as covered promenade and means of access in bad weather between the buildings making up the monastery.

The verandah as an external corridor joining the rooms of a colonial bungalow and appearing in some of the more charming of our Regency villas, was universally employed by the Romano-British villa-builders for the same purpose. Recalling the pillared porticos of nobler architecture and called *porticus*, these verandahs were also attached to the rural temples and their successors the early Christian churches erected following St. Augustine's mission. They must have formed a notable feature of the architecture of Roman Britain and may well have survived in the memory of men well into the Dark Ages. If the remaining timber churches of Norway, which are believed to date from the eleventh and twelfth centuries, give any indication, the wooden churches of Anglo-Saxon England may well have also been surrounded by verandahs presumably also to protect the planked screen walls from becoming too saturated. (See Figs. 3 and 4.)

We are all familiar with the type of building known as a 'lean-to' (in the West *linhay*, pronounced 'linney'), a secondary class of structure attached to the side of a parent building and having a roof which leans against its high wall. One sees them everywhere today in farmyards housing the tractors which have supplanted the farm cart.

In medieval days the lean-to was widely used for two purposes. In its temporary form as a shelter for masons working upon a building it was called a 'lodge'—possibly an abbreviation of 'lodging'—but the general term in use was *pentice*—short for *appentice* and seeming to signify an appendage.

The pentice was used as an external corridor. The rambling palaces of the twelfth-century Court in this country comprised a complex of scattered 'King John' houses, a number of which were flanked by pentices between the ends of which persons in fine clothing might dash when hoping to escape a wetting.

The abbey cloister had pentices passing along the east and west sides giving access to the various rooms and joining them to the 'processional' doorways leading into the nave of the church. A south pentice passing between them beside the high refectory wall would be an obvious convenience, and once the masons had finished with their lodge beside the church on its site could be converted into a sunny north walk. In this fashion the cloister court became provided with a covered promenade.

The walks of the cloister also served as corridors joining the various buildings of the abbey, entrances to the more important apartments being indicated by doorways of high architectural merit.

First and foremost of these came the entrance to the chapter house, always set near the centre of the east walk of the cloister and its principal feature. As the west front to the most important apartment in the monastery it was always given special treatment and had a fine doorway flanked by a pair of two-light windows, the whole elaborately ornamented with carving. (See Plates 14 and 19.)

Close to it, at the end of the east walk, was the processional doorway to the church (see Plate 14), again indicated by a fine piece of architectural detail such as remains among the ruins of the Augustinian abbey of Lilleshall in Shropshire.

Where the west walk of the cloister reached the church there was a similar doorway, the western processional doorway.

Particular attention was always given to the frater doorway near the west end of the southern walk of the cloister. Having no windows to set it off, unlike the chapter house doorway, it was always elaborated to a superlative degree and was probably the most architecturally splendid doorway outside the church. (There is a doorway in Malmesbury near the bridge which must surely have been once the frater door at the abbey.)

If we followed the route of the processional way from the church around the cloister we should first pass on our left the entrance to the inner parlour or 'slype' leading to the infirmary and the cemetery of the monks, after which would come the entrance façade of the chapter house. At the end of the walk would probably be the day-stair to the dorter but beside it at its foot might be a doorway leading into the monks' 'warming-house' beneath the dorter and next to the chapter house. Turning right into the walk opposite the church we should reach the fine doorway to the refectory, probably with its elaborate 'laver' or washing-place in the wall beside it. Turning the angles of the cloister once more we should keep along the western walk back to the church, passing on our way the echoing tunnel of the outer parlour leading to the great court beyond.

The original cloisters probably had the eaves of their roofs carried on timber posts like any other 'linhay' (Fig. 19a), but by the twelfth century this was being replaced by miniature arcades. These were so low, owing to the high pitch of the roofs, that the arches had to be small and the colonnettes supporting them very slender. As the minimum thickness of a masonry wall in those days was close upon three feet, the colonnettes had to be set in pairs athwart the wall. The result was a charming miniature arcade.

These cloister arcades with the miniature arches carried upon coupled colonnettes, seen so frequently today in the twelfth-century cloisters of Continental abbeys, have suffered so badly in this country that hardly an example remains. A short length may be seen in the arcade of the little cloister of the cathedral priory at Canterbury and another rather pathetic fragment has managed to survive in the galilee porch to the church at Fountains Abbey.

An angle of the cloister at Rievaulx Abbey in Yorkshire has been rebuilt as a sample of what has been lost.

One finds fragments of the colonnettes and specimens of their interesting variety of caps scattered everywhere about monastic sites, most of which must be from twelfth-century cloister arcades never rebuilt during the Gothic era. On the village green at Alderbury in Wiltshire a drinking fountain has been made up with colonnettes from the cloister of Ivychurch Priory, the ruins of which may be seen close by.

Similar miniature arcades, only one colonnette deep, may be found used as dados along walls, in particular the slype leading out of the cloister at Gloucester and inside the gatehouse of Evesham Abbey in Worcestershire.

The cloister walks began as covered ways the roofs of which were steep lean-to's attached to the walls of the buildings surrounding them. With the coming of lead roofing and the resultant reduction in roof pitch the outer walls of the cloister could be raised and designed as fine arcades with more spacious arches. (Fig. 19b.)

But such cloister arcades are not common, for their wide openings would have detracted from the comfort of the cloister rather than improved it. It was not until the fourteenth century, the era of the great traceried windows, that the cloister became completely transformed. With its wall no longer open arcades but protected by glazing as with any other building, the cloister alleys became promenades of considerable distinction. Stone-vaulted ceilings soon followed, and these eventually developed into the lovely stone fans which were the delight of the masons during the twilight of the age of the abbots. Outside in the cloister court, ranks of pinnacled buttresses began to appear to support the vaults within.

The cloister was the centre of the abbey's daily life. The east walk was the main thoroughfare passing the chapter house and the inner parlour leading towards the little cloister and infirmary. It was in the little parlour that the rule of silence was relaxed in order that the officers of the abbey could meet and discuss its affairs. In the east walk, also, were buried the abbots for whom no room could be found beneath the chapter house. (Fig. 18.)

Opposite the east walk was that into which the outer parlour opened and where the novices were instructed by the novice-master.

The south walk having in it the abbey laver was the site of the ceremonial Maundy washing of poor men's feet.

The sunny north walk, most loved by the monks, was the *scriptorium* where the books were laboriously written.

At Gloucester one can still enjoy the architectural skill with which the masons turned each bay into a study or 'carrel' lit through the tall tracery by the sunlight coming over the frater roof.

The walling of the abbey cloister, which was almost entirely formed of glazing, was quickly destroyed at the Suppression for its leadwork. The building was then useless, even as a house for calves. The roofs came off for fuel and the stonework was easily pulled to pieces. Thus there are very few of the abbey cloisters remaining today.

We are of course exceedingly fortunate in having had saved for us some of the magnificent cloisters of the cathedral priories. Some of the cathedrals also provided themselves with cloisters. We can still walk in the austere cloister of Salisbury Cathedral and compare it with the more developed Gothic of Norwich Cathedral Priory. The splendour of Gloucester's fan-vaulted ceiling is of course in a

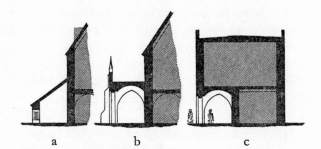

a          b                    c

Fig. 19   *Development of the cloister*
(a) shows the twelfth-century cloister
with its steeply-pitched shingled roof
supported by a low arcade of small
arches. At (b) is shown the vaulted
cloister covered with a lead roof and at
(c) the final phase of the cloister where
it becomes absorbed into the undercroft
of the claustral buildings

class by itself and represents a glorious swan-song to the English cloister.

One of the most perfect of the Gothic cloisters remaining is that of a nunnery. Few medieval nunneries have survived in this country. A notable exception is the Augustinian nunnery of Lacock in Wiltshire which has completely lost its church but retains a good deal of its claustral building including the cloister.

The church was aisle-less but from the trace of it left upon its north wall appears to have been of stately proportions.

The cloister adjoined it to the north. Round its whole perimeter the undercrofts remain, together with most of the upper storey though its apartments have been largely remodelled. The chapter house displays the usual attractive entrance features but is unusual

in having two pillars along its axis which may have proved somewhat obstructive to vision when the chapter was in session. The
stair to the dorter is in the thickness of a nearby wall.

The cloister is one of the best preserved of any belonging to a
small monastic house. It is of late date, with spacious windows and
vaulting supported by many ribs, the intersections of which are
covered with carved bosses.

During the fifteenth century many attempts were made to convert the cloister from a mere vaulted corridor into a fine apartment
—that of Forde Abbey in Dorset, for example, was reconstructed
in splendid style just before the Suppression. But the most efficient
type of cloister design may be seen in those constructed by the new
Orders of friars that entered this country during the thirteenth
century.

The development of the cloister alley from a lean-to pentice
into a proper building having a low-pitched roof enabled it to be
absorbed within the buildings against which it had been hitherto
set. The result of this discovery was a revolutionary type of
cloister completely changing the plan of the adjoining claustral
buildings. For whereas these had been constructed with a central
row of pillars down the middle this was now replaced by a medial
wall which formed the back of the cloister. Behind this wall was
the ordinary vault carrying the 'stone soller' over, while the other
half was the cloister with its fine stellar vaulting. (Fig. 19c.)

A valuable fragment remains of the south-west angle of the
cloister at Muchelney Abbey in Somerset which has been preserved through having been absorbed into the lower storey of an
abbot's house built late in the monastic era and saved to be a farmhouse. As befits all Somerset work its vaulting is elaborately
attractive and gives us an idea not only of what has been lost at
Muchelney but how much English architecture suffered when these
splendid promenades were swept away.

The remains of wall-arcading, some of it of high architectural
quality, on the walls of claustral buildings remind us continually
of what was pulled away from them with their cloisters. How
attractive must have been some of the late cloisters such as those
of Romsey Abbey which were two-storeys high, as were those of

15. Beaulieu

16. Easby

Polsloe Priory by Exeter, a most surprising expression of Gothic architecture the loss of which is sad indeed.

Very strange indeed are the great cloisters of the Carthusians which enclose areas more like paddocks than cloister courts. These were used as cemeteries and behind the surrounding walls were the small cottage-like cells, each with its garden. (The Carthusians were in fact the gardeners of the Middle Ages.) Beside the cloister was a diminutive but gracious church with a central bell-tower set between nave and choir, both aisle-less, and flanked by a chapter house. Not far away were the small frater and its kitchens.

The cloister must have been an architectural feature much loved by the medieval churchman—representing perhaps a haven of dignity and peace away from the ugly medieval world of poverty, squalor, and violence. The largest, that of Salisbury, belonged to a chapter of secular canons who were not enclosed but still felt they needed a cloister in which to meditate. The cloister of Westminster Abbey survived the destruction of some of the buildings surrounding it. Most of the cathedral priories managed to keep at least their cloisters at the Suppression.

In English monastic architecture one cloister today stands out above all the rest, that of the Benedictine abbey of Gloucester, since the Suppression Gloucester Cathedral. The church itself is a structure of great interest, its interior vastly impressive, the tower rising above its roofs architecture at its noblest. The amazing nave with its towering pillars, massive imitations of the Classical Orders, have no equal anywhere though nearby Tewkesbury Abbey and the lost nave of Pershore were attempts to emulate them.

What is so particularly interesting about the interior of Gloucester Cathedral is the excessive contrast between this original work and the exquisite sophistry of the vaulted ceiling rising above them, product of the twilight of monastic architecture. The whole presbytery, culminating in what is conceivably the largest window in England, forms a splendid swan-song to the age of the abbots.

North of the church—the town lay to the south—is a cloister contemporary with the fan vaulting in the church and of the same elaborate character. The walks are protected from the weather by ranges of stately windows. The equipment of the cloister, its 'carrels' for study and book-production, its long laver for washing, are all products of the mason and stone-carver at the culmination of their centuries of experience in making of our abbeys things of beauty, some of which, at least, have been suffered to remain for us today.

# The Chapter House

The monks hall, changed though it was out of all recognition from the contemporary secular hall, was nevertheless a modification of an apartment which had been known to architecture for centuries. But we now arrive at an apartment entirely foreign to medieval Europe. A democratic institution—a conference hall.

An abbot was elected by the community and governed subsequently in conclave with it. From the first St. Benedict, not unmindful of the fact that he was instituting into the feudal world an Order to be organized upon democratic lines, set out provision for an assembly hall in which each community could discuss both matters concerned with religion and problems connected with administration.

From the start it was not anticipated that the buildings would be anything other than rectangular rooms of no great architectural merit. But by the time the monastic plan reached this country the chapter house had become the building next in importance to the church itself and always sited next to it, usually as a direct attachment to the south or cloister transept except that the inner parlour leading to the infirmary separated the two, perhaps as an acoustic lock. Sometimes, as at Cluniac Much Wenlock Priory in Shropshire, the two shared a common wall.

By the eleventh century the chapter house could probably have been matched in internal dignity with the great halls of the royal palaces, but these would have been of the ordinary domestic type cluttered up with pillars and carrying an open timber roof, whereas it was possible in most cases to cover the Benedictine chapter house with a good vaulted ceiling.

Bristol Cathedral, before the Suppression a church of the Augustinians, has a splendid twelfth-century chapter house adjoining it.

As an apartment designed solely for conferences the interior of the chapter house was seized upon by the medieval builders as an opportunity for trying their hand at interior decoration. The walling was sometimes lined internally with interlacing arcading embellished with the same carved motifs encountered within the churches themselves. The chapter house of Much Wenlock was elaborately ornamented in this fashion; one of its walls remains as the outer face of the south transept, the rest has disappeared.

At the foot of an elaborately arcaded dado was ranged the chapter seating, centred upon the raised seat of the abbot enthroned, flanked by his officers, at the upper end farthest from the entrance doorway, leading out of the cloister.

Externally the west front of the chapter house was always developed into an impressive architectural presentation, taking the form of a fine entrance doorway flanked by a pair of two-light windows. The ordinance of this particular feature must be of some antiquity and the strange massive arcade at Winchester Cathedral which is all that remains of its chapter house has a very primitive Byzantine appearance.

The interesting feature about the chapter house façade in the abbey cloister is that it was almost entirely concealed at the time of its erection by a cloister roof of very steep pitch and as a result very low eaves. Only a very foreshortened view was thus possible of the architect's design; only now that the cloisters are down can we see any number of these attractive frontispieces exposed to view at last. (See Plate 14.)

All the Orders, even the somewhat pedestrian Cistercians, followed the universal practice. The façade at the Augustinian abbey at Haughmond in Shropshire is notable, and at the Premonstratensian abbey at Torre in Devon one of the principal features remaining is the triplet of openings indicating the chapter house.

Of the once-mighty Cistercian abbey of Hayles in Gloucester-shire, with its great church ending in an elaborate French-type *chevet* built to contain a drop of the Holy Blood and consecrated in the presence of the King and all the notables of the land . . . nothing is left except three lonely arches which indicate the entrance to the chapter house.

One of the most impressive medieval elevations, fortuitously displayed through the destruction not only of the cloister but the refectory, is the west front of the monks' house at Furness Abbey in Lancashire (Plate 14), a house founded under the auspices of Savigny but transferred with the rest of the English houses of that Order to Cîteaux in 1147.

The ruins today form an impressive group of monastic remains warm red in colour from the use of sandstone. Splendid in their ruin are the presbytery and transepts of the great church, with the immense sweep of the monks' house, the longest in this country, seeming to reach interminably towards the south.

The aisled chapter house, spanning forty feet and sixty feet in length, must have been a splendid apartment. (Plate 20.) It was approached through a porch-like vestibule—like that at Hayles but a century earlier—before which three elaborately ornamented arches led from the cloister. The dignity of these features is emphasized by its setting in the whole magnificent elevation, and expanded by the addition of two smaller arches leading to the inner parlour and the slype leading to the infirmary which in Cistercian houses were two different apartments.

On the upper floor of this long house were the dorter of the monks and-half-way along its length, on its eastern side, the rere-dorter connected to it by a bridge.

The great ruin of Furness still retains a vital atmosphere not only illustrating the tremendous achievements of twelfth-century architects but forcibly reminding the visitor of the commercial brilliance of the hard-working Cistercian monks. For as early as the thirteenth century the abbey was already working the local iron deposits and by the end of the century was running an active smelting industry exporting iron by sea. Thus the Black Death which spelt ruin for the entirely pastoral abbeys of Yorkshire left

Furness still gainfully employed. And at the Suppression the monks simply handed over their industry to the founders of the great port of Barrow.

Some impression of the effort which was constantly being made to neglect no opportunity for enhancing the dignity of the monk-made abbot and developing him into a personage of weight may be gained when one finds that some of the twelfth-century chapter houses actually have apsidal ends to them. The apse at this period was normally reserved as a setting for an altar, but this seems to have been enthroning the abbot with the dignity of a magistrate in a Roman basilica.

Practically the only notable relic of the once-powerful abbey of Reading in Berkshire is the wreck of its apsidal chapter house, an apartment so lofty that its façade was in two storeys, the uppermost of which appeared above the cloister roof.

The foundations of other apsidal chapter houses may be seen in a number of places; Castle Acre Priory in Norfolk and Kenilworth Priory in Warwickshire are examples. At Rievaulx Abbey in Yorkshire are the remains of a large apsidal chapter house entirely surrounded, including the apse, by an aisle. The reason for this remarkable addition will be explained when we come to examine the glorious ruins at Rievaulx. For the time being we will look at an early chapter house of simpler design.

The impressive range of buildings which today represents the Cistercian abbey of Forde in Dorset is likely to attract the eye of the traveller on the main line of the Southern Railway if he looks southwards when leaving Chard for Crewkerne. Forde Abbey today represents one of the most successful of the post-Suppression conversions, for its last abbot, Thomas Chard, who may be remembered as one of the great builders of his era, created for his abbey one of the most sumptuous abbatial residences remaining today.

From the antiquary's point of view Forde is most interesting as it retains one of the few monastic chapter houses still in use as an apartment, in this case a private chapel. It is an early building of the twelfth century, vaulted in two large bays without any central supports—thus a rarity in Cistercian chapter houses—and presents an excellent illustration of the kind of assembly hall which played such an important part in the daily life of a medieval abbey.

Northwards from the chapter house stretches the monk's house with its long dorter above the usual vaulted undercroft. The abbey church has utterly vanished; it lay to the south of its cloister, the north range of which forms the nucleus of the present mansion. The cloister walk is a lovely fragment of Abbot Chard's rebuilding project, and thus represents one of the last cloisters ever to be built in this country. Fragments of the original twelfth-century laver may be recognized, for we are close to the frater which still stands above its vaulted undercroft, as does its kitchen, still used for its proper purpose in the house of today.

Westwards of this are some remains of the house of the lay-brothers—those inevitable companions of the Cistercian monks—and still farther west is the abbey's proudest building, the great hall of Abbot Chard, one of the most beautiful creations of the medieval domestic architect begun less than twenty years before the destruction of the abbey. At the lower end of the hall is its slender porch-tower with a storeyed oriel window reaching to the battlements from above the entrance archway. At the upper end of the hall is a block of apartments, said to have been remodelled by Inigo Jones, which were designed to provide lodgings for the abbot and his guests. The whole building might be described as an architectural treat.

It will be readily understood that the architectural dignity of the chapter house made it desirable for it to be provided with a vaulted ceiling so that the normal jumble of medieval roof timbers could be decently concealed from view. But with the building's increasing size and importance it became apparent that vaulting above a low apartment such as can be seen at Forde created an oppressive atmosphere. Vaulting over a wide span requires height to remove the crushing effect engendered by a massive stone ceiling so close overhead.

Subdivision of the span would have been the normal solution, but a line of pillars down the centre of an assembly hall depending for its effect upon a view along a central axis towards the seat of the abbot might have appeared obstructive. At the large chapter house of Roche Abbey in Yorkshire this system was adopted.

But not long after the Conquest some of the larger Benedictine abbeys were abandoning the axially planned rectangular chapter house in favour of a circular form having a central pillar from which vaulting could spring across to the side walling. This ingenious solution to the vaulting problem was to bestow upon our abbeys and cathedrals some of the most beautiful memorials of the Middle Ages in England.

It was not until late in the medieval period that the Gothic engineers began to form some notion of the proper fashion in which to manage the abutments to their high vaults. The early barrel vaults relied for their support upon walling of massive and most uneconomical thickness. Even though the rigid adherence to the system of design by bays spread to the elevations of the buildings so that each bay came to be represented by pilaster strips passing up the external face of the walling, these had no structural significance and were useless as abutment. Even as late as the thirteenth century when the pilasters began to increase their projection until it equalled and even exceeded their width and assert themselves as features of architectural punctuation, they still were not designed to exert a thrust against the pressure of the vaults behind them. Not until the fourteenth century brought the more sophisticated era of the High Gothic with its strong Continental affiliations did the English engineers begin to realize that their vaulting systems, springing as they did from isolated points in the wall, derived no support from the walling between these points; from this realization was born the splendid fenestration of the era with its vast expanses of glazing set between mullions and beneath an arched head filled with intricate tracery. At last the wall between spread outwards from the building to form true buttresses each capped with a tall pinnacle as a counterpoint to the internal thrust.

The polygonal chapter houses then became stone lanterns filled with painted glass—apartments which for beauty and light can compare with anything in architectural history.

A number of our cathedrals yet retain their superb polygonal chapter houses. Such are those of Salisbury and Wells, Lincoln and

Worcester. But the abbeys long ago lost their lantern-like structures in an age when their beauty had ceased to impress, they served no longer any useful purpose, and their materials were coveted for use in more practical structures.

At Cockersand in Lancashire all that is left of a Premonstratensian abbey is a small hexagonal chapter house isolated in the middle of a field.

Worcester Cathedral Priory and neighbouring Pershore Abbey started the fashion for circular chapter houses before the end of the eleventh century. The idea soon became popular and the larger Benedictine abbeys followed suit, to be followed soon after by the Augustinians and even the Cistercians. Bolton in Yorkshire, Whalley in Lancashire, Thornton in Lincolnshire had octagonal chapter houses of which the last has a fine fragment remaining. Bridlington Priory in Yorkshire had a ten-sided chapter house, while a similar one at the great abbey of Evesham in Worcestershire was fifty feet across; its twenty-five foot vaulting spans must have made it a very impressive apartment internally.

It will be remembered that the aim of the monastic planner had been to try to attach the end of the monks' house directly to the church transept in order that the monks could pass between these during the night hours by an internal stair without having to pass through the cloister. A tall chapter house intervening at this point would have the effect of preventing this connection, and so the device was often employed of forming a vestibule beneath the monks' dorter where the original chapter house had been, with the new chapter house beyond it, eastwards of the monks' house. These vestibules were generally vaulted in nine small bays from four slender pillars, the architectural façade of the chapter house becoming transferred to the vestibule preceding it.

Probably the best-known polygonal chapter house in this country is that at Westminster Abbey, the royal foundation which became the burial place of England's kings.

The abbey church was rebuilt by Henry III during the thirteenth century in the style of a French cathedral. It has a nave twelve bays long covering the site of the nave built by Edward the Confessor before the Conquest; the monks' choir occupies the four easternmost of these bays. The presbytery has three bays and ends in an apse which is surrounded by an ambulatory, out of which originally led a *chevet* of five chapels of which the centre one has been removed to make way for a lady chapel added by Henry VII at the end of the fifteenth century.

The cloister is on the south, the river side. The monks' house reached from the south transept of the Confessor's church and was attached to its successor. Its eleventh-century vaulted undercroft is pierced by a vestibule leading to the fine octagonal chapter house with its central pillar and a high vault supported externally by a ring of flying buttresses.

Next to this vestibule the day-stair to the dorter separates it from the abbey treasury known as the Chapel of the Pyx. Afterwards the undercroft continues as the warming-house of the monks, an apartment which will be described later in this chapter. The monks' house continues well south of the cloister the east walk of which continues alongside it until it reaches the slype or inner parlour—the 'Dark Entry' of the Westminster school-boy—leading to the little infirmary cloister and the remains of the infirmary chapel now built up into post-Suppression houses.

Looking back from the little cloister one can see high up a solitary window remaining from the monks' rere-dorter.

The long east passage ends southwards at the site of the prior's lodging.

The large frater which lay beside the south walk of the cloister has disappeared. The walk itself, however, continues westwards as the outer parlour past the site of the west range and into the great court of the abbey known today as Dean's Yard. Close by, separated by a court from the old west range, is the abbot's house comprising his hall with the kitchen at one end and his chamber—the 'Jerusalem Chamber'—at the other.

Towards the end of the monastic era the Augustinians, true to their reputation for enterprise, erected at some of their priories—Kirkham in Yorkshire and Lanercost in Cumberland are examples—large rectangular chapter houses with strongly buttressed walls suggesting high walls and large windows. They would appear to date from the fifteenth century. Certainly lead-roofed, they were most probably finished with one of the splendid timber ceilings of the period which had made the high vault no longer necessary. Canterbury Cathedral has a vast chapter house of similar proportions but is covered with a West Country cradle roof of doubtful antiquity.

The original Cistercian concept of austerity in all things caused them to set their chapter houses beneath the dorter in the area occupied by the vestibule in the Benedictine plan. The Cistercian chapter house was vaulted in the same 'four-poster' fashion so as to enable the dorter to reach the church and a night-stair. This type of chapter house remains intact at Buildwas Abbey in Shropshire and Valle Crucis Abbey in Denbighshire.

One of the great abbey ruins in this country is that of the Cistercian church at Kirkstall in Yorkshire, its perfect nave overtopped by the wreck of its lantern tower, beyond which stretches the presbytery with a great gap in its eastern wall marking the site of a large fifteenth-century window. (Plate 4.) Among the remaining claustral buildings is the chapter house with its pillars centrally arranged and in consequence a pair of entrance arches instead of the usual central one.

At Lacock Abbey in Wiltshire, however, which also has central pillars, the central doorway is retained.

Still used for domestic purposes are the chapter houses of Birkenhead Priory in Cheshire and Beeleigh Abbey in Essex.

In a previous chapter it was noted that the enclosure of the cloister yard on the west side by the cellarer's range necessitated the provision of a passage through this called the 'outer parlour' by which the cloister could be reached from the world outside. Some communication was also needed between the cloister and other buildings which were part of the monastery but not claustral. Chief of these was the infirmary, an isolated building to which sick monks were transferred. Beside this, at the east end of the church, was the monks' graveyard.

The vaulted undercroft of the monks' dorter provided a site for another passage, sometimes known as the 'slype' and serving as the symbolic exit from the cloister corresponding to the outer parlour through which it was entered. It was known as the 'inner parlour' and in it speech was permitted between abbey officers discussing administrative matters. (See Fig 18.)

Both parlours were cut through the undercroft of their respective ranges immediately adjoining the church so as not to waste space, the inner parlour thus normally coming between the chapter house and the transept. Cistercian builders, however, evolved their own plan for this part of the east range which will be discussed in Chapter 14.

Houses which embarked upon unconventional planning had to adjust the siting of their inner parlours to suit. The Augustinians, who were apt to set their infirmaries in unusual positions, fitted in their inner parlours to provide easy communication between them and the cloister.

During the Middle Ages the normal form of domestic space-heating was the bonfire of logs in the middle of the hall floor with the smoke drifting upwards and leaking out through a vent at the top of a gable wall, or in later days a louvered turret perched upon the roof timbers. It was an excellent system allowing no loss of heat as with a flue. But the introduction of a second storey, as with a private house or castle keep, demanded the provision of a fire-hearth set in the wall with a flue passing up through the wall as a vent. The first vents were slots set vertically on either side of a projection like a pilaster strip so that the smoke could escape from the leeward one if the other was temporarily blocked up with straw. Chimney pots or 'tunnels' came in with the end of the twelfth century.

Essential to the great house was the cooking fire on its cavernous hearth with a wide flue leading upwards through the heart of a great masonry chimney stack. Every abbey would have a main kitchen attached to the frater and by about 1200 the abbots' houses and perhaps the infirmary would have their own kitchens in which meat could be cooked.

As early as the ninth century it had become accepted that if the monastic way of life was to be introduced into this country some kind of heating would have to be provided to enable the Anglo-Saxon monks to survive the winter. Thus each abbey was permitted to prepare a 'warming-house' where a fire would burn in winter to thaw out monks who had been engaged in manual work or craft or meditating in the cloister. As these apartments were sited on the ground floor of a two-storeyed range a wall fireplace and flue had to be constructed.

In the standard monastic plan the warming-house was established in the undercroft of the monks' dorter immediately next to the chapter house. It would have been entered from the east walk of the cloister near the foot of the day-stair.

An interesting warming-house heated by a central fire may be seen at Tintern Abbey. Above the hearth a pair of wide-span arches carry two sides of the great flue while smaller internal arches support the other two sides, the whole no doubt capped originally by a stone turret similar to that at Glastonbury. Access to the Benedictine Abbess of Shaftesbury's huge barn at Place near Tisbury in Wiltshire was through two gatehouses each of which had a lodging attached to it. That adjoining the inner gatehouse has a small hall heated by one such device; the arches and the turret itself may still be seen.

The houses of the abbots, used as they were constantly for the entertainment of important travellers, had to be provided with fireplaces in hall and chamber. As the first halls were on an upper storey, stall-fireplaces had to be arranged.

The only surviving chimney of the thirteenth century may be seen above the prior's house at Abingdon Abbey in Berkshire; it is a miniature copy of a tower-top having two opposing roofs set crosswise as above the chapter house of the Carthusians of Hinton in Somerset.

The fraters do not appear to have been heated until the wall fireplace became a standard feature of the domestic hall during the fifteenth century. The charming little frater of Cleeve Abbey in Somerset has a fireplace near its upper end.

Since any kind of fireplace would have been unsuited to the monks' choir, heating there was probably by braziers. Where the standard position for a warming-house under the monks' dorter is found to be without a fireplace it is likely that this too was heated by braziers.

With all these fires to feed it is no wonder that one of the 'obedientaries' or abbey officers was the woodward.

The foregoing pages have described the standard plan of the eastern claustral range as employed by all the monastic Orders except the Cistercian, which developed along different lines from the start as will be explained in Chapter 14.

The east walk of the cloister was the principal thoroughfare of the abbey, joining as it did the day-stair from the monks' dorter with the church passing the inner parlour and the chapter house. (See Fig. 18.) It was farthest from the outer parlour and in the heart of the living-quarters—the frater and the dorter.

The monasteries had to guard their valuables, and often those entrusted to them by lay folk. The ground floor under the chamber of the private house was the 'wardrobe' or treasury of the owner. There is some case for suggesting that the northern end of the dorter undercroft, between the warming-house and the chapter house—the position, in fact, of the Chapel of the Pyx in Westminster Abbey—may have been the treasury of the medieval abbey.

# II

# The Little Cloister

─────

Once a monk entered an abbey he left it only through the inner parlour or 'slype' to lie with his brethren in the cemetery. There might however be a transitional stage, for at the end of the parlour was the abbey hospital or infirmary where monks who were sick, either temporarily or suffering from such chronic conditions as old age, were taken to relieve them from the austerities of the monastic life.

The infirmary consisted of a hall, often of the aisled domestic type, having the beds set along the sides as in a hospital ward. At the eastern end was usually a chapel.

The infirmary had to be provided with a special kitchen where nourishing food could be prepared. For patients who were out of bed there was often a small refectory—a flesh-frater or misericord. For the monastic idea, originating in a far warmer clime than that of this country, may well have been hard to sustain on a vegetarian diet.

All medieval buildings were of a type known as single-span, which is to say that basically they were designed as two parallel walls with a roof spanning between these and the ends filled in with gable-ends. Excessive length was of no consequence, but lateral expansion was only possible by carrying the roof over to eaves at a lower level, either directly or by means of lean-to appendages. Only with great difficulty could roofs be set alongside each other because the collection of snow between them would be almost certain to cause internal trouble. For the craft of plumbing was as yet in its infancy and the sealing devices of today were unknown.

Hence the addition of a building to another would suggest setting the two at right angles; thus we get an ordinary L-shaped structure. Two such additions might result in the original building developing wings; were these of considerable projection and their ends joined by a light wall a courtyard would appear.

Thus the courtyard becomes a natural solution to all medieval planning problems.

The development of the pentice principle which had resulted in the invention of the monastic cloister encouraged the introduction of small courtyards into a large planning complex where persons had to pass around the various apartments in indifferent weather.

The kitchen court was a common adjunct to a large medieval house. Round it were gathered storerooms for foodstuffs, granary, bakehouse, brewhouse—water was an unsafe drink in the Middle Ages—and the day-to-day stores known as the pantry and buttery.

Any house-owner with an aversion to wind-borne rubbish would be glad to have it restricted to a court in which it could be allowed to rot away clear of his nose. The great Cistercian abbey of Byland had one such kitchen court set out between the frater—which being a Cistercian one ran north and south—and the long house of the lay-brothers.

The houses of the more powerful of the Benedictine abbots were sometimes arranged round courtyards. The abbots of Westminster and St. Albans were thus accommodated, their courts being, as one might have expected, west of the cellarer's range. These however were exceptions to the normally less presumptuous plan of the normal abbey.

The department of the abbey which made good use of a small courtyard was the infirmary. The infirmary hall was always an impressively large building, having at most times a large number of patients in various states of health. The original hall of the infirmary of the cathedral priory of Canterbury is aisled and its ruins today show the large circular pillars of 'Romanesque' type. The remains of its chapel may still be seen at its eastern end.

17. Rievaulx

18. Fountains

The great Cistercian abbeys continued to build large aisled infirmary halls right into the thirteenth century, indicating that they were fully prepared to use such archaic structures where they were suitable for the purpose required. The infirmary hall at Fountains was aisled at the ends as well as the sides, a modification probably unknown in the secular hall. The thirteenth-century hall at Buildwas was aisled in seven bays.

Generally speaking, however, by the Gothic era the infirmary had settled down as an ordinary hall similar to the dining-hall of the abbey but not of equal height. It was fully equipped with its chapel, kitchen, misericord or flesh-frater, and it often had a lodging attached to it for the infirmarer in order that he could keep a closer watch over his patients.

The little or infirmary cloister is found in the abbeys of all the Orders except those of the Carthusians who lived and died in their own cottages and had no infirmary. The best-known example in this country is that at Westminster Abbey approached by way of the Dark Entry.

One of the principal aims underlying the provision of an infirmary cloister was to enable the convalescent patients to have their own covered promenade for exercise. Another purpose was to provide the pentice system of circulation so that persons could pass from room to room of the infirmary department under cover.

As will be seen later in Chapter 14, the houses of the Cistercian abbots were sited in the vicinity of the infirmary and it was often so arranged that the abbot could also use the little cloister as his promenade and pass by way of it to both the cloister and the presbytery of the church.

The sites where one can best study today the complicated plans of the medieval abbeys are those of the Cistercian abbeys lying desolate in the Yorkshire dales.

After the great ruin of Fountains (Plate 18), that of Rievaulx Abbey (Plate 17) may be placed second in interest and beauty of situation, but unequalled in the perfection of its Gothic architecture. Not so complete as Fountains in that it has been more seriously burrowed into by the spoiler who has removed the nave of the church and the great house of the lay-brothers, it lacks the splendid façade which makes the western approaches to Fountains so memorable. (Plate 18.)

Of the central tower only the east wall remains but flanking it are two massive transepts lacking nothing but their roofs. Eastwards stretches the matchless presbytery, in ruin seeming more perfect for the loss of its outer walls leaving the six splendid Gothic bays open for all to see. (Plate 10.)

The remarkable chapter house, apsidal and completely surrounded by an aisle, has been reduced almost to ground level. The remarkable design of this building may be explained by recalling that the abbots were at first buried in their chapter houses—later in the east walk of the cloister—and that Rievaulx's first abbot, who had been secretary to the founder of the Cistercian Order, St. Bernard of Clairvaux, was after his death canonized as St. William so that a shrine had to be raised over his tomb and the chapter house became a religious building requiring architectural recognition as such.

Following the monastic processional route along the east walk of the cloister one next reaches the inner parlour—here and in all Cistercian houses a separate apartment—and next the day-stair leading to the destroyed dorter. Next is the slype through which one reached the little cloister. The south end of the monks' house, which was of considerable length, was first used in the normal manner as a warming-house, but after the south range of the claustral buildings had been rebuilt on what was to become standard Cistercian lines and the warming-house moved elsewhere, the old one became the novices' room.

The original frater in the south cloister walk had been placed in the usual Benedictine fashion parallel to this, but after the review of Cistercian planning which had resulted in the adoption of a new arrangement, the frater was pulled down and rebuilt at right angles to the cloister, separated from the monks' house by a new warming-house which filled in the gap between the two. West of the frater lay the great kitchen serving both it and the long house of the lay-brothers which lay beside the west walk of the cloister.

With its ranges of immensely tall lancet windows (see Plates

15 and 17) the towering mass of the new frater represents today the wreck of what may well have been the finest medieval domestic building ever to have been erected in this country, certainly in so far as that century of great buildings, the twelfth, is concerned.

Completing the processional journey round the cloister on the way back to the ravaged nave of the church, we find that the long house of the lay-brothers has been reduced to sorry ruins.

Returning along the west walk to the south walk and following this to its eastern end, passing en route the twin lavers by the frater door, we continue past the east walk and go on through the slype leading towards the little cloister. With memories of the vanished dorter which once lay overhead we should think of the slype as a vaulted tunnel, emerging into daylight and continuing along the north walk of the little cloister.

The south side of the little cloister was formed by the monks' rere-dorter which projected eastwards from their house. Facing us to the east is the one-time infirmary hall, impressive in ruin, The decline of the Cistercian abbeys, deprived of the services of their lay-brothers by the Black Death, increased with the approach of the Suppression which possibly only anticipated their bankruptcy. Conditions at Rievaulx were such that the abbot, finding his infirmary hall too large for the present number of patients, converted it into his own hall of residence so that he and his guests could share the rere-dorter of the monks. A new building called the Long House was erected along the north side of the little cloister to accommodate the reduced number of patients.

The above description of Rievaulx Abbey employs for compass directions those of the normal monastic plan. In fact, however, the narrow valley in which it was built forced the planners of the great church to align it north and south so that all the monastic buildings are ninety degrees out.

From the rural Cistercian sheep-farmers we pass to the more sophisticated black canons of St. Augustine, the ruins of whose abbey at Haughmond in Shropshire form one of the most interesting relics of the monastic occupation of England.

Of its great church practically nothing remains but a fine twelfth-century processional doorway indicating the fine architectural quality of the lost building which is, moreover, borne out by the magnificent façade to the chapter house, almost all that remains of the claustral buildings.

The interest of the abbey ruins resides in the buildings surrounding the little cloister which here lies to the south of the greater one, separated from this by the frater which has been almost destroyed though the great fireplaces of its kitchen are still standing.

At the east end of the hall is the abbot's house with a tall bay window. Diagonally athwart the end of the abbot's house and the monks' house in the east range, which was distorted as it passed the little cloister so as to allow for this, is the rere-dorter shared between the monks and the abbot.

The reason why the abbot's house and infirmary hall at Haughmond are so well preserved today is that they were converted into a hall, parlour, and chamber for the post-Suppression grantee; the mansion was, however, burnt out during the Civil War and never rebuilt.

A rather smaller monastic house than Haughmond may be seen at Finchale in Durham where the Benedictine priory church stands complete to its roof. It is an unusual building with all four limbs unusually long, and, having no aisles, appears a trifle lean compared with the usual wide monastic churches. It is a Gothic building with large windows which probably made up with their opulence for the meagre lines of the plan.

The cloister lacks its walks but the buildings around it are of interest notwithstanding the fact that it never seems to have had a cellarer's range to the west but simply a wall closing the cloister on this side.

The frater is nearly complete to its eaves and is a fine building approaching in dignity the Cistercian halls of Fountains and Rievaulx.

To the south of the long presbytery of the church is a court which resembles a little cloister and is entered in the normal manner from the east walk of the main cloister. Along its south side passes the rere-dorter of the monks, and attached to this is the elaborate house of the prior. To the east of this court were the domestic offices including a kitchen, a bakehouse, and a brew-house, apparently the same as those which served the frater but more convenient for attendance upon the prior. As the prior's lodging is of late date and the court is so similar to the normal infirmary cloister it may be that the prior took over an earlier infirmary and converted it into a house for himself and his guests.

The remains of the Cistercian abbey of Whalley which lie beside the River Calder in Lancashire can still illustrate a number of features peculiar to the plans of that Order. Its great church with the splendidly buttressed fourteenth-century presbytery is now nothing but traces in the turf; its octagonal chapter house is in similar state. The undercroft of the monks' house, today lacking its vault, extends to an impressive length and ends in a detached rere-dorter set at the south-east angle of the building. The Cistercian warming-house, sited west of the monks' house between it and the vanished frater, stands to a considerable height. On the west side of the cloister, most of the lay-brothers' house remains roofed and in use.

To the east of the monks' house and parallel with it are the remains of the infirmary hall, an aisle-less apartment forming the eastern side of a court with the abbot's house adjoining it to the south convenient for the rere-dorter of the monks.

At the Suppression the infirmary hall at Whalley was converted into the long gallery of a new mansion, but it is now roofless. The aged John Paslew, last abbot of Whalley, was hanged in 1537 for resisting the suppression of his abbey.

The Cluniacs could always have been trusted to produce an interesting display of architecture wherever they might settle. Their priory of Much Wenlock in Shropshire forms no exception.

Their great church is gone, except for one huge transept the impressive style of which enables one to form an opinion of the scale and beauty of the lost building. Against the transept may be seen part of the elaborate interior arcading of the chapter house of which the usual three-arched façade remains.

The cloister is nothing but a bare yard with all its buildings swept away. At its south-west corner, however, are the remains of an unusual type of circular laver covered by a canopy.

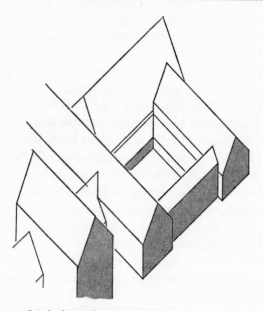

Fig. 20   *Little cloister from south-west*
A common Cistercian plan is shown. Beyond
the frater is the monks' house with the slype
within (see Fig. 25) leading out of the great
cloister into the little cloister. The arrangement
shown has the great hall of the infirmary to the
north, the abbot's house to the east, opposite the
house of the monks, and the cloister closed to
the south by the rere-dorter accessible to both
houses

It is the little cloister to the east of the main cloister which
forms one of the most memorable examples of monastic architecture in this country. Its western range, which was the monks'
house, has been swept away so the little cloister stands open on
that side. On its north side is the twelfth-century infirmary hall,
an interesting building lit by two storeys of windows and having
its chapel at its eastern end.

The east side of the little cloister is occupied by the building
for which Much Wenlock is famous, the fifteenth-century prior's
lodging with its stone-panelled façade, one of the best examples of

domestic architecture of its period remaining today. The northern end of this building contained a lodging for the infirmarian who was able to visit his hall by descending a spiral stair.

The south side of the little cloister would have originally been closed by the monks' rere-dorter also accessible to the prior and his guests.

This may well have been a form of standard plan for the little cloister of the abbeys (see Fig. 20), except that the abbatial houses of the Benedictines were always situated at the western side of the cloister near the outer parlour. For the Cistercians, who preferred to site their abbots' houses east of the cloister, the little cloister formed an ideal arrangement.

The mass of the infirmary hall to the north of the cloister performed the same sheltering service for it that the church did for the great cloister. Then with the abbot's house set north and south along the east side of the cloister and the court closed to the south by the rere-dorter, a highly efficient planning complex was achieved by which the abbot, his guests, and patients all had the use of the little cloister for exercise in wet weather and for access to the rere-dorter as occasion required.

The little cloister was entered from the great cloister along the slype passing under the dorter from the east walk of the latter. This was difficult when the slype adjoined the church as it did in the Benedictine plans, but the Cistercians and others set the slype practically opposite the south walk of the cloister which suited the situation much better.

Those enterprising planners, the Augustinians, sometimes set their infirmary cloisters to the south of the frater in what seems to be on paper a very orderly design, with the little cloister forming a kind of echo of the main one. The most notable example is that at Haughmond already examined, but the same arrangement can be suspected at Llanthony in Monmouthshire where the infirmary hall is now a church, and at Thornton Abbey in Lincolnshire where a farmyard now occupies what may be the site of the little cloister.

The great Cistercian abbey of Byland in Yorkshire is best known for the ruin of its west front with the fragment of a large rose window, and for the strange sight of the whole of the large perimeter of the aisle walls—even the transepts are fully aisled—surrounding a void whence the whole of the main structure has been completely removed. (Plate 29.)

At the south-west angle of the claustral buildings is a kitchen court, and farther east, on the farther side of the monks' house is the little cloister with the abbot's house attached to its north-east angle. Along the western side of the court the east wall of the monks' house has been carried on five arches opening on to the court. The rear wall occupies the site of what would normally have been the row of pillars down the centre of the monks' house.

The same feature occurs at Buildwas Abbey in Shropshire where, however, the infirmary hall is aisled and the cloister as a result rather narrow, allowing for only three arches in place of Byland's five.

These loggias are very remarkable features indeed to find in medieval England. The device is of course the same as that which was eventually to be followed by the designers of the later cloisters who set their alleys entirely within the claustral buildings, a system which could not have been followed prior to the raising of the frater upon an undercroft to match the rest of the buildings.

Unless a monk had been temporarily indisposed through the effects of malnutrition or the periodic blood-letting he left the infirmary, as we have said, for only one destination—the graveyard. This was sited at the east end of the church, near to that part of the great building which had been the embodiment of his life as a monk, and away from the domestic and commercial bustle always taking place around the opposite end of the church.

Amongst the many fine buildings making up the medieval abbey the great hall of the infirmary must be given a high place. Vast ruins such as those at Canterbury Cathedral or the remains of another aisled hall at Gloucester cannot be overlooked, and the hall at Haughmond was clearly regarded as worthy of conversion to a Tudor banqueting hall. The foundations of the hall at Fountains indicate a notable medieval building.

It is a great pity that not one remains intact, except for the small hall at Llanthony Priory in Monmouthshire which is now a church, the infirmary chapel serving as its chancel.

One of the most attractive of architectural compositions is the courtyard, especially if it should be enhanced by the play of light and shade encouraged by the presence of a surrounding arcaded walk. While we could never have expected anything of an oriental nature or even dispensing the charm of a Mediterranean cloister, what the monks built for us was something this country has never again seen since their labours were brought to nothing.

# 12

# Abbots' Houses

We have some knowledge today of bishops, who appear in our midst from time to time at confirmation or induction ceremonies. But the removal from the English scene of the abbots who had for so long formed an important part in the government of the country and could be seen from time to time on their journeys about their wide estates must have deprived us of personages whose places have never been filled.

The abbot was a personage wielding great power. And it has to be appreciated that the difference in social position between the ordinary members of a monastic community and their abbot was immense, not as privates to a captain but rather to a general. The abbot—or in the case of priories the prior (and the powerful Cluniac monasteries were only priories, owing allegiance to the Abbot of Cluny)—was a feudal lord, head of his hall. The rest of his community were faceless.

Philosopher or saint, the abbot had wide estates to manage. He had to be in constant touch with advisers concerning the administration of these. He had to provide elaborate hospitality to travellers of importance. He was inevitably involved from time to time in political issues. Were he a mitred abbot of episcopal rank—the heads of such abbeys as Westminster, St. Albans, Glastonbury, St. Edmundsbury, Evesham, St. Augustine's Canterbury, were mitred abbeys—he actually had to take his seat in Parliament.

Thus it will readily be seen that elevation to the abbot's stall had the result of lifting the monk right out of the community and bringing him close to the peerage. By the end of the twelfth century this had become so obvious that the abbots and the heads of important priories had given up the pretence of living in their dormitories and were being found lodgings in the west range; by the next century they were launching out into proper houses with hall, chamber, chapel, and kitchen.

The extra-mural responsibilities of the abbot have been noted in Chapter 1. Theoretically the democratically elected head of a humble community, he had become of such national importance that his election had to be confirmed by the Crown. He could not possibly have carried out his duties and maintained his political position while sitting on his bed in the dorter.

From a proper house he could administer his abbey, interview his bailiffs and other representatives, discuss external affairs with his colleagues the lay lords, and entertain those important travellers who regarded the abbey as the hotel of the period.

But such a proposition as an abbot's house would have presented problems new to contemporary experience. For the traditional Anglo-Saxon residence, apart from the hut 'built of poles and thatch at every lane end', was the feudal hall. The 'King John's' houses which appeared at the end of the twelfth century were not complete houses but were attached to the end of a hall and merely served as private chambers for sleeping in. By itself the house plan made no provision for meals and no kitchen existed other than that attached to the hall below. In fact everyone who owned a private house owned a feudal hall as well.

The abbot had his high table in the frater so there was no problem as regards his meals. The entertainment of guests could be considered in the future. For the time being all that the abbot needed was a privy chamber, where he could sleep and in which he could interview visitors from the outer world in a less public place than the outer parlour.

In the end it was decided that the situation of this apartment, the abbey's 'front door', would govern the siting of the abbot's lodging and that room on the upper storey of the cellarer's range would be set aside for him. He was set above the parlour and next to the church so that he could if he wished have a window looking into this.

But the problem of housing visitors remained. For the chamber was essentially a privy apartment. One did not entertain in it. Entertainment of any sort in those days meant the provision of a hall, not necessarily the large aisled ground-floor hall of feudalism but the apartment on the *piano nobile* representing the daytime counterpart to the sleeping-chamber. This was probably originally provided by simply allocating a few more bays of the cellarer's range and attaching it to the abbot's chamber, so that he no longer had to entertain in this or perhaps even, on the arrival of important travellers, give up his bed in it to them for a night or more.

For the introduction of the separate house for the abbot had the inevitable result that he was expected to extend the original monastic idea of hospitality to travellers to providing what amounted to hotel accommodation for personages journeying about the country, perhaps in the course of 'eating out' their distant manors.

The *bona fide* traveller was entitled to be fed and housed for two days and nights but nothing was laid down as to the style in which he was to be so accommodated. But a personage arriving at an abbey would have almost certainly laid it down as to how he was to be entertained. If the abbot had only a chamber it would have to be evacuated; possibly even if he had a hall this might not be good enough for the noble guest.

If the King or Queen should be arriving the situation became a crisis. Abbots such as those of St. Edmundsbury or St. Albans had on occasion to turn the whole of the abbey maintenance teams to *building* a house for the visit, which might even be called a 'palace'. Such expense however was not expected of the ordinary abbey.

Nevertheless the attitude towards the hospitality expected of the medieval abbot—who after all had an establishment far in excess of anything in the country other than half-a-dozen royal palaces—encouraged him to build a house for himself which as well as advertising his dignity enabled him to exercise hospitality comparable with this.

By the end of the monastic era an abbot such as Chard of Forde Abbey in Dorset was building a great hall equivalent of the contemporary banqueting hall. And Forde, be it remembered, was only a Cistercian house, which serves to remind one how far these one-time rustic abbeys had been developing along lines similar to those of the Benedictines and Augustinians.

The abbot's guests would certainly reject the vegetarian food supplied to the monks. Hence the provision for the abbot of a special kitchen such as forms the impressive memorial at Glastonbury.

Once the idea of a separate house for the abbot had been agreed upon by the principal Orders at the close of the twelfth century, the development of this feature of the abbey proceeded apace and during the thirteenth century abbots of such important houses as Battle in Sussex erected fine houses complete in every particular.

From the start the abbot's lodging had been planned as a house set out entirely upon the *piano nobile*. The hall was so situated; it was not a large apartment and was simply the day-room and dining-room of the abbot. Next to this was the abbot's chamber, entered from the hall. The idea was for every house to have a private chapel or oratory. And close at hand, though probably on the ground floor, was the kitchen.

The house was entered up a wide stair leading into the hall, and the foot of this stair was generally close to the entrance of the outer parlour.

The remarks above, however, do not apply at all to the houses of the Cistercian abbots, who from the beginning had entirely different ideas on the subject.

The Cistercian abbots enjoyed a freedom from the anxieties which troubled those of the other Orders. Their outlying estates were efficiently administered by a system which will be explained in Chapter 14. They played no part in the political life of the country—only three of the twenty-nine mitred abbots were Cistercian—and one suspects that their hospitality may well have been avoided wherever possible in favour of less austere hosts.

Their Order laid it down that Cistercian abbots were to sleep in the dormitory with the community. Nevertheless the abbot's duties made this requirement too inconvenient for it to be continued, and the abbot first had a separate cubicle in the dorter and then—it is believed, for so many of the Cistercian monks' houses have disappeared—a chamber built out from the upper end of this.

What is certain is, however, that the houses of the Cistercian abbots were never built near the outer parlour as was the case with every other Order, but always on the east side of, and close to, the monks' house. With this eastern situation established, however, the Cistercian abbots eventually began to build proper houses in the same fashion as those of the abbots of the other Orders. The decision to take this revolutionary step corresponded with that to abandon the old austerities of the twelfth century.

The choice of site would have been affected by circumstances other than the proximity to the dorter. The situation at the Cistercian abbeys differed fundamentally from that at the houses of the other Orders. Their outer parlour was not the same busy scene of social and commercial activity. Moreover that part of the abbey was in close proximity to the house of the lay-brothers, probably regarded as of an inferior class to the professed monks and unsuitable neighbours for the abbot and his visitors.

A house for the abbot situated to the east of the monks' house would have been a long way from the kitchen quarters at the south-west angle of the cloister. But in the same area was a building which needed a kitchen—the infirmary. Thus it is found that the abbot's house and the infirmary often shared a kitchen.

Where the Cistercian plan had an advantage over the Benedictine was that the latter set the abbot's house very far away from any of the sanitary arrangements. We have seen in the last chapter how well the little cloisters were designed to obviate this.

The abbots' houses, especially those at the more public western end of the site—and the house at Forde is an example of Cistercian departure from their strict rule—were steadily developed in accordance with the fortunes of the abbey concerned. A ground-floor parlour might be introduced as a form of estate office for the abbot and, as we have seen at Forde, there might in the end be a great hall of secular type.

The abbey church of the Benedictine house at Sherborne, another Dorset abbey, is one of the most beautiful buildings in this country. Of great antiquity, it was originally the seat of the Wessex bishops, but almost all memories of this past life seem to have been effaced by the glory of the present building with its breath-taking high vault of stone fans.

The cloister is on the north away from the ancient town. Of its east walk only the slype remains with a fragment of the dorter above it.

The west range remains with lodgings for guests above its cellarage. The frater, which has vanished, was in a range which was carried westwards beyond the cellarer's range, a reversal of the usual practice. On the upper floor of this western projection was the abbot's hall.

The outer parlour was in the unusual position of being in the northern or frater range and continued the line of the western alley of the cloister; this may have been the reason for the distance of the abbot's house from the church. One is of course bound to observe the similarity between the arrangement at Sherborne and that at Forde.

The abbot's house at Sherborne—the whole region has a great tradition of fine medieval building—was during the fifteenth century developed into a fine residence fortunately surviving within Sherborne School which uses part of it as a chapel. The abbey kitchen was in the angle between the house and the frater.

To the east of the cloister was the prior's house, retained at the Suppression as a private residence but removed during the eighteenth century.

The ecclesiastical residence had the advantage over the secular counterpart by having available a team of highly skilled masons who could turn their hand with enthusiasm to the design of any beautiful feature desired by the abbey.

In the secular hall, its aisles abandoned and its height vying with the naves of the churches, the principal architectural feature was the tall bay window lighting the dais. The abbots also began to build fine windows for their halls, but these being on an upper floor were not generally bays but projecting oriels supported upon elaborately moulded brackets.

The oriel window might be described as the monastic version of the great bay window. A fine example may be seen at the abbot's tower at Cerne in Dorset. Although also suited to the secular 'upper chamber' it always seems to have a somewhat ecclesiastical presence.

The prior's house at the Cluniac priory of Castle Acre in Norfolk has two oriels of different periods. One of these looks over the 'parvis' which lies before the twin-towered west front of the priory church with its elaborate twelfth-century interlaced arcading. Some massive fragments of the church remain, but the eastern arm has long been levelled with the turf, as has much of the claustral work.

The chapter house was apsidal. The monks' house was a lengthy one and terminated in a large and impressive rere-dorter set athwart the south gable with the great drain passing below its seats.

There were two infirmary halls; instead of an infirmary cloister there was a series of long passages connecting these halls with each other, the choir of the church, and a latrine set above the great drain east of the rere-dorter.

The frater has almost disappeared but west of its site are the foundations of a square kitchen with the bases of four sturdy pillars.

The north end of the cellarer's range was converted into the prior's lodging and from this developed a fine house—bearing in mind the absolute stonelessness of the region—with chamber and chapel, taken over at the Suppression to serve as a farmhouse and still roofed.

The particular attraction of this house lies in its oriel windows. The earlier, on the north side overlooking the west front of the church, is projected so far from the wall that it has to have a kind of buttress propping it up. On the west gable of the house, however, is a very sophisticated oriel, clearly completed only just in time to watch the entry of the commissioners come to sack the place.

An important feature of all houses of abbots and priors which for obvious reasons has almost entirely vanished today was the private chapel, of no use to the lay grantee and therefore either demolished or converted at the Suppression. Only in an establish-

19. Cleeve

20. Furness

ment remaining in ecclesiastical hands might one expect to discover a survivor of what might well have been a charming series of little Gothic structures.

The cathedral priories have been fortunate in having kept a number of their monastic buildings when so much has disappeared from the more powerful abbeys. One of the most comprehensive groups of monastic domestic structures is that which was provided at the south-west angle of the cloister at Ely Cathedral for the use of the cathedral prior. Much of it seems to be concerned with hospitality in that dreary region. The prior's guest hall runs north and south and has two wings, that to the south being a lesser guest hall and that on the north parallel to it the hall of the prior himself. At the upper end of this is the prior's chapel, a particularly charming example of the Gothic in miniature.

In striking contrast to this imposing medieval house still forming part of a great ecclesiastical compound, we find a number still remaining of abbots' houses which have been preserved through having been used for the last four centuries as farmhouses. One of the most valuable of these is the abbot's house at Muchelney in Somerset.

Across the marshland from Glastonbury stood the two abbeys of Athelney and Muchelney, the first founded by Alfred the Great after his irruption from the mound upon which it stands to hammer the Danes at Ethandune, and now utterly vanished. Muchelney looks even more forlorn as it gazes out over the misty swamps of the Parret.

The abbey site has been much robbed to metal the tracks across the marshes, and the great church has completely disappeared. The east range has gone too, but on the south side a single wall, panelled in stone in the lavish Somerset style, remains as a memorial of the frater.

The south-west angle of the cloister has been preserved as a part of Muchelney's principal architectural display, its abbot's house. This interesting building was constructed partly above the screens area of the frater and partly above the cloister adjoining this. It dates from the fifteenth and sixteenth centuries and comprises two wings built out to the west and south. A staircase leads up to the abbot's hall with its elaborately carved fireplace and a carved contemporary wooden settle with linen-fold panelling surrounding the upper end as though on a dais.

The south gable of the house is a most charming composition quite late in date but still in perfect medieval style though the almost Elizabethan design of its windows indicates the shape of things to come.

Amongst the farm buildings to the south of the house is one which upon inspection turns out to be the ten-seater rere-dorter of the monks.

The cloister at Muchelney lies to the south of the abbey church and to the north of this, in the usual position, stands the parish church which lifts its Somerset tower today no longer rivalled by its once mightier neighbour, above the bleak landscape of the Parret marshes.

With notable exception of the house at Much Wenlock Priory, most of the abbots' houses situated to the east of the cloister—which includes, of course, practically the whole of the Cistercian houses—have been destroyed.

One of the best known of the less dramatic Cistercian ruins is the abbey of Buildwas in Shropshire. The church makes an impressive ruin now that the outer walls of the nave have been removed and one can obtain an uninterrupted view of the ranges of sturdy 'Romanesque' pillars leading up to a central tower flanked by the remains of its transepts. (Plate 21.)

Beside the northern of these is the chapter house, its vault still carried upon four pillars. Beyond is the slype leading to the little cloister, a narrow court at the western end of which one can see the remains of an arcade of three arches that represents a loggia constructed under the dorter and facing east along the infirmary court.

Across the northern end of this lies the abbot's house, now in private occupation, while beside it on its north side the south arcade of the infirmary hall can be seen. Passing along the south side of the little cloister is the rere-dorter shared between the monks and their abbot.

The more compact area of the abbot's houses might well have

appealed to the Tudor farmer where a great house like that at Forde with its banqueting hall would have been pulled down. Thus it seems probable that many of the most elaborate of the abbots' houses perished with their great churches. Nevertheless one of the finest of the thirteenth-century houses survives at Battle and is now a girls' school.

But it is the smaller houses such as the prior's house at Ewenny Priory in Glamorgan which are the most likely to be found intact in whole or in part.

The house of the Premonstratensian abbot of Blanchland in Northumberland and that of the Augustinian prior of Llanthony in Monmouthshire are today hotels.

One of the most interesting features of the abbots' houses upon which a good deal of skill was lavished was its chamber fireplace or, if it had a hall, the fireplace heating this. After the Suppression a good many of these fireplaces were salvaged—in the days of lime mortar this was not a difficult matter—and transferred to the internal chimney stacks of the farmhouses which were being built everywhere on the abbey estates. Some of these new chimney stacks were still being built in their medieval position in an out-side wall, but the practice at the middle of the sixteenth century was to set fireplaces in pairs back to back in a central stack so that this could serve both kitchen and parlour.

Everywhere one comes across the fine old fireplaces, many of them nowadays filled in with a modern range or a parlour 'interior' grate. But every now and again one may discover a splendid fifteenth-century feature with an elaborate—perhaps heraldic—overmantel.

In which case one may perhaps look for the site of a lost abbey not far away.

# 13

# The Great Courts

Beyond the cloister and the little cloister, and perhaps a kitchen court and an abbot's court, there was still another area covered by the buildings of the abbey in addition to the large enclosure formed by the gardens, orchards, and perhaps vineyards of the abbey.

The abbey site was extensive and its existence was based upon a water-supply. The abbey's life-line was the abbey stream. This was usually an artificial watercourse led from some nearby stream and used entirely by the monastery. Its first task was to turn the stones of the abbey mill, vital to the community which lived largely upon bread.

As the stream approached the claustral area it would enter the kitchen region where its water would be drawn off for cooking purposes and for washing the pots and pans. This was also the area in which the guest houses were situated; their kitchen too had to be supplied and possibly that of the abbot. Water would also be needed for the bakehouse and brewhouse.

Water would be carried in lead pipes to the laver in the cloister by the frater door, and eventually to the infirmary and the abbot's house if this was east of the cloister.

From the kitchen led the great drain, carrying away kitchen swill and going on to the monks' rere-dorter. In Cistercian abbeys, where the lay-brothers' house with its large population lay along the west claustral range, water to the kitchen would need to be tapped upstream of their rere-dorter.

Water-supply was such a vital necessity to the life of these huge communities—perhaps more than six hundred at Fountains, for example—that the twelfth-century hydraulic engineer had to know what he was about. A contemporary drawing exists setting out the plan of the water-supply to the cathedral priory at Canterbury.

The lead water pipes of the medieval abbey would have been one of the first items of loot. But the great drain—the 'underground passage'—yet remains.

What happened to the effluent has not been ascertained. The water, however, presumably returned to its parent river.

It is when one considers such matters as water-supply, cooking, and sewage disposal that one begins to realize the very considerable administrative problems surrounding the abbey and the number of lesser works there descending from the great church to the woodshed.

The centre of the non-architectural building effort of the abbey was its outer court. The outer parlour giving access to the cloister through the cellarer's range did not open directly into the public street. Before it was spread a large forecourt known as the great court or *curia*, which was walled about and inaccessible to the members of the public having no business at the abbey. (See Fig. 21.)

The only part of the abbey accessible to the public was the nave of the abbey church, entry being by the west front or by a north porch corresponding to the south porch of a parish church. Where access to some shrine in the eastern end of the church was required entrance to it would probably be through the north transept.

Thus generally speaking the north side of the church—assuming the cloister to be in its normal position—and its west front with the 'parvis' (Paradise) before it, were exposed to public access, the rest being within the abbey grounds.

This means that the normal points of attachment of the precinct wall were the north-east angle of the presbytery or the transept and the southern end of the west front.

This last angle closely adjoined the outer parlour so that the precinct wall had to be squeezed rather tightly between the west front and the parlour entrance. Thus anyone facing the west doorway of the church would have the precinct wall close to his right hand.

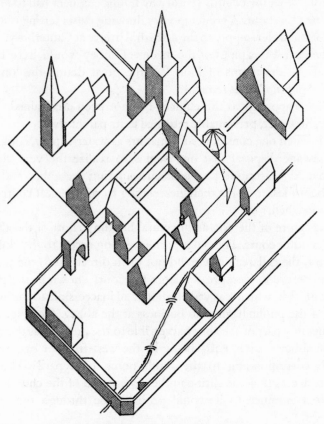

Fig. 21 *The abbey court from south-west*
The Benedictine curia is seen spread before the outer
parlour set in the cellarer's range which has been
expanded by wings forming the abbot's house and the
guest-house. A gatehouse leads out of the parvis before
the west front of the great church across which is the
parish church standing amongst its graves. The court
contains various buildings connected with the administration of the abbey; through it flows the abbey
stream which as it reaches the claustral buildings
becomes the great drain. By the polygonal chapter
house projecting from the monks' house on the east
side of the cloister is the inner parlour from which a
path leads to the infirmary hall with its chapel, kitchen,
and flesh-frater. Beside this at the east end of the great
church is the graveyard of the monks

182

From the parvis, through this wall, and close to the church, was the outer entrance to the abbey represented by its great gate.

The *curia* of the abbey was a kind of semi-secular enclave in which the operations commonly associated with the maintenance of a large house with its residents, staff, and guests were conducted. A granary was needed to be kept stocked from the abbey barns situated on its various estates. Kitchen offices such as scullery, bakehouse, brewhouse, pantry, and buttery were needed. These were situated in the great court—unless, exceptionally, there was a special kitchen court—together with maintenance workshops such as masons' lodges, carpenters' and glaziers' shops, and plumbery. Of supreme importance was the smithy, where in the days before factory fabrication everything in the nature of hinges and locks, bolts and bars, window ironwork, and cooking devices was made; the smith also sharpened the tools of the masons and carpenters and the tools used in farming operations. As all transportation, whether of goods or persons, was dependent upon the horse, the smiths had to be always on call for shoeing. Stabling always formed part of the court of any large house.

Prominent in the *curia* was the guest house, sometimes projecting as a wing from the cellarer's range which dominated the scene. Another wing might contain the abbot's house, perhaps with an oriel window surveying the activities below.

The almonry would be one of the buildings to be found in the great court, attended at certain times of the day by the indigent local peasantry.

At the great abbey of Wilton, the *curia* of which is today called Kingsbury and forms part of the town, the only building remaining of the famous Wessex nunnery is the counting-house, the 'checker' in which presumably the exchequer board was kept, and accounts submitted to the cellarer for supplies of foodstuffs, cloth and so forth were examined and settled.

The great Wessex abbey was situated on the north side of the ancient county town and its cloister seems to have been on the north side of the church next to the River Wylye. South-west of the abbey lay the market place where one may still see the ruins of the principal parish church, sole survivor of a number of others now vanished.

In the case of all the Orders save the Cistercian and Premonstratensian whose lay-brothers used the nave of the church as their choir, the local people were allowed to worship at the nave altar and sometimes even used the nave or one of its aisles as a parish church.

They would use the north side of the church for burials.

Many abbeys took to building a parish church thereabouts for the sole use of the parishioners so as to make them independent of the abbey church. This was especially the case where the village had grown around the abbey as at Muchelney and thus had no original parish church, or on the other hand where an abbey had in early days taken over the parish church and had to allow its parishioners to worship in the nave of the abbey church.

The parish church of an abbey town is nearly always found to the north of the abbey church. Great abbeys such as St. Edmundsbury or Evesham sometimes provided two churches, and both in these two cases are still standing.

It is an interesting fact that some parish churches remain, when all else has gone, and give no inkling of their origin.

The lovely parish churches of Cirencester in Gloucestershire and Blythburgh in Suffolk tower today above the countryside while beside them nothing whatever remains above ground of the great abbey churches which in the past had soared above them.

Perhaps the best known of the 'monastic' parish churches is that of St. Margaret lying beside the great abbey church of Westminster.

The Cistercian arrangement was quite different from that of the Benedictines. The public was not admitted to the nave of the church which formed the choir of the lay-brothers. So the church came entirely within the monastic precinct and was enclosed within its wall. The Cistercians on principle built on sites 'far from habitation' so there was no question either of any parishioners being dispossessed or of any village forming about the new abbey. Nor was there any lay burial ground. So the abbey remained aloof within its precinct wall, entered through a gatehouse set across the route by which the site was approached.

At Dunkeswell in Devonshire the abbey gatehouse is sited immediately in front of the doorway to the outer parlour.

This plan was followed by others of the non-urban monastic houses where the church was not much used by the local people and in particular where there was no burial ground for the laity.

The Cistercian abbey usually built for the laity a small chapel just outside the main gate to the precinct. The 'chapel at the gate' may be seen at Croxden Abbey in Staffordshire where it has become a church. Others remain at Furness in Lancashire, Merevale in Warwickshire, and Coggeshall in Essex. At Tilty in the same county the gate-chapel now forms the chancel of the parish church.

It has been noted that the precinct wall of the Benedictine abbey usually left the north side of the church with its burial ground open to the public. But the great abbey of St. Edmundsbury in Suffolk was entirely enclosed. Its great church, about five hundred feet long and probably the longest church in the world, has vanished entirely save for the stupendous ruin of its west front, so vast that a large dwelling-house has been accommodated within its nooks and crannies.

The precinct wall—a view of which probably offers the grandest display of medievalism still discoverable in England—passes before the west front on the axis of which is an old gate-tower like that of a Norman castle but very elaborately ornamented. This gate leads into the abbey parvis flanked by two parish churches for the town parishes.

In the normal Benedictine plan, the visitor arriving in the parvis before the west door of the abbey church would find himself confronted by two imposing examples of medieval architecture, one ecclesiastical, the other military.

Facing him would be the west front of the abbey church, either covered with arcading as at Castle Acre or Dunstable, or showing the later refinements of Lanercost (Plate 13), or with the coming of the High Gothic imposing west windows such as those of Binham or the sad relic of once-mighty Thorney.

On his right hand would be the great gatehouse of the abbey, leading into the activity of its *curia*, and through it to the humble entrance to the outer parlour and the abbey cloister.

The great gatehouse of the abbey was a feature of great architectural significance.

The first gatehouses were probably just gate-towers of the type giving access to the bailey of the contemporary castle as may be seen at Exeter. These towers were just square structures with a large arch on opposite faces like the central tower of a transept-less church.

The gate-tower of the twelfth-century abbey, however, would very likely have been displayed as a fine architectural structure elaborately ornamented like that at St. Edmundsbury.

This very large and powerful abbey differed from the general run of monastic houses in having round it a large fortified pre-cinct forming a sacred area enclosing the original burial place of St. Edmund, very much venerated in Anglo-Saxon times. Within this area were originally seven parish churches two of which were demolished to make room for the huge abbey church and rebuilt flanking the abbey parvis. This court with its two churches came within the abbey precinct wall and it was to give access to this from the town that the tall gate-tower of St. James was built.

It is interesting to note that we have at St. Edmundsbury a medieval parvis planned on monumental lines with its two flanking churches, entered through St. James's Tower, and leading to the broad frontispiece of the abbey church with its tall western bell-tower supported by long transepts in a style today only represented by Ely Cathedral.

At St. Edmundsbury the cloister lay to the north of the abbey church and the great court was situated as usual west of this, north-west of the church. But instead of being entered in the normal fashion from the parvis before the abbey church the *curia* was reached by way of another gatehouse, this time a fine Gothic work, set in the precinct wall north of St. James's Tower. The long west wall at St. Edmundsbury with its two gatehouses still presents an impressive spectacle from medieval England.

The powerful abbots of St. Edmundsbury were seldom popular with the townspeople and their walls and gates were somewhat indicative of the uneasy relationship between abbey and town. In 1327 the latter sent a party of three thousand rioters to sack the abbey and burn the buildings of the great court, a conflagration which lasted for three days at the end of which the sheriff coming to quell the disturbance had to stable his horses in the outer parlour, all else having been destroyed.

When one considers the castles of the early-twelfth century and what poor things they were compared with the magnificent monastic houses, one is not surprised to learn that during the anarchy of Stephen's reign some abbeys were well able to stand a siege—generally on behalf of the Empress—which put the castle of the period to shame.

Even the nunneries joined in. The abbess of Wherwell in Hampshire held out against Stephen from behind her precinct walls while close at hand at Stockbridge a bloody battle was fought and lost by her party. The castles of that period were either still stockaded or had at best low walls even though these were reinforced by deep-hewn ditches.

The great bishop Roger of Sarum, chancellor of the realm but also in revolt against the King, himself built a number of castles in a style more palatial than military. Having seized Malmesbury Abbey on its height he built a castle in its *curia* within a few yards of the abbey church, the ruins of which in their strange acropolis seem today so menacing despite their pathos.

Bishop Roger's castle availed him nothing and did not survive the failure of his cause so the abbots of Malmesbury were able to continue their peaceful rule. But less than a decade ago the Castle Inn by the west gate closed its doors to the wayfarer.

During the Gothic era, the abbey gatehouse developed into a very beautiful feature which although by nature para-military was really intended to be regarded as an architectural introduction to a building of the highest aesthetic merit.

It is always well to remember that the government of medieval England was far from being the orderly establishment with which we are familiar. From the time of the Conquest the power of the Crown was for ever being threatened by that of the massed nobility, and every few decades civil war broke out with disastrous effect upon the safety of the ordinary man and his property.

During the 'Edwardian' period of castle building, cities also built walls round themselves for protection against marauding bands of soldiery. Between the end of the thirteenth century and the end of the next all the cathedral closes were actually granted 'licences to crenellate', that is to say to surround themselves with walls which could actually be defended against assault. The abbeys did the same with their precincts but their walls were not crenellated—that is to say battlemented—and could not have been defended against serious attack.

Entrances through such walls of *enceinte*, whether of castles, cathedrals, or abbeys, were invariably covered with gatehouses which were made to look to some extent awe-inspiring, but in the case of ecclesiastical establishments were also treated as important architectural structures presenting an imposing aesthetic frontispiece to the outside world.

The chief feature of the gatehouse, its great arch, made it an easy structure to provide with an impressive architectural treatment, and during the thirteenth and fourteenth centuries the Gothic gatehouse became a structure comparable aesthetically with the façade of the great church.

Most of the monastic gatehouses remaining today are isolated examples set in the precinct walls of rural monasteries such as those of the Cistercians.

The very rich Cistercian abbey of Kingswood in Gloucestershire has so completely vanished that even its site is uncertain. Its only memorial is a very lovely Gothic gatehouse.

One of the latest of the monastic gatehouses must be that which may be seen at Abingdon Abbey in Berkshire.

A feature often found in the great gate of the abbey was the small wicket gate set beside the main arch so that the great gate could be kept closed if it was thought desirable and only the small one used to let individuals in and out. The rear arch of the gatehouse remained a single span. It may well have been the experience of the abbey of St. Edmundsbury in 1327 that encouraged the abbots to take their defences more seriously. In 1381 St. Albans Abbey was besieged and captured by rioters.

Some of the abbey gatehouses appear as military structures. The Augustinian gatehouse at Thornton Abbey in Lincolnshire

(Plate 25) formed in 1382 the subject of a licence to crenellate; it is a tremendous structure with a hall above its entrance passage in the style of the great 'Edwardian' gatehouse of the contemporary castle.

The powerful-looking gatehouse of St. Albans Abbey was used as the abbey prison.

The Continental type of fortified abbey is unknown in this country. But in Glamorgan, its countryside thick with castles, stands the fortified Benedictine priory of Ewenny, entirely surrounded by a towered *enceinte* provided with gatehouses at the north and south angles of the west wall of the precinct which is also that of the great court of the monastery.

The nave of the church is small, having been from its foundation assigned to the parish as its church and the monks restricted to their choir in the crossing, above which rises a massive fortress-like tower. The presbytery is covered by a wide barrel vault—a real *volta di bombe* which makes the building look more like a fortress than ever. The north transept has gone, but in its fellow is the fine tomb-slab of the founder, Maurice of London.

The east range has been destroyed, but the frater in the southern range forms part of a modern house. The western range, occupied as usual by the prior's lodging, has also in part survived.

Ewenny Priory is a rare example in this country of the fortified monastery. Only on the Border and in the Marches might one expect to find a religious establishment presenting such a military appearance.

The last type of monastic gatehouse, the large turreted tower of the Tudor era, was not intended for defence but simply as an advertisement of abbatial power and pomp. The great gatehouse of Battle Abbey in Sussex is an example. The stately gatehouse of St. Osyth Abbey in Essex, with its long flanking wings, forms a mansion in its own right and was taken over as such at the Suppression. It remains one of the most impressive memorials of the age of the abbots.

When one considers the six hundred and fifty suppressed monasteries and recalls that each was surrounded by a precinct wall, and that each opening through this wall was covered by a gatehouse, one can appreciate that there were a very large number of monastic gatehouses scattered about the countryside.

Many of them remain. Not worth the trouble of pulling down, they made excellent gateposts for a farmer's field.

In scores of places, in villages where once the abbots ruled, two lumps of masonry, breaking the lines of roadside walls and opposing each other across the way, will show where once the lofty arch of a gatehouse passed above the head of the wayfarer.

But some of them made good houses. Palace House at the great Cistercian abbey of Beaulieu in Hampshire is simply its great gatehouse. Mighty Thornton gate is a house, so is the charming gatehouse of Butley in Suffolk.

At Cistercian Dunkeswell in Devon half the gatehouse is a dwelling to which the ruins of the other half form a queer neighbour.

In any building its most important exterior feature is its entrance. It should always be inviting. If funds allow it should imply the opulence of the interior to which it leads. This was the purpose of the monastic gatehouse, offering an antithesis to the great gate of the castle the purpose of which was to inspire fear.

The entrance to any great house should always be as splendid as the architect can devise. Thus the entrance porch of the abbot's house had to receive elaborate architectural attention.

The porch before a doorway is a feature demanded by the English climate which makes it impossible to live in an apartment opening directly into the open air. A porch would shelter the interior from anything but a tempest blowing directly into it.

Under the influence of Gothic architecture which tended to draw all architecture upwards the medieval porch developed into a tower—a purely monumental structure doing nothing more than advertising the entrance below it. Towards the end of the monastic era the abbots' towers were springing up everywhere, rising ever higher than those of the secular halls and the porch towers of the parish churches.

The abbot's tower at the Premonstratensian abbey of Torre in Devon is simply the porch of his house raised above the roof. Abbot Chard's graceful porch-tower at Forde in Dorset has an oriel window passing right up its face from the crown of the arch to the battlements; the abbot's tower at Cerne in the same county has a similar example of this lovely type of window, so peculiarly monastic.

The abbey cloister, despite late attempts to brighten up its décor, must at all times have been a solemn place, calm and peaceful. By passing through the outer parlour the scene must have changed completely, socially and architecturally. The façade of the western range, with perhaps its projecting wings for the abbot's house and guesten hall, must have appeared like the forecourt of any other large house, and have been the scene of very considerable activity of many descriptions.

Pass on through the great gatehouse to the parvis before the church and reach the public world beyond the abbey *curia*. A busy establishment accommodating perhaps fifty monks and an equal number of servants must have attracted numbers of people, hangers-on, some of them, and genuine visitors to the abbey as well.

Imagine the west front of a great Benedictine abbey and hard by it the great gatehouse leading into the outer court of an establishment voracious for foodstuffs, cloth, and building materials—a thoroughfare alive with the constant passage of visitors arriving with many purposes in view.

Such an area as this parvis would be likely to become a magnet for market stalls and more permanent structures until the head of the street leading to the abbey would have become the high street of a market town. In this way many of our ancient towns, Reading and Abingdon for example, have owed their origins to some vanished abbey of the Middle Ages, represented today by perhaps a forlorn fragment of walling . . . or perhaps not even by a memory.

# 14

# The Rural Abbeys of the Cistercians

The Cistercian Order shows today two phases in relation to the English countryside. And its chequered career forced it through a third.

At first it was a reformed Order, determinedly setting its face against all evidences of wealth including architectural display. Thus its architectural presence during the great twelfth century, the century when this country played such a notable part in the architecture of western Europe, was simple and austere to the verge of grimness.

The second phase which came at the close of the century appears as a realization of the fallaciousness of supposing that worship must necessarily be joyless, and a conversion to the view of the oldest Orders that God is worthy of the best in everything. It was during the thirteenth century that the Cistercian architects were able to develop their attitude towards the integrity of religious architecture with the aim of achieving a style realizing the transcendent. This is the era of the noble Cistercian presbyteries which expanded eastwards from the grim old twelfth-century naves.

The last phase is one of almost complete collapse due to the appearance of a plague, the Black Death, which struck at that element in their mode of life, the complement of lay-brothers, without which their abbeys could not properly function.

The differences between the Cistercian Order and the Benedictine stemmed not only from the former's puritanical views but as a result of the system adopted by the Cistercians for making their abbeys financially independent. This was husbandry, leading to their settlement in areas 'far from habitation'. As their abbeys were always sited in what was virtually waste land they were able to enjoy a site free from any restrictions imposed by existing buildings. But they employed large numbers of lay-brothers to work the farms upon which their incomes depended, and these lay-brothers had to be housed and fed in addition to the professed monks who maintained the offices in the choir. This not only made their abbeys very large indeed but introduced the complication of dichotomy.

The abbeys of the Cistercians were founded on a rigid system entirely different from that followed by the other Orders. When the Benedictines began to build an abbey they sent an advance party to the new site and set them to work first organizing temporary accommodation and then consolidating their position by replacing this with permanent structures. How it worked seems difficult to understand when one bears in mind the tremendous complications of the abbey plan and the size and character of the buildings.

The Cistercian system was entirely different, for the abbey buildings were completely finished before the monks moved in. Not until everything was ready for him did the new abbot and his twelve monks take up residence.

Such an operation, in the twelfth century, suggests a remarkable knowledge of systematic organization. It was in fact only possible through the formulation of a standard plan for all Cistercian abbeys. This is very advanced architecture, most remarkable when one considers that the men who carried it out could not add two and two together without the use of a chequer-board. For Arabic numerals were four centuries away from this country. It is also fascinating to realize that the Order had worked out the plan of each building and also a standard elevation for each. And of course they had actually agreed upon an optimum site-plan; true, this was based upon the experience gained from the Benedictines, but the whole scheme had to be set out to a set of fixed dimensions.

The Cistercian church (Fig. 22) followed the basic design of the original Benedictine churches. The nave was also of considerable length, for although in the rural areas no lay congregations were to be catered for, the nave had to serve as the choir of the lay-brothers who worked on the abbey estates but were not admitted to the choir. This was arranged in exactly the same fashion as with the other Orders, with the same two screens, the nave altar being that used by the lay-brothers. The eastern arm and the transepts were of moderate projection; the latter invariably had an eastern aisle containing chapels. (Plates 12 and 26.)

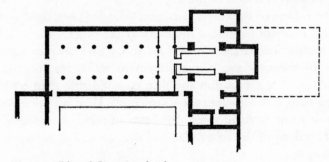

Fig. 22  *Plan of Cistercian church*
Note the short eastern arm and the transept aisles
containing the chapels. The broken line indicates
the thirteenth-century enlargement of the eastern arm

The arrangement of the interior of the church varied considerably from the Benedictine plan in that the nave, despite its length, had to accommodate the lay-brothers and no more than one or two of its easternmost bays could be assigned to the monks' choir. The retro-choir of course took up yet another bay. Thus the Cistercian choir occupied the crossing, the stalls stopping short of its eastern arch so as to allow for the lateral choir doorways leading into the transepts.

The early Cistercian churches would have been far from attractive internally. Since vaulted ceilings were regarded as a luxury the main spans were open to the roof timbers; the aisles, however, could be vaulted, probably for the reason that their vaults were traditionally regarded as an essential part of the structural system carrying the main roof. The Cistercians arrived late in the era of post-Conquest architectural development. The heavy 'Anglian' piers had given place to circular pillars built up in masonry in an attempt to imitate the 'Roman' Classical column. (Plate 21.) The arches of the main arcade had become pointed but those of door-ways and windows remained round-headed. There was a small clearstory, but no gallery over the aisle, and the lantern above the crossing was simply a section of the clearstory raised above the ridges of the roofs impinging upon its walling. As the Cistercians were not allowed bells, they made no allowance originally for a bell-tower, but this rule was relaxed later.

The Cistercian nave was lined by the seats of the lay-brothers. Sometimes they were backed against low screen walls set between the pillars. (Plate 24.) With the seats facing each other across what must have been an exceedingly bare prospect, the nave would have presented a strange spectacle to the visitor used to the spacious galleried naves of the churches of the other Orders. But of course no visitor was allowed in a Cistercian nave.

As the Cistercian abbey had to be laid out in advance by a pioneer team of tradesmen helped by lay-brothers, everything had to be worked out in the parent abbey before this party left for the new site. Thus a standard plan was adopted which with slight variations due to site conditions or perhaps whims of the emigrant abbot would take care of everything and enable even the church to be built without too much argument or misgiving.

An examination of some Cistercian abbey churches of the middle of the twelfth century has enabled the writer to discover something of the system upon which the planners worked. The pole of sixteen feet appears to have been employed. A centre line was marked out and the outline of the nave set out two poles' length on either side of this giving an overall width of sixty-four feet.

The outer face of the west wall was then marked out across these two lines and its thickness set out. Nine poles away to the east—one hundred and forty-four feet—the length of the nave was marked out and again the thickness of the wall set out on the farther side of this. The side walls of the nave were then marked out internally within the four-pole limit.

The centre lines of the nave arcade were then set out two poles apart and their widths lined up. The nine bays of the nave were set out across these lines. The plan of the nave was now complete. The width of its main span was from twenty-six to twenty-seven feet according to the nature of the materials and craftsmanship and the thickness of walling decided upon.

A square of this span gave the crossing and transept width. Each transept and the short presbytery projected from the crossing two poles. The eastern aisles of the transepts were worked out to produce square vaulting bays.

The system of construction to be employed for the building would have been left to the expert tradesman with a knowledge of local materials and practice.

The elevational design of the church was quite unsophisticated. The circular pillar formed the basis of the nave arcades and carried simple pointed arches with flat soffits in the Roman rather than the Byzantine fashion with 'orders'. The nave had an exposed timber roof covered with 'close-couple' rafters—set close together in pairs—covered with shingles probably fixed to boarding. The aisles had lean-to roofs and might be vaulted but had no galleries above them; there was no intermediate arcade between the main arcade and the simple clearstory which had no cleaning gallery as in the Benedictine churches.

It is interesting to note that the Cistercians of the twelfth century were building churches on a 'do it yourself' principle. As the buildings they produced were humble in architectural style, this could be followed by the 'local builder' engaged in erecting a parish church. Thus the type of parish church arcade with circular pillars and cushion capitals Corinthianized with scallops or tall cones possibly represents help from the Cistercians.

Until the end of the twelfth century when they revised their attitude with dramatic results, the Cistercians remained indifferent towards architecture other than as required by problems of construction. They then introduced the most attractive features into their buildings, relying for ornament, however, upon delicate systems of mouldings rather than the elaborate carved motifs developed from the Anglo-Saxons which were being so enthusiastically employed by the Benedictines, Cluniacs, and Augustinians.

21. Buildwas

22. Haughmond

It may well have been their original attitude towards ornament and the resultant interest taken by them in the development of systems of moulding which enabled the Cistercian architects to create their beautiful Gothic presbyteries during the thirteenth century.

For the time being, however, the Cistercians were content to restrict the use of ornament to the embellishment of doorways of special importance. These, by the way, were the west doorway to the church, its east and west processional doorways leading into the cloister alleys, the frater door, and, above all, the façade of the chapter house.

Returning to the lay-out of the Cistercian plan we find that the width of the claustral buildings was usually about two poles, from the centre of one wall to the centre of that opposite, which for practical purposes meant from the inside of one wall to the outside of its fellow across the span. In a small abbey such as Valle Crucis in Denbighshire the width was reduced to a pole and a half.

The monks' house was set out as a projection from the south transept of the church and of approximately the same width. This completed two sides of the cloister.

Opposite the monks' house, across the cloister to the west, the house of the lay-brothers had to be erected. This was where a decision had to be made which affected the size of the cloister. If the lay-brothers' house were to be lined up with the west front of the church this would give a cloister approximately one hundred and twelve feet across, but the effect would be that the west front of the church was being squeezed behind the lay-brothers' house.

At Fountains Abbey the Cistercians took the middle course and made the cloister a hundred and twenty-five feet square. But they added two bays to the nave—making eleven in all—so as to be sure that its west front would 'master' the long west wall of the house of the lay-brothers. In this fashion they created the finest medieval frontispiece remaining today in England (Plate 18), a spectacle which must have made a tremendous impact upon the twelfth-century visitor used to the great gatehouse with its jumble of buildings which he would have experienced at the houses of the other Orders.

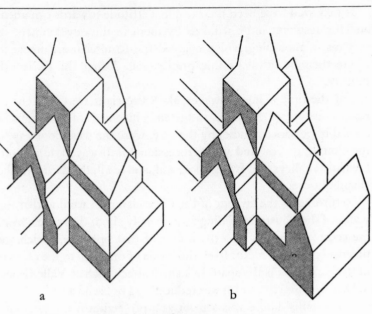

a                                        b

Fig. 23   *Cistercian east ends*
(a) the aisles carried across the east end to
form an ambulatory. (b) an eastern transept
having an ambulatory giving access to eastern
chapels. (This may be seen at Abbey Dore; at
Hereford Cathedral it was lengthened
laterally, and at Fountains Abbey it was
raised to the full height of the building)

As a matter of fact the west front of Byland Abbey may well
have been even finer than Fountains. The church façade contained
a large circular 'wheel' window and the lay-brothers' house
extended from it on the same line. The church had been extended
in the same fashion as at Fountains, but the lay-brothers' house had
been set back one bay from the cloister wall so as to provide a
'lane' for their exercise and at the same time bring the long house
in line with the church. The south end of the lane was continued
into the kitchen court. It is indeed unfortunate that this fine front
is now reduced to a line of broken fragments of walling.

So much of English monastic architecture has been destroyed
that we have forgotten just how splendid these great houses were,

and how far advanced they were during the twelfth century in the design of monumental frontispieces. Our idea of monastic architecture may be limited to the lateral aspect of the great church, but it was the western elevation, prototype of the great frontispiece of the Escorial, which was the real loss to English architecture when the abbeys came down in 1539.

It may be noted in parenthesis that there are indications, for example at Jervaulx in Yorkshire, that a house for the lay-brothers was the first to be erected, so that they might be housed while the abbey was being made ready for the draft of twelve monks and their new abbot. It may well have been that a building of such an immense size—nothing approaching it in scale could have been found elsewhere in domestic architecture—erected upon a free site uncomplicated by the presence of other structures may well have been regarded by the twelfth-century mason as a canvas upon which to display his skill at domestic elevational presentation. Which is a reason to deplore the loss of almost every one of these Cistercian western buildings with their frontispieces.

That at Jervaulx is down to its foundations and so is its church, described at the Suppression as 'one of the fairest'. But a wealth of claustral building remains including much of the monks' house, the abbot's house, and the infirmary.

Jervaulx has a special claim to our respect. The Cistercian Order founded the pastoral wealth of this country, and made it great. And while the Benedictine monks were sitting in their cloisters writing books the monks of Jervaulx were breeding the hardiest and soundest horses in the North.

The abbot of Jervaulx died at Tyburn. But his horses, no doubt, still scamper in the pastures of the North.

At Basingwerk Abbey in Flintshire the cloister was reduced in width from east to west in order to line up the west front of the abbey with a rather short nave. Normally, however, the cloister was a square.

The cloister once marked out, the sites of its buildings followed a standard plan, so much so, in fact, that it was said any monk visiting a strange abbey would know exactly where each apartment was situated. (See Figs 24 and 25.)

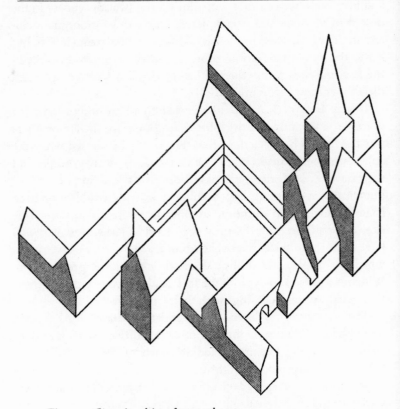

Fig. 24   *Cistercian cloister from south-east*
The monks' house and rere-dorter follow the Benedictine arrangement but the slype has been moved
farther away from the church. The frater is set at
right angles to the cloister and separates the warming-
house from the kitchen. Closing the cloister on the
west is the very long building housing the lay-
brothers, with their rere-dorter at the end

The chapter house was sited in its usual position near the centre
of the east walk next the south transept. Instead of the Benedictine slype, however, the bay separating the two was divided into
two by a screen. Its eastern half, entered from the church, was the
sacristy while its western portion, entered from the cloister, was
the abbey book-store. (See Fig. 25.)

The slype leading to the infirmary, and possibly a little cloister connected with this, were sited on the side of the chapter house farthest from the church and generally more or less continuing eastwards the south alley of the cloister. Between it and the chapter house was the inner parlour, in Cistercian houses a room separate from the slype, in which abbey officers could discuss administrative matters in more suitable conditions than in the middle of a passage.

The southern end of the dorter undercroft was not, as in the houses of other Orders, the warming-house but appears to have been assigned to the novices, their normal schoolroom in the western parts of the abbey having been taken over by the Cistercian lay-brothers.

The west range was the house of the lay-brothers, the outer parlour passing through its undercroft in the normal position next the church. Its accommodation was variously arranged, the most frequent arrangement being to assign the end nearer the church to their dorter and the farther end near the kitchen to their frater. This left the cellarage available for its normal use as storerooms. But alternatively the frater was sometimes sited under the dorter, both being at the southern end of the range, which left some of the cellarage intact and provided upper chambers for guests or possibly the prior.

As originally set out, the Cistercian standard plan sited the frater of the monks alongside the south cloister walk in the same fashion as with all the other Orders. But the Cistercians found this site inconvenient. Since its ends were jammed between the two long houses of the monks and the lay-brothers it could not be enlarged as the abbey expanded as it was always intended it should. So the Cistercians soon began siting their fraters at right angles to the cloister so that they could extend it southwards without any difficulty.

This arrangement enabled the main kitchen to be sited between the frater and the lay-brothers' house where their frater was situated.

Between the frater and the monks' house was built the warming-house, a ground-floor apartment with nothing above it and thus easy to heat. (See Fig. 24 for the Cistercian claustral lay-out.)

The arrangement of the little cloister with its infirmary hall and chapel, kitchen and flesh-frater has been discussed in Chapter 11, also the development of the abbot's house to the east of the cloister instead of on its west side as with the other Orders.

There was no *curia*. The various out-structures were scattered about the rural site within reasonable access of the kitchen quarters

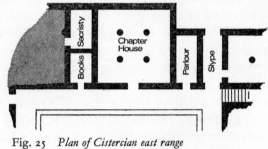

Fig. 25   *Plan of Cistercian east range*
May be compared with Fig. 18 indicating the Benedictine arrangement of
this important range. Note position of
Cistercian slype and the private parlour
adjoining this

and the outer parlour. There was no great gatehouse as such, though the precinct was entered through a gatehouse of architectural quality.

There was no parish church beside the Cistercian abbey.

The abbot lived far away to the east of the house, for he, like his professional colleagues who gave their loyalty to Cluny, had little to do with the outside world and played no part in politics or government.

Behind their long façades the Cistercians lived out the twelfth century.

But sheep-farming must have been a perilous way of earning a living in those days, especially during the Anarchy when followers of both factions would have taken turns at eating the Cistercians' sheep. This situation would have improved a little during the uneasy peace of Henry II, but this was followed by another phase of campaigning as King John and his barons fought it out across the countryside. This King was ever contemptuous of the Cistercians and with his characteristic ruthlessness thought nothing of raiding their flocks and even their houses.

But when peace followed the accession of Henry III the Cistercians entered into a phase of comparative tranquillity and were able to build up their flocks, only suffering a little from the Barons' War. Thereafter until the Wars of the Roses—when the country was approaching the twilight of monasticism—England, free from the dreadful marching and countermarching of the armies in France, discovered herself to be a graziers' paradise, well able to go ahead and build up the flocks which were to make her great. For 'it was the sheep . . . Cistercian sheep . . . that paid for alle.'

However, the Cistercians cannot but have been conscious of their financial insecurity when compared with the powerful Benedictines, the pompous Cluniacs, the sophisticated Augustinians. They must have wondered whether the time was now ripe for them to abandon their non-conformist attitude and begin collecting the same revenues as the rest, even advertising their affluence and perhaps potential power by improving their churches.

There may have been many Cistercians who were wondering whether it was truly appropriate to ignore the long-established common belief in the adage 'the best for the highest'.

And it may well have been galling for the Cistercian architects to see the money being poured out on the great churches of the other Orders, and a glorious architectural style being established in the land.

In any case, the first phase in the improvement of the Cistercian churches was the removal of the pathetically insignificant presbyteries of early days, and their replacement by an aisled presbytery several bays in length with an ambulatory behind the high altar and a row of chapels leading out of this. The central lantern would probably have been rebuilt in the same style, and also the transepts with their eastern aisles, the whole structure, of course, in that splendid style of architecture which has come to be called Gothic.

This phase of rebuilding the eastern ends of churches with a new crossing, transepts, and presbytery absorbed the whole country and affected all the monastic Orders and the cathedrals. The movement is also reflected in the parish churches which removed their early chancels and built new cruciform east ends in imitation of the monastic presbyteries. If they could not afford all this they just built a new long chancel.

The Benedictine churches on the whole were content to extend existing presbyteries eastwards. The Cistercians, however, possessed the advantage in that their original east ends were so contemptible by modern standards that complete rebuilding was the only solution.

To this period belongs one of the most charming examples of Cistercian architecture and the only eastern arm of that Order still in use as a church, the choir of Abbey Dore in Herefordshire. (Plate 8.) Its east wall as rebuilt has no apse but is carried upon three graceful arches which lead into a double-aisled structure passing north and south across the east wall to form an ambulatory and a row of eastern chapels (see Fig. 23b). The original roof which ended in two small gables has been lost. The device forms a peculiarly English reply to the great semicircular *chevets* of the Île de France, though in fact this flamboyant type of east end eventually appeared in the Cistercian churches of Hayles in Gloucestershire, Croxden in Staffordshire, and Vale Royal in Cheshire.

But these were exceptions to the general architectural practice of the Cistercians who concentrated upon a style which by its utter rejection of the apse in any form seems to be setting aside the Byzantine and 'Romanesque' styles and seeking to develop a system of building design based upon first principles, with the gable as the only acceptable termination to any building. They soon rejected the clumsy circular pillar in favour of a modification of the Anglian 'ordered' pier which became the clustered pillar, fitting in pleasantly with the elaborately moulded arches above.

During the thirteenth century most of the Cistercian abbeys rebuilt their eastern arms in the Gothic style (see Plates 10 and 17), and some, such as Tintern, rebuilt the whole church. (Plates 23 and 24.)

The Cistercian chapter house, the most important apartment architecturally after the great church, was equally standardized. It occupied three bays of the dorter undercroft which meant that two of the pillars supporting the upper floor came within it. The east

23. Tintern

24. Tintern

wall of the monks' house was removed for this length and carried upon another two pillars, so that the chapter house had four pillars obstructing its floor area (see Fig. 25). A new east wall with its lateral return walls completed the apartment.

The Cistercians' abandonment of their original austerity campaign led them to give up their cramped old 'four-poster' chapter houses and build on a more commodious scale. Some of the thirteenth-century chapter houses were long apartments which might continue, however, to be low as before, in order not to break into the dorter above. Others, however, such as that at Rievaulx, were large buildings paying no attention to this requirement and cutting off the dorter from the church. Then again planners might avoid this inconvenience to the monks by building east of their house altogether, perhaps even a polygonal chapter house such as at Whalley Abbey in Lancashire or Margam Abbey in Glamorgan. Where this was done the old chapter house was left as a vestibule; this is probably the origin of the chapter-house vestibule such as one finds at Westminster Abbey.

There is a noticeable refinement of approach to their task by the Cistercian architects differing from those of the more urban Orders, the former without doubt affected by the beauty of the rural sites upon which they were building. For although it might seem strange to credit the men of the Middle Ages with any appreciation of natural scenery, it must surely have been the effect of this which inspired them in building their votive achievements, fearful perhaps of defiling the visible presence of the majesty of God.

In order to see a superb monastic ruin in a setting of rare beauty one must go to the valley of the Skell in the West Riding of Yorkshire.

The great ruin of the abbey of Our Lady of the Fountains (Plates 18 and 27) is too vast, and too complete, for it to be more than cursorily noticed in a general book of this nature. One can spend hours in it and in the end come away from it with the sensation that one has been a guest in a Cistercian abbey. For it only lacks its roofs, and on a sunny day the loss of these seems to add to, rather than detract from, its atmosphere of hospitality.

The west front with the seemingly endless panorama presented by the long house of the lay-brothers is a monument to twelfth-century architecture not easily forgotten. (Plate 18.)

The church is vast—it was intended at the Suppression to preserve it as a new cathedral—the nave very primitive and Cistercian with its massive pillars and complete lack of Gothic ornament. Its central lantern has fallen but at the end of the north transept rises a beautiful bell-tower—the Cistercian swan-song—added just before the Suppression. (Plate 27.)

The presbytery is a hollow shell, but is terminated by the tremendous Chapel of the Nine Altars, an eastern transept which set the seal upon the development of the English *chevet* seen in humble form at Abbey Dore.

The cloister has lost its arcades as well as its roofs but is still a noble court surrounded by the church, the lay-brothers' house, and in the north-east angle the towering mass of the south transept, contrasting with the low façade of the chapter house. On the south side is the great ruin of the frater, a spacious hall thrusting between the kitchen and the warming-house.

All along the banks of the Skell which washes the south side of the claustral buildings lie the remains of the infirmary, the abbot's house, the guest halls, and many other structures connected with the operation of a great Cistercian abbey.

But perhaps those huge ruins which drowse in the valleys of Fountains, Rievaulx, and Byland are not so typical of the Cistercian conception and the Cistercian contribution as are found among the ruins of the rural abbeys of humbler character. One of the loveliest of the Cistercian sites is that of Valle Crucis in Denbighshire. The thirteenth-century church displays all the Cistercian charm of its era with none of the splendour of the greater buildings. Its east and west ends are triplets of lancets in the most perfect Gothic tradition.

Its eastern range having been used as a farmhouse since the Suppression is today perfect. There is the usual vaulted chapter house flanked by sacristy to the north and parlour and slype to the south. Above are the monks' dorter and rere-dorter, all to a small scale.

With the larger abbeys and the smaller dividing up the English countryside between them into wide pasture covered with grazing sheep, one wonders how the Cistercian settlement might have progressed had not a national disaster brought it all to a sudden halt.

The Black Death of 1349 which almost halved the population of England and left wide agricultural areas desolate for lack of hands to work them struck a fatal blow to the Cistercians, for their lay-brother system broke down completely, never to be replaced.

A touching memorial to this terrible disaster to medieval England may be seen on the site of the Lancashire abbey of Sawley where the monks walled off the lay-brothers' nave and left it to go to ruin.

Throughout Cistercian England the long house to the west of the cloister knew the lay-brothers no more. Its lower storey became cellarage; the upper a guest house. This is probably the reason why considerable portions of the lay-brothers' houses at Beaulieu in Hampshire and Whalley in Lancashire, presumably found useful at the Suppression, have survived intact to this day.

The impact of the Black Death upon architecture would have been comparable with that on the country as a whole. The vigour of the twelfth century had developed into the achievements of the thirteenth. The fourteenth century had begun with the revolution created first by the general introduction of lead roofing, then the expansion of fenestration, and the beginnings of a sense of appreciation of the true nature of abutment. But after a blow which halved the country's population a decline in production was to be expected.

It may then have been discovered that churches of the size so recklessly embarked upon during the twelfth century were now costing a great deal to maintain in a state of repair. Certainly no church on anything like their scale was ever built again. Thereafter the tendency was to plan a church compactly, more in Continental fashion, with perhaps a splendid presbytery but a nave not very much longer than this. The last abbey church to be built in this country, that of Bath, occupies with its whole length the site of the earlier nave.

Indeed, even before the Black Death and the subsequent collapse of the lay-brother system the Cistercians had given up building long naves. Perhaps the best-known Cistercian abbey today, though a far from typical one, is the famous ruin of Tintern which rises so splendidly beside the River Wye in Monmouthshire. Its site is very Cistercian, but the abbey church which forms the most striking part of the ruin is quite untypical, as it was entirely rebuilt during the latter part of the thirteenth century. (Plates 23 and 24.)

Largely intact except for its roofs and its lantern tower, it is characteristic of the new type of church which replaced the long sprawling structures of the twelfth century. Tall and compact, it composes architecturally into a complete entity only lacking completion by a central feature.

Its nave is only six bays long instead of nine to eleven as before. A choir of four bays has replaced the old stumpy presbytery but again is only two-thirds of the length of the great presbyteries of half a century earlier. But three-bay transepts help to stabilize a well-balanced composition typical of the great church of the High Gothic era.

The cloister is to the north, next the river and water-supply. The plan of the eastern range can clearly be seen. Next to the transept is the sacristy with the book-store at its western end and beyond this the chapter house projects as far east as the transept aisle and has its eastern part vaulted over; four pillars remain. Next come the inner parlour and the slype to the infirmary continuing the north alley of the cloister.

Continuing the east cloister walk are the day-stairs to the monks' dorter, the long pillared undercroft of which was probably the novices' schoolroom. West of the day-stairs is the warming-house with a central fireplace having its flue carried on arches over.

The frater is the usual long hall set in Cistercian fashion at right angles to the cloister. The remains of the pulpit can be seen, and beside the entrance is the laver. In the south-west angle is the hatch leading into the kitchen which still exists between the frater and the long house of the lay-brothers beside the west walk of the cloister.

The slype from the north-east angle of the cloister leads into the south walk of the little cloister and along this to the west door of the large infirmary hall. The north side of the little cloister is formed by the monks' rere-dorter running eastwards from their house. The east walk of the little cloister is continued to the presbytery of the church. The line of the great drain can clearly be seen joining the kitchen and the monks' rere-dorter.

The abbey church of Tintern is memorable for having much of the tracery of its great windows still in position. And as a reminder of the monks who in the dark hours crept down into its choir, high up in the north transept can be seen the small doorway from which the night-stairs led down to the church.

We are all familiar with the so-called 'tithe barns'—the finest of which is that which belonged to the Abbess of Shaftesbury and may still be seen at Tisbury in Wiltshire—which are in fact barns erected on their estates by the monastic houses. The Cistercians made each of these establishments into a miniature monastic house called, from the Norman word signifying barn, a 'grange'. Each grange was staffed by two monks who lived in a small house of 'King John's' type such as remains, with its charming little twelfth-century window, at Hazeldon near Cirencester in Gloucestershire; the great barn has, however, been largely destroyed.

It is interesting to recall that the 'moated grange' of the Victorian romance never in fact existed as a mansion but took its title from a little stone house about twenty feet by thirty.

But the ubiquity of these 'granges'—some of which are presumably genuine—gives one an idea of the completeness of the Cistercian colonization of England during the Middle Ages.

The most remarkable relic of a Cistercian grange is that at Leigh in South Devon once belonging to the abbey of Buckfast. With dorter, frater and kitchen set round a courtyard some twenty-five feet square and approached through a fine gatehouse with a chamber above it seems an abbey in miniature.

Scattered throughout the sheep-pastures of our countryside, the Cistercian abbeys must have been admirably situated for a life of contemplation among the 'choirs where the birds sang'. It is difficult to imagine their ever having played the part of a St. Albans, St. Edmundsbury, Malmesbury, or Gloucester in the political life of the country. At the Suppression they were already fading away, the majority failing to meet the 'means test' of 1536 which meant for them closure and the distribution of their communities among the more affluent abbeys.

The Dales of Yorkshire seem to be sown today with amazing ruin-fields, vast in area and complicated in plan, appearing as relics of another civilization . . . of Sumer, perhaps, or the Sassanians.

These are the great monuments. But tucked away everywhere are the lost Cistercian abbeys. Dunkeswell in Devon, with a plain little Victorian church built amongst ruined walls, surrounding its churchyard, which in their day were the tall walls of the abbey choir. Barlynch in the same county, now just snags of walling in a farmyard.

We should not forget, as we watch the descendants of the sheep their lay-brothers folded among the hills and valleys of England, that the true Cistercian memorial is . . . the Woolsack!

# 15

# Friaries and Smaller Priories

The preceding chapters have dealt with the monks, black and white, urban and rural, who lived in enclosed communities, and the canons regular, black and white, who went about their priestly duties among the parishes but lived in communities as one might in a residential college. All followed a disciplinary Rule. Although in theory professing renunciation of worldly goods, some of their houses were exceedingly rich and powerful.

During the thirteenth century another kind of religious Order began to appear in England. These were the so-called Mendicant Orders whose friars were not enclosed in cloisters nor worked regularly at parochial tasks but travelled about the country in a kind of missionary capacity, preaching the Gospel and performing charitable duties towards the poor and sick. Their mission made them wanderers. But each had to have some kind of home. Those homes were their beds in the dormitories of their friaries.

There were four major Orders of friars. There were the Dominicans or friars preachers, usually called black friars, who entered this country in 1221. They were followed by the grey friars, the Franciscans, and finally by the Carmelites, white friars, in 1240. The other major Order of friars was the Augustinian or Austin friars.

There were various minor Orders. One of these which built a most attractive church, that of Edington in Wiltshire, was the Trinitarian, which had been founded originally during the twelfth century for the purpose of rescuing the captives of the Moslems taken during the Crusades. After the end of the Crusades the Order changed its purpose to that of the care of the sick.

The friaries were nothing like the size of the monasteries built by the older Orders. The friars used the cloister as a nucleus, however, and set their buildings—house, hall, chapter house—in much the same fashion as the Benedictines. With past experience of planning problems and developments, however, the friars were able to introduce new features into the arrangement of their houses.

One of these devices helped considerably with the compacting of the claustral plan and enabled the friars to fit it into the confined spaces within towns frequently occupied by their houses. This was the cloister absorbed within the ground floor of each of the three cloister ranges, the corresponding outer halves of the undercrofts being divided into rooms and the whole of the upper storey occupied by a large apartment—dorter, frater, guest hall—all of which were thus finally accommodated upon the *piano nobile*. This had the effect of making the dimensions of the cloister the same as the square of the buildings surrounding it instead of the buildings having to retreat beyond the cloister arcades. (See Fig. 19c.) Aesthetically the effect was most attractive, as may be seen today at the Carmelite friary of Aylesford in Kent where the western and frater ranges remain, and an advance upon the old pentice type of cloister which, even when translated into terms of traceried windows and fan vaulting, was still an appendage rather than an integral part of the building. It was, in fact, the first internal corridor.

The little cloister for the infirmary was adopted by the friars as normal to their plans; at the black friars' house in London it was attached in the usual fashion to the south-east of the cloister and entered by way of the usual slype continuing the line of the main south alley.

The Franciscan friary at Walsingham in Norfolk adopted what might be called the Augustinian plan of setting the little cloister alongside the main one, the frater lying between the two. But the Franciscans went one better by letting the frater undercroft absorb both cloister walks, its medial wall separating the two.

Generally speaking the friars followed the same arrangement for their house and the chapter house and seem to have given the east cloister walk the same importance as it held in the houses of the monks.

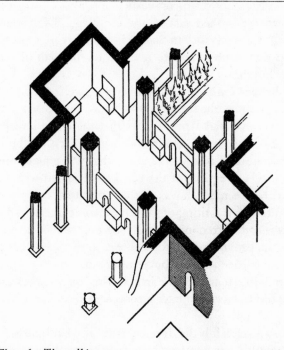

Fig. 26 *The walking space*
After the withdrawal of the monks' choir into
the eastern arm the whole of the crossing with its
transepts became a large retro-choir known as
the walking space

The entrance to the friary was at the northern end of this walk
instead of by the outer parlour in the western range. Its doorway
was thus in the northern side of the cloister where normally the
church would have existed; in fact it occupied the same position
as the eastern processional doorway into the nave.

But the north side of the friars' cloisters was built separately
from the church, possibly in many cases preceding its erection,
for the friars were poor, and had no money to squander upon a
fine church when they were in need of somewhere to live.

The link with the outside world was this doorway in the north-
eastern corner of the courtyard of the cloister. To it led a lane
which in many cases survives today as the Friary Lane. (Fig. 29.)

The transference of the monastic choir into a complete church of its own established east of the crossing, as introduced from Cluny into Lewes Priory in Sussex in about 1140, represented the first step towards a complete revision of the plan of the greater English church.

At Salisbury Cathedral, begun in 1220, we see the plan for the episcopal choirs of the future.

The move created a problem in that the choir screen with its central doorway, being set in the eastern arch of the crossing, lacked the normal retro-choir and, what was equally important, could not take the place of the usual rood-screen with its pair of doorways between which was set the nave altar.

Consulted on the siting of the nave altar at Exeter cathedral the writer was forced to conclude that the only solution to the problem was the provision of a rood-screen in the western arch of the crossing, as existed at Canterbury until 1750.

Is it possible that all cathedrals having their choirs east of the crossing did in fact once have a rood-screen set across its western arch?

The abbeys certainly did. It remains at Crowland and St. Albans.

This would have converted the crossing with its transepts into a retro-choir, a revolutionary change in the monastic church plan. For this would have meant leaving an area some hundred and twenty feet in length and thirty feet wide as an ante-chamber to the monastic church and entirely separating it from the church of the laity now occupying the whole of the nave.

The central area, filled with altars and tombs, was known as 'the walking space'. (Fig. 26.) It was entered from the cloister through a new doorway formed in the west wall of the transept.

Thus the final appearance of the monastic church in this country was in reality a tee-shaped building having the choir and presbytery in its long eastern stem and the cross-bar filled with the walking space.

One might wonder whether any churches were in fact built on this plan. It is apparent that the college chapel of the Oxford college adopted it, the monastic choir being represented by the chapel and the walking space by the ante-chapel. (Fig. 27.)

A pleasant impression of the appearance of the walking space may be received from a visit to Abbey Dore where the crossing and transepts are today empty and a charming chancel screen dating from 1633 occupies the eastern arch of the tower.

The churches of the friars were all laid out to a standard plan of nave and choir separated by a walking place which replaced the crossing of the monastic church of the period. Its width from east to west was reduced to a single bay instead of occupying the width

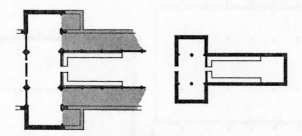

Fig. 27 *Walking space and college chapel*
With the nave of the great church
entirely abandoned to the laity, the
monastic church became reduced to a
tee-shaped area having the cross-arm as
its ante-chamber. The university colleges
of Oxford adopted this plan for their
college chapels

of a transept, for this is always absent from a friars' church. In the centre of the walking space rose the usual lantern tower, but only one quarter of the size of the earlier feature. As it rose it became octagonal, and it was completed with a tall steeple. The Grey-friars tower at King's Lynn is one of the best known of these steeples; Coventry's triplet includes one.

The no-man's-land of the walking space under the tower was the entrance passage to the cloister of the friars and was thus set before their cloister doorway on the line of 'Friary Lane'.

On the east side of the walking space the friars built their choir, and to the west the public nave. (Fig. 28.) The choir was usually aisleless, but the increasing popularity of the friars and in particular the mounting desire to use their choirs for sepulture encouraged some of the larger urban friaries to build aisled choirs.

The nave of the rural friary church was generally aisle-less. But one of the principal activities of the friars was the delivery of sermons, hitherto a minor feature of church services but adopted by the friars as an important element of their missionary duties.

Thus we find introduced into medieval architecture a new ecclesiastical apartment, the 'preaching nave', an entirely different feature from the long covered processional ways of the twelfth

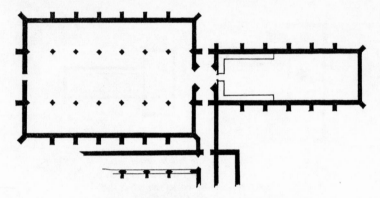

Fig. 28  *Plan of friary church*
The walking space, much reduced in area and
surmounted by a slender campanile, forms the
basis of the plan. East of it is a fine but
aisle-less choir, westwards is spread a spacious
preaching-nave

century. They were to be planned on the 'auditorium' system—later accepted by Christopher Wren—of making length and width as near as possible equal so that no one would be too far away from the pulpit. Thus great width was now needed instead of length.

The increased use of lead for roofing had made it possible to form storm-gutters out of this material and thus risk the setting of buildings side by side, hitherto inadvisable in a climate which produced deep snow. This meant that a building such as the nave of a church could be repeated indefinitely on either side. The replacement of low aisle walls with those of any height desired made it possible to provide enough illumination to render a clearstory unnecessary. Roofs supported each other laterally so the need for sturdy supports was eliminated, and thus no heavy pillars obstructed the view of the preacher.

Churches with wide naves and aisles of equal width and height were known as 'hall' churches. Naves of this description were ideal for the reception of sermons and thus formed the 'preaching naves' of the urban friary. (Fig. 29.) Tradition, however, dictated that the naves were always a little wider than their side-aisles.

By replacing the old monastic attitude of aloofness in favour of getting amongst the people the friars made themselves popular with all classes. This, coupled with the impression their trained preachers made upon everyone, attracted many of the nobility towards making arrangements for interment within friary churches. This in turn encouraged the friars to enlarge their churches by adding aisles to the choir, but even then these structures were so very small as compared with the presbyteries of the great minsters that the tombs and the monuments above them had to be tightly packed in the aisles.

Nothing is left today of the monumental art which during the Tudor era filled the choirs of the urban friaries and even those set in the countryside. The church of the Trinitarians of Easton Royal in Wiltshire became the burial place of the Hereditary Wardens of Savernake Forest; the monument to the last of the pre-Reformation wardens was left abandoned in the ruins until his son rescued it and re-erected it in the parish church of Great Bedwyn.

Above the centre of each friary church rose its slender steeple with at its foot the doorway leading to the cloister. Unlike the greater churches of the monks and canons the friars seem to have made the lateral elevation of their church more important architecturally, no doubt because their best feature would have been the steeple, barely visible from the west.

Public access to the nave of the church was by the west door but no parvis lay before it and no access to the cloister was possible from that side. The friary entrance was on the north along the lane and where this passed through the precinct wall a gatehouse was usually provided. It was at this point that contact with the outer world was maintained, so that if a friary could be said to

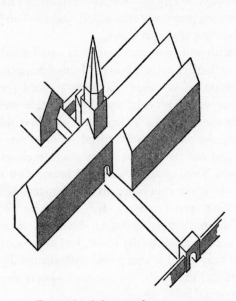

Fig. 29 *Friary church from north-east*
The friary lane is seen leading from the
gatehouse to the doorway into the
walking space, above which is the
campanile. To the left is the aisle-less
choir; the wide nave is roofed under
three separate roofs in the style of the
'hall church'

have had an outer court it would have been here on the north side
of the church.

The lane passing through the friary gate to the doorway at the
foot of the steeple must have been something of a busy route with
friars passing to and fro along it as they left or returned, engaged
upon their pastoral duties. Local tradesmen would presumably
have also used it when calling at the friary door for the delivery of
supplies. It is a noticeable feature of the sites of friaries—the
majority of which have been completely obliterated by urban
development—that the friary lane has nearly always survived as a
memorial.

At the Carmelite friary of Aylesford in Kent the whole house was enclosed within a precinct entered by a large gatehouse. This friary has a large outer court, still perfect, to the west of the cloister, entered by an inner gatehouse in its north-east corner close to the west front of the vanished church. To reach the inner gate from the outer, one would have passed the north front of the church and the cloister entrance.

Diagonally across the outer court was the water gate leading to a wharf on the River Medway, so that there was an alternative approach by water to the friary. A cellarer's entrance leads from the outer court into the west range of the claustral buildings.

Opposite the outer gate the lane would have led to the cloister doorway at the foot of the central tower. The church had aisles to its nave and as an aisle-less choir. Walking space and eastern range have disappeared and with the church the northern side of the cloister has vanished also. The south walk with the frater above it is, however, perfect and provides perhaps the best surviving example of an internal cloister; it returns to the west beside the cellarer's range which probably had the prior's lodging on its upper floor.

If we make an assessment of the monastic settlement in England at the height of its supremacy we shall find that we have besides the great Benedictine abbeys a considerable number of priories which, although of lesser rank through having been colonized by some parent abbey, nevertheless subsequently achieved considerable architectural dignity. We also have the Cluniac priories— none of them abbeys since they all owed allegiance to the Abbot of Cluny—most of them of the first class amongst monastic houses. The Augustinian canons founded priories some of which became abbeys but most of which remained priories equal to all but the greatest of the Benedictine abbeys.

But there were a considerable number of priories of nothing like the scale of these great houses. Some of these were 'cells' of large English houses, while others—the 'alien priories' which caused so many misgivings during the Hundred Years War—were colonized from Continental abbeys.

Such priories as these were on an infinitely smaller scale than anything we have hitherto been considering. They all had churches or parts of churches, but for the most part had no cloisters or anything resembling the claustral building complexes of the large monasteries.

Each had its monastic choir, though this might have been no larger than was required to accommodate seats for up to a dozen monks which was the statutory minimum but might in fact be even less than this.

At Bungay in Suffolk the nave of a Benedictine nunnery has been rebuilt in the fifteenth century and now forms a parish church. Eastwards of it are the ruins of the nuns' choir, little more than an ordinary chancel of unusual length.

Some were very old Anglo-Saxon abbeys which had been left behind at the Conquest and had never been taken over and re-organized with the more favoured abbeys. The once famous abbey at Horton in Dorset is represented today by a large north transept of distinct architectural merit attached to a parish church which appears to be of somewhat mediocre eighteenth-century origin but has some very thick walling.

When thinking of priories one immediately imagines them based upon churches which, if not on an impressive scale when compared with those of great abbeys at least rise in size above the parish church. But some of the daughter houses of great monasteries were founded with the intention of providing visible evidence of ownership of some large or valuable estate. The Benedictines had no system of 'granges' as did the Cistercians.

These small priories were monastic houses in that their monks had a house to live in and a chapel in which to pray, but nothing in the way of a cloister or its usual buildings.

Accommodation could well have been a simple house, two-storeyed certainly, with a dorter and frater end to end on the upper floor or a dorter above a frater. This would be the 'priory'.

The manor of Ipplepen in Devon was held by a foreign abbey and the parish priest appointed by them. The manor house was known as the priory and the priest was called the prior but no actual monastic house existed in the village.

Some of the cloister-less churches may have been of considerable size and dignity, such as those of Stogursey in Somerset and

Stanley St. Leonard in Gloucestershire, both of them plain twelfth-century cruciform buildings with aisle-less naves, though the choir of Stogursey is aisled. This was the church of an alien priory and may well be typical of the type of building, parochial in architectural style, which the foreign monks founded on their English estates.

The alien priories were suppressed more than a century before the general Suppression of 1539, at a time when there was no thought of complete obliteration to remove any threat to the permanency of the movement. Thus the churches of these priories could simply have been taken over by the parishioners who in any case would probably have been using the nave and had merely to walk into the choir.

There are numbers of these small priories scattered about the countryside. Their choirs could either have been separate buildings, no larger than a rural chapel, or attached to a parish church in the form of an isle or even a transept.

The parish church might well have belonged to the priory, so that the monks might either have adapted a portion of it for their choir or, more reasonably, have attached this to the parish church either as an addition or as part of a rebuilt structure.

The monks' choir might be sited in an aisle to the chancel, alongside the nave or partly so in the form of a wing or transept. Such additions might well have been on the south side with the parish porch transferred to the north.

At Upavon in Wiltshire the parish church has a magnificent west tower of more than parochial scale. The south aisle of the nave has been destroyed, leaving a blocked arcade; it may have been the choir of an alien priory removed in 1414 when the monks were ejected.

Had the aisle been taken over by the parish no one would ever have suspected its former use. Or had it been separated from the parish nave by a solid wall and joined to it in 1414 by an arcade, this would have looked just like any other church arcade of the period and again would have given no apparent clue.

Where the existence of a monastic addition to a parish church is suspected one might try to discover the date of such a structure.

The toothing of a vanished wall or the scars from extracted quoins might disclose the existence of a vanished aisle. A blocked-up doorway indicating the monks' entrance might be visible. It is unlikely that a monastic choir, however small, would have been covered by a lean-to roof. It would probably have had its own double-pitch roof, possibly a lead flat.

It was not uncommon for the monks of a priory to provide accommodation for the laity in an aisle built beside the nave of their church. At Weybourne in Norfolk one such aisle is now the parish church and has the nave of the priory church as its north aisle.

The later story of the development of the monastic church in this country is one of gradual absorption of the building by the laity.

The parish churches of Hatfield Broad Oak and Hatfield Peverel in Essex both appear to have quite normal parish naves except for the fact that their chancels have had to be fitted into their eastern ends by surrounding them with screens. They are in fact the naves of Benedictine priories of which the transepts, crossings and eastern arms have been destroyed.

These naves were originally of the twelfth century and probably having been small and without aisles were rebuilt by the monks during the fifteenth century. But because they have been rebuilt in parochial style they give no hint of a monastic origin.

It is clear that in medieval England there were two classes of building, on the one hand that of the monastic teams and on the other what might be described as that of the 'local builder' who ran up the parish churches. (There was nothing much else to build.)

As we approach the end of the monastic era we begin to appreciate that we are witnessing the rise of the parish churches. As the fourteenth century wore on it could be seen that the great monastic churches were all completed and now only required maintenance. Architecture on the grand scale was on the decline, and the 'local builder' was becoming far more active.

The 'parochial' movement may have derived partly from the fact that the monastic builders had really nothing much more to

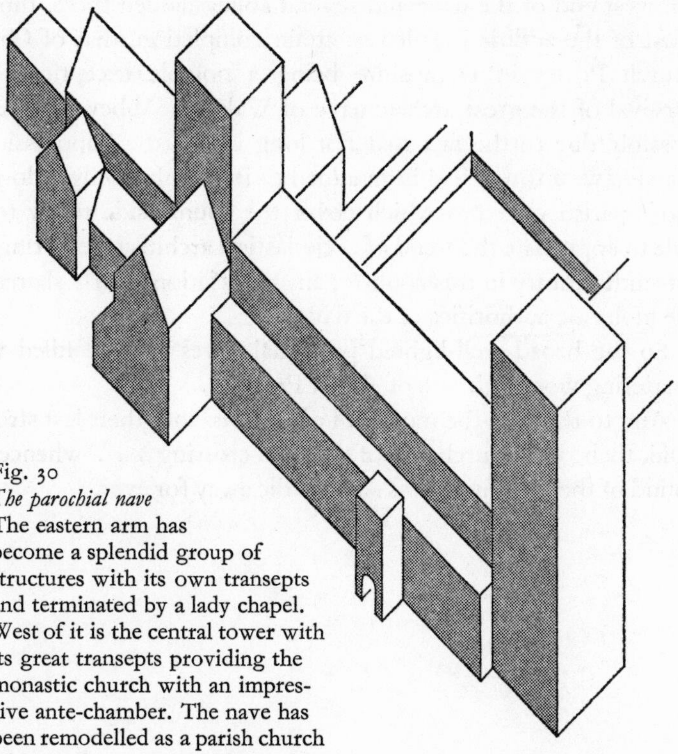

Fig. 30
*The parochial nave*
The eastern arm has
become a splendid group of
structures with its own transepts
and terminated by a lady chapel.
West of it is the central tower with
its great transepts providing the
monastic church with an impressive ante-chamber. The nave has
been remodelled as a parish church
with a tall west tower of parochial
type.

do than to rebuild some of the more primitive naves, and partly
from the fact that this rebuilding was being carried out in the style
of the great parish churches which were rising everywhere
throughout the country, especially in East Anglia and Somerset.
(See Fig. 30.)

A glance at the nave of Wymondham Abbey in Norfolk will
show that it is just the nave of a fifteenth-century church complete
with the inevitable western bell-tower. It may well be that it was
for this reason it survived the Suppression, for there is nothing
monastic about it. The choir has of course been destroyed, the
ruin of the central tower remaining.

The twilight of the abbeys saw also the era of the bell-tower at the west end of the nave and several abbeys added these, though most of the additions failed to attain completion, that of Christchurch Priory in Hampshire being a notable exception. The survival of the great archaic nave of Waltham Abbey in Essex is possibly due to the fact that not long before the Suppression a massive west tower had been added to it. One has only to look at those parish churches which cover the countryside today to be able to appreciate the trend of ecclesiastical architecture during the fifteenth century in this country, an appreciation clearly shared by the monastic authorities of the day.

So the broad well-lighted parochial naves became filled with chattering wool-rich folk of Tudor England.

And to the east, the monks of old moved into their last stronghold, their own church east of the high crossing . . . whence the sound of their chanting was soon to die away for ever.

# 16

# The Suppression

It is of interest to speculate as to how the English abbeys might
have developed had they been allowed to continue for another few
centuries as on the Continent. For notwithstanding the weakening
of the absolute hold the Roman Church had upon the medieval
population, the monastic concept continued to flourish across the
Channel until atheistic prejudices accumulating at the end of the
eighteenth century drove the French monks from their abbeys as
from the English houses three and a half centuries earlier.

Regarding the probable development of the plan of the abbey
church one intention seems predominant—the desire to abandon
the nave and withdraw into the privacy of a separate monastic
church situated east of the crossing.

The cost of maintaining a great nave must have been discouraging to an abbey with an extensive complex of domestic buildings to
keep in repair. England's last great abbey church, that of Bath,
seems to point to the situation as seen by the monks. At the end of
the fifteenth century the huge church was in a state of utter dis-
repair. Rather than repair the nave they pulled it down completely,
building on its site a complete new church. This was a compactly-
planned building with a nave of five bays, a presbytery of three,
and small insignificant transepts, the whole surmounted by a
splendid central bell-tower of Somersetshire type.

But as this church was not completed until after the Suppression
we do not know how it was intended to be used. Surely the choir
would have been sited west of the short eastern arm. Was it perhaps to leave been west of the crossing—perhaps just leaving a

short western annexe to hold a small congregation of the laity? Was it in fact to have been a return to the plan of Romsey?

When one examines the church of Bath Abbey closely one discovers that the crossing is not a true one in that the transepts are not the same width as the east/west part of the church and that in fact they are in the nature of eastern or choir transepts, the tower being in fact rectangular. Thus it seems very probable that the church is in fact a monastic choir lacking its nave.

Bath was a rich abbey and its church held a bishop's throne. It seems unlikely that many houses would have been able to build entirely new churches, especially when one considers the architectural magnificence now to be required of the great church. It seems more likely that had the Suppression been delayed for another century we would have seen many of the abbeys, especially those of the bereft Cistercians, pulling down their naves and retiring into their splendid eastern choirs.

However, the lovely 'Lantern of the West' with its great windows and intricate vaulted ceilings, might show us what a new abbey church of the sixteenth century was like.

And it is in this compact cruciform presentation that the great church enters into the Renaissance.

The new churches would presumably have soon shed the Gothic trappings of pinnacles and tracery. With better constructed roofs all aisles would have disappeared.

It would have been interesting to know whether England would have followed the rest of Europe in reverting to the Byzantine dome as a central feature. From parish church examples it becomes clear that the insular English architects were content to raise Gothic-type church towers well into the eighteenth century. It seems not unlikely that the Baroque *campanile*—belatedly introduced by Wren—might have continued the English tradition of the 'whispering spire' rather than an introduction of the lumpish dome.

Who knows what might have happened to English monumental architecture had the monks been left in control of the incomes derived from their great estates. Their work at Bath indicated that English ecclesiastical architects retained their skill to the very end. There seems to be no reason why they should not have accepted the Renaissance and made of it in the passing of time a style as English as the house of the Georgian squire. It is a pity that the Suppression caught them in a state of unpreparedness for a sudden changeover not only to a new type of building but also to a revolutionary architectural style.

The abbeys which survived the Act of 1536 still had the use of a very large proportion of the national income to spend on fine buildings, in this respect being far better able to support a national architecture than the Church in Europe.

Nevertheless the Continental abbeys continued to flourish, concentrating for the most part, however, upon the improvement of domestic accommodation.

Thus we are able to obtain from the Continent a glimpse of how the English abbey, allowed to continue without interference, might have developed.

As the age of the abbots drew to its close in this country we can notice a tendency to abandon the communal life in favour of some degree of privacy in separate rooms. The early ward-like dorters had been divided into cubicles by boarded partitions or 'brattices' as early as the fourteenth century.

By building their strange cloisters surrounded by cells which were in fact small cottages each with its garden, the Carthusians had set a fashion for individualism in the guise of cenobitism. For simplicity of catering they met for meals in a common frater, but their daily lives could have been planned under conditions far more suited to contemplation and study than under what must all too often have been the irritating communal existence within the houses of the major Orders.

The friars, latest recruits to the monastic life, were including their cloister alleys within the ground floors of the claustral ranges. The development from this was to divide up the back portion of each range into small rooms which in the end replaced the communal dorter. Each 'cell' had in fact become a bed-sitting room.

By the mid-sixteenth century the novelties of Renaissance architecture had become well-established and were rapidly spreading—albeit in strange forms—throughout this country. The multistorey building had now arrived and would have replaced the old two-storey ranges of the cloister of medieval days. The Gothic limitations of a style designed in bays had been set aside and architects were experimenting with the '*palazzo*' type of façade.

The awe-inspiring spectacle once provided by the lateral elevation of the interminable medieval church had been entirely lost. Only a somewhat restrained west front feebly supporting a dimly-seen dome was left to the ecclesiastical architects.

For the architecture of the Renaissance was keyed to the production of what had for so long been ignored—the construction of domestic buildings.

The *palazzo* was the key building of the Renaissance world. And beside the now rather unimportant west front of the church stretched a building which could provide an excellent canvas upon which to apply a Renaissance façade.

Thus by the close of the sixteenth century what had been the cellarer's range had become transformed into an apartment block, possibly containing, as of old, rooms connected with the lodging of the abbot and his guests.

For such a building its presentation as a fine Renaissance elevation became inevitable. Thus we find the new type of west elevation developing as a long façade of some height reaching southwards from the entrance front of a church, beginning soon to show signs of the arrival of the Baroque.

May we ascribe to that grand west front of Fountains the privilege of introducing the theme from which was to develop the splendid mission architecture of New Spain?

But all such interesting developments were denied to us in this country by the fall of the royal axe in 1539.

\* \* \*

There can be no doubt that monasticism in this country had been for some time on the decline. A more liberal attitude which the ordinary man was displaying to the more superstitious beliefs had checked the flow of foundations and endowments, and as early as 1279 the Statute of Mortmain had put a brake on the wholesale handing over of English land to the voracious abbeys.

The most serious objection to the monastic system was the

25. Thornton

26. Roche

feeling that it was wrong for the insular Englishman to be in any way bound to a foreign potentate. The English abbots had long formed an important section of the country's nobility. Appointed by the King of England, it might have seemed intolerable that they should be dividing their allegiance between him and the Pope of Rome.

This country has always been passionately concerned for the preservation of its insularity and the King of England gladly stood firmly behind his people in encouraging this vital characteristic which has ever carried his country through its darkest hours. It may well have been the hidden memories of Hastings which enabled us to hold fast against the Armada.

To a country with such a strong sense of independence the existence of a shadowy sovereign far away in Italy may have often seemed repugnant.

The medieval English pastime of waging war on France made the presence of a large number of French monks in this country a source of concern. That 'second Pope', the Abbot of Cluny, was far from being *persona grata* with Englishmen and in 1376 Parliament petitioned that the Cluniac priories over here should be purged of Frenchmen and only English monks admitted. Then in 1414 all the alien priories were summarily suppressed and their houses left desolate.

The person who struck the first blow at the inviolability of the English monasteries was none other than the Papal legate himself, Cardinal Wolsey, who in 1519 had been empowered by a Bull to reform them. This he did by seizing twenty-five monastic houses with fewer than the long-ignored statutory minimum strength of twelve monks, receiving Papal authority for this step in 1524. The Cardinal's real aim was to finance the endowment of his college, now called Christ Church, at Oxford which he based upon the Augustinian priory of St. Frideswide, the church of which is now Oxford Cathedral.

This rehearsal for the final suppression, which was carried out with complete banditry and without any protest from the Crown, left men in little doubt as to the ultimate fate of the country's monasteries.

It has often been said that it was due to Henry VIII's wish to divorce Queen Catherine that the English monasteries were suppressed. This is not strictly true. For Henry was only according royal support to the view of the great majority of Englishmen that they could not have a foreign sovereign dictating to their king.

The task of suppressing these vast concerns which between them held a quarter or so of the land in the country and had long exercised a political power incomprehensible to us today was a formidable one and needed to be planned with care. Fortunately for the Crown some of the abbeys and priories were themselves offering a pretext.

Maintenance of their buildings and the increased expenditure of the abbots in connection with their social and political activities were landing some of the monastic houses in debt, so that sooner or later they seemed to be headed for bankruptcy; the Cistercian abbeys had been almost ruined by the loss of their lay-brothers following the Black Death.

So the first act of the final suppression was the closing down of houses having an income of less than two hundred pounds a year; this wiped out over three hundred of them, mainly Cistercian, whose monks were absorbed into more affluent abbeys. Thus on financial grounds themselves the ancient abbeys could have been presented as dissolving themselves. It was indeed a sound move, for the brethren affected could hardly complain at having their financial cares transferred from their shoulders and themselves accommodated in better-administered and probably more comfortable houses.

But the Crown had not allowed for the complete disorganization of the pastoral areas which followed and a serious rebellion, the Pilgrimage of Grace, followed the suppressions. This was put down with medieval savagery and abbots were hanged.

After such a serious rebellion, which brought forty thousand under arms against the Crown, there was only one course for Henry to adopt.

So in 1539 the order went out for the total suppression of the English monastic houses.

The business was inevitably an ugly one which reflected little credit upon those who carried it out. Nor is it looked on, in the main, as a period of history without shame for the perpetrators. All that one could say is that it was long overdue, an immense operation to undertake, and that it is doubtful whether anyone else could have done it better.

To operate the machinery of suppression there were commissioners to be appointed, and it is generally agreed that they were just the kind of unscrupulous knaves one would in fact have had to employ for such an obviously disreputable task. For desirable though it may have been politically, the operation was in fact simply one of theft, the seizing of legally-owned property and its distribution amongst persons having no right whatsoever to it.

The persons who were ejected were eventually quite well treated, all evicted monks being accorded pensions and the more important of the abbots being translated to thrones in a few of the abbey churches which were being retained to serve as cathedrals of new dioceses. Monastic servants were given a year's wages.

The pity was that those who resisted, almost invariably through conviction, were treated so savagely. The King could never have had any illusions as to the gravity of the step he was taking. And, curiously enough, no one more than he was conscious of the spiritual power of Holy Church. For far from being the atheist he is still presented as, Henry intended to make as little change as possible, to avoid casting any doubt upon religious beliefs, and to press for the continuance of church worship as before. Indeed he gave himself personal responsibility for the future by making himself head of the English Church. What he would no longer tolerate was any adherence to a foreign Pope. Thus any opposition to the monastic suppression was simply regarded as high treason and dealt with accordingly.

Thus abbots, some of them aged men, unable to throw off suddenly the beliefs of generations, were hanged, drawn and quartered in the barbarous fashion which still obtained even as late as the seventeenth century. The cry of treason against the English realm justified the application of any punishment.

After the Act of 1536 had wiped out scores of the poorer houses all the friaries meekly surrendered. The final Act of 1539 brought the total of houses suppressed to over six hundred and fifty.

The circumstances connected with the surrender of the monasteries seem to have been wholly disreputable. The smaller priories were simply entered upon by gangs of thugs calling themselves commissioners and their occupants told summarily to move out. Given an elderly and terrified abbot to bully, the commissioners seem to have been able to empty an important abbey such as Roche in minutes.

Then the local peasantry, gathered together waiting for the signal, would rush into the ancient place and loot it of everything immediately portable left by the commissioners, who had, however, locked up certain items to preserve them for the Crown. The booty, both private and official, was of course of immense value.

It has been computed that the Suppression brought to the Crown alone goods and land to the value of a hundred million pounds of today's money. Some of this was of course returned to the monks in the form of pensions.

The measure of Henry's real concern for the preservation of the insularity of his realm is indicated by the amount of money he spent upon coastal defence. Walmer, Deal, Southsea, St. Mawes and Pendennis are among the Renaissance artillery forts he built around the Channel shores.

The monks had been removed from their long-held strongholds, now empty and despoiled. The last stage in the Suppression was the complete eradication, as far as possible, of every vestige of the centuries of monastic occupation of England.

It is reckoned that of the six hundred and fifty houses suppressed about one-third have been completely obliterated.

The King's commissioners had definite instructions to destroy physically the buildings of the abbey. Structures specifically listed were the church, steeple, cloister, frater, dorter, and chapter house. The King did not wish to leave standing any structure which might provide a basis for monastic revivalism.

The church and steeple were particularly singled out to be destroyed. Henry might possibly have reflected on the discredit which would have been brought upon the Church of which he was now the Head if scores of magnificent religious buildings were abandoned to sink into squalor and decay.

The grantees were of course only too eager to turn the buildings into cash by demolishing them for their materials. But those who had not done so at the accession of Queen Mary might well have been alarmed at her attempts to bring about a monastic renaissance. The owner of Repton Abbey in Derbyshire, leaving nothing to chance, gathered together a host of masons and carpenters from all over the shire and spent with them a whole Sunday in 'plucking down, in one day, a most beautiful church'. This attitude helps one to appreciate why so very few abbey churches falling into lay hands were suffered to remain.

'The nest has been destroyed', said one of the grantees 'lest the birds should build there again.'

Thus the tale of the abbey churches following the Suppression is one of desolation. Yet some of them are perhaps even more splendid in ruin now that their one-time interiors are no longer darkened by the heavy vaults long fallen from them. The great ruin perched upon the cliff-top at Whitby in Yorkshire (Plate 28) might have seemed in its heyday just another large church among many.

Even in ruin the immortal Gothic glorifies those stately Cistercian memorials rising among the Yorkshire dales.

Rievaulx is far more than just a ruined church. (Plate 17.)

The Abbey of Fountains is one of the world's great ruins. (Plate 18.)

The Cistercians seem to have been determined to leave their mark on England. Hampshire's Netley Abbey has survived conversion into a mansion, discarded the sacrilegious accretions and emerged as lovely as ever from the interlude. (Plate 30.)

But against all this, how many once great churches fail today even to break the surface of the turf. Looking through the fascinating series of aerial photographs in Dom David Knowles's *Monastic Sites* one sees page after page of abbey churches only visible today as light imprints upon the fields and pastures of England.

*Delenda* are Lancastrian Whalley and Barlings beside the Cambridgeshire fenland. For the abbots of both died in their defence.

Many are the Cistercian and Augustinian churches seen today only as phantoms appearing for an instant when the land which carried them is drying out after rain. They have taken their places beside those other English ghosts—the painted pavements of Roman Britain.

The church was the first to go. Throughout the centuries a great deal of valuable building material had gone into the construction of the monastic houses. Chiefly there was lead, greatly in demand now that the new low-pitched roofs were everywhere replacing the old steep shingled ones. The churches were covered with lead, so their roofs had to go, soon to be followed by the fraters with their fine fifteenth-century roofs.

Gothic architecture, erected with such great difficulty, was found to be all too easy to bring down again. Its arcuated construction, in which so much depends for support upon the presence of a neighbour, made it a prey to that ancient enemy of the strong-walled castle, the miner. A mine was dug under one of the crossing piers, the masonry above shored up, and a fire lit amongst the shoring. When the pier sank the arches above it collapsed; deprived of their abutment there was a good chance that the adjoining arcades would also fall bringing down in ruin the heavy vaults they had safely carried for so long.

When the great sheets of lead were rolled up from the church roof and hurled down to the ground it had to be melted in cauldrons and cast into ingots or 'fothers'. The roof timbering was too massive to be cut up for fuel, so the much handier timber represented by the stalls and screenwork of the choirs was used to stoke the fires.

As the bells came down from the tower they broke into more or less portable pieces for transportation to the foundries where they were cast into bronze cannon for the new coastal castles.

The metalwork was thrown down into the church where the cauldrons were set up close to their fuel supply. This activity resulted in the demolition of the tombs of 'divers noble men and women'. For, as the chronicler mused, there was no sense in keeping these intact 'when the church over them was spoiled'.

There were two attitudes towards the destruction of the abbey churches. For while there were plenty who approved the orgy for the booty which accrued, there were others who were genuinely ashamed, even in those rough days, at the sight of so much loveliness wantonly and contemptuously 'spoiled'. Such individuals may not have been so much affected aesthetically as deploring an exhibition unworthy of a civilized nation, for it was in this guise that Tudor England was beginning to regard itself. The suppression of the anachronisms represented by the medieval abbeys was in reality an expression of this attitude. But this deplorable orgy of destruction proceeded at a feverish pace, the eradication of the hundreds of monastic houses appearing almost as a national pastime with every abbey the focus of a horde of 'spoilers'.

Those excavating the sites of abbeys today are not involved in much carting away of fallen stonework. There is little burying of the lower parts of walls in material fallen from above. This is because the stones of the abbey were useful material. They could be used for three purposes.

They could be burnt for lime, more in demand than ever now that the most common building material was brick which uses more mortar than dressed stone.

Another use for the stone was for building houses for private persons, farmers and the like, who had taken over portions of the abbey lands and needed homes from which to work them.

An interesting form of building technique was invented for the use of second-hand stone, walls being built honeycomb fashion on both faces with the tails of each facing stone matched by a void on the opposite face of the wall. When the voids on either side were filled in with rubble, brickbats or flint, a chequerboard effect was created. This looks attractive today; in the sixteenth century it formed an ingenious method of using the stone from the abbeys.

The third use of abbey stone was for the metalling of roads. The huge abbey of Glastonbury in Somerset stands in a marshy countryside which was very much in need of roads having a sound bottom. The Presbyterians who succeeded the monks erased the building almost completely and sold the stone for this purpose, and the work of generations of Somerset masons and carvers was sunk forever into the mire of the Parret.

Amongst valuable items of salvage the abbeys supplied paving stones, in many parts of England hard to come by and greatly in demand for the floors of houses.

It is interesting to note that the verb used in describing the destruction of the abbeys was always 'to *pluck* down', which seems to suggest some kind of tensile assault. So possibly ropes and ox-teams were used to topple the walls.

Amongst the disappearances of great churches one seems quite incomprehensible, that of a whole cathedral priory, complete with its cathedral church, at Coventry; it has vanished so utterly that all one can see of it is the base of a crossing pier deep at the bottom of a hole, sole relic of a great church of the twelfth century.

The powerful Prior of Lewes, representative in this country of that 'second Pope', the Abbot of Cluny, had his great church singled out for an all-out assault, the progress of which was enthusiastically recorded by one John Portinari, foreman of the demolition squad, who brought seventeen men all the way from London to assist him.

Ten masons 'hewed the walls about' after which three carpenters fixed the shores to 'underset where the others cut away'. Two smiths were employed in keeping the tools sharp. Two plumbers attended to the stripping, melting down, and casting of the lead from the roofs; a local man 'keepeth the furnace'. The recipient of this report was Thomas Cromwell, Chief Commissioner for the Suppression, to whom the great priory and its estates had been granted by the King.

So down came the great church of Lewes with its two sets of transepts and its elaborate French *chevet*.

'Nothing was spared save swine-cots and other houses of office that stood without the walls.'

The aesthetic loss to the country resulting from the Suppression was far greater than that from any other event connected with historical architecture. But the practical result was revolutionary and wholly beneficial to the country. For a start there was the release

27. Fountains

28. Whitby

of almost the whole of a national building potential, for centuries mewed in the *curia* of the abbey and engaged on maintaining and adding to hundreds of virtually useless structures and unable to perform the much-needed function of improving the domestic architecture of a country still living under medieval conditions.

England was now a rich country, firmly seated upon the sheep's back. Its domestic architecture, however, had been forced to lie dormant until such time as the building trade of the country should have been liberated from its long ecclesiastical servitude. But with medievalism, long nourished and preserved in the gloomy cloisters of the past, finally brought to a halt, the country was now ready to accept the stimulus of the Renaissance.

With the flight of the abbots appeared the Tudor wool-baron to lay the foundations of a new England—Shakespeare's England —the Merrie England of Elizabeth.

# 17

# Survivals

The English countryside must have presented a strange sight during the fifth decade of the sixteenth century when the tall towers of the Middle Ages were everywhere toppling away into oblivion. Only a few of the Benedictine towers such as those of Gloucester, Evesham, Bath, Sherborne, Pershore, Milton, and of course the grand old campanile at Ely, remain of the scores swept cleanly away.

The huge church of St. Albans Abbey, sharing with Westminster the premiership of the English abbeys, and centuries later to become a cathedral, was bought by the town for four hundred pounds. Ancient Tewkesbury (Plate 2), reduced to parochial status, still impresses thousands of visitors yearly by its dim nave lined with gigantic circular pillars. The Benedictine nunnery church of Romsey in Hampshire, bought by the town for a hundred pounds, remains as perhaps the finest example of a period when England was leading the world in the perfection of its architectural style.

The parishioners of Pershore in Worcestershire could not afford the sum required to save the whole of their great church with its long nave in the style of neighbouring Tewkesbury. But they were able to buy the eastern arm with the crossing which gave them not only a western bell-tower of great beauty but what is possibly the most lovely parish church in England. (Plate 1.) Across the Severn the priory church of Great Malvern, humble miniature of Tewkesbury, still survives as a parish church.

The great church of Selby in Yorkshire is well-known while

at the other end of the country is the lovely church at Sherborne in Dorset. Romsey Abbey in Hampshire stands in a class by itself in the perfection of its antique architecture while the same may be said, at the other end of the story, of the last of the great churches, that of Bath Abbey in Somerset. The Augustinian church of Carmel Priory in Lancashire was saved for the parishioners. One of the most delightful of the survivors is the charming priory church of Brinkburn in Northumberland (Plate 3), among the most perfect examples of the early Gothic in the country.

One great Augustinian church, that of Christchurch Priory in Hampshire, remains to give us a clearer impression than we deserve of a monastic church in its heyday. Its choir is situated east of the crossing; in it the stallwork, which seems to have been renewed just prior to the Suppression, is complete to its screens and looks as though the canons had just walked out of it. At the eastern end of the choir stands the remains of what was once a magnificent reredos but the niches are bare of the figure sculpture they originally held.

The east end of the presbytery is complete to its terminal lady chapel. West of the crossing and transepts stretches the parochial nave which had a lofty bell-tower added to its west end just twenty years before the Suppression.

The choir screen is in the eastern arch of the crossing and the choir entirely east of this. The lantern above the crossing has disappeared and the internal effect of what might have been the most impressive part of the building—the 'walking space'—has been spoiled through the obstruction of the south transept by a large organ on a gallery. It is a church, nevertheless, which provides a very valuable memorial of the age of the abbots.

The abbey church was the first building singled out for destruction, partly for its lead and partly because the obliteration of what was the heart and soul of the abbey would preclude any possibility of its resurrection. There were certain difficulties, however, where a great nave had been so extensively used by the local people that it had become to all intents and purposes— possibly even incontrovertibly so—a parish church. Thus we fortunately find a considerable number of cases where the monastic nave was spared from the general destruction which almost invariably, however, befell that indisputably monastic part of the church, the choir of the monks with the crossing and transepts.

It would probably have been easier to have saved the nave if the monks' choir had moved eastwards out of it. At Malmesbury Abbey in Wiltshire the cloister was on the north and the parish church to the south of the abbey nave. But a very long east end was built onto the abbey church and the monks' choir transferred to it out of the nave, the new rood screen being set across the western arch of the crossing. The monks having thus virtually abandoned the whole of the nave to the laity it was much easier for the parish to claim this at the Suppression.

The Augustinian priory church of Bolton in Yorkshire (Plate 32) is an example where the crossing, transepts, and presbytery were simply unroofed without being actually pulled down and thus remain as splendid ruins east of the parish nave which is still in use. 'Bolton Abbey', as it is called nowadays, is a magnificent building of the mid-Gothic era with a fine west front partly obscured by the lower storey of what was to have been a huge bell-tower left incomplete at the Suppression. The cloister is still recognizable as well as some of the buildings around it.

The massive Anglian-style nave of Binham Priory in Norfolk survives west of the pathetic ruin of transepts and presbytery. At Blyth in Nottinghamshire another massive nave stands short of its eastern termination. The nave of Wymondham Abbey in Norfolk, which must have been brand-new at the Suppression, reaches between a stately bell-tower and the ruined lantern of the monastic choir. At Elstow near Bedford the remains of the grim old nave of a Benedictine nunnery stand beside a detached belltower similar to those of Chichester Cathedral and the vanished one at Salisbury. The preservation of such rebuilt naves as those of Hatfield Peverel and Hatfield Broad Oak in Essex have been noted in the last chapter.

The Augustinian canon seems to have been more successful than any of the old Orders at obtaining exemption for their naves. The great nave of Dunstable in Bedfordshire remains, also that of Bridlington in Yorkshire and Worksop in Nottinghamshire. At

Thurgarton in Nottinghamshire part of what must have been a splendid twin-towered Gothic nave remains in use as a parish church.

The mitred abbey of Waltham in Essex, burial place of King Harold and the last abbey to be suppressed, still retains its mighty nave.

At the other end of the scale such little churches as those of Stogursey in Somerset and Stanley St. Leonard in Gloucestershire were preserved complete as parish churches, probably because they had been built on a parochial scale.

The destruction of the monastic choirs was so savage that it is a wonder that any are left. The lovely choir of Pershore must be the finest survival from the great days. To compare with the austere choir of Pamber Priory in Hampshire we have the charming little church of Little Malvern which is the priory choir. Sussex has the fascinating choir of Boxgrove Priory (Plate 7), eight bays long and of unusual design.

A really magnificent structure is the great choir of Milton Abbey in Dorset, preserved to be the parish church not of a town but to serve the needs of a tiny village which in its turn has been erased, at the whim of a Georgian squire, leaving as its memorial the stately choir, transepts, and tower of a great church.

Of sterner quality are the fine choir and transepts of Hexham Priory in Yorkshire, while in London itself we can still stroll round the ambulatory of St. Bartholomew's Priory in Smithfield.

Of the glories of canopied stallwork which once filled these and the hundreds of lost choirs only three places have preserved these magnificent examples of the carpentry of the Gothic era. Pride of the parish church of Wolverhampton is the stallwork rescued from the fires of the Augustinian abbey of Lilleshall in Shropshire. The most beautiful of all are the stalls in Lancaster church which came from the choir of the Premonstratensian abbey of Cockersand of which nothing is left save a hexagonal chapter house in a field.

The stalls of the Premonstratensian abbey of Easby in Yorkshire are preserved in the chancel of the parish church of Richmond nearby.

Stalls were not used in parish churches only requiring a seat for a single priest, so the preservation of these three sets of stalls is nothing less than miraculous and must represent the devotion of some Tudor parishioners of the churches giving these lovely examples of medieval carpentry room in their chancels.

The fine choir stalls at Chester Cathedral form a memorial to the days when it was the church of a Benedictine abbey.

Portions of the choir screens may, however, have been saved for use in parish churches, especially those needing to form chancels at the ends of newly-acquired monastic naves. There may be many unsuspected pieces of monastic screenwork yet to be discovered in our parish churches.

Fifteenth-century roof timbering with its underside marvellously wrought as a ceiling was certainly salvaged and transferred to the side chapels of churches; Marnhull church in Dorset has a ceiling believed to have come from Shaftesbury Abbey. Still more likely is the suggestion that such timbering was reused in the new mansions which were being constructed everywhere out of abbey salvage.

Here and there we may enter some parish church to find it incorporating some fragment of glorious Gothic obviously far in advance of parish church standard. Such a church is that of Little Dunmow in Essex which is discovered to be the south choir aisle of an Augustinian priory church.

Of mighty Crowland, deep in the Fens of Lincolnshire, a lonely tower broods over a vaulted aisle of its nave which is all that is left of a great abbey church founded before the Conquest.

The rural Cistercian churches have been left with only slight fragments still in use. But place the nave of Margam church in Glamorgan at the west side of the crossing at Abbey Dore in Herefordshire and the result would be a complete Cistercian church.

Some abbey churches have survived in very strange guise for one would hardly have supposed them capable of being converted into houses. Yet the abbey church of Buckland in Devonshire has been thus transformed; it is a curious encounter to be wandering along an upper floor to be confronted by large round arches indicating that one is in the lantern of a central tower.

Still stranger is it to discover the nave of an Augustinian priory being used as a nursery with the adjoining choir serving as a dining room with a fan-vaulted pantry beside it. Above is a drawing room ceiled with all the glories of Gothic. That is Stavordale Priory in Somerset. In the same county is Woodspring Priory with its once magnificent nave turned into a farmhouse along the north side of which one may see the phantoms of its splendid windows. At its east end is a desolate tower vaulted with all the brilliance one expects from its county.

At Denney in the Cambridgeshire fens the nave and transepts of a nuns' church have been converted into a farmhouse and at Alberbury in Shropshire a farmhouse known as White Abbey is mainly formed from the church of a priory belonging to the French Order of Grandmontines.

At Mottisfont in Hampshire even the visible presence of monastic undercrofts fails to prepare one for the surprise of encountering a stone screen from the church in the kitchen regions of the present house.

Most curious of all is the barn at Latton in Essex which upon inspection turns out to be the complete crossing of what was once a priory church.

Central towers standing upon their four vulnerable legs seldom survived the Suppression, though strange fragments still remain at such places as Maxstoke Priory in Warwickshire and Talley Abbey in Carmarthenshire. The more sturdily-built western towers, however, often added to 'parochial' naves as the Suppression approached, still stand in several places. The splendidly situated Premonstratensian abbey at Shap in Westmorland is mainly represented today by the ruin of a bell-tower at the west end of the remains of the church while at Ulverscroft in Leicestershire a slender *campanile* still watches over the ruin of a small Augustinian church.

The parish church of Beaulieu in Hampshire was once the frater of the Cistercian abbey as its lovely pulpit clearly indicates.

At Llanthony in Monmouthshire the parish church was the infirmary hall of the priory.

Of the great array of claustral building which once formed the domestic portions of the monasteries there are considerable remains.

In an age of great courtyards there must have been some temptation to convert the abbey cloister into a domestic court. Actually, however, this does not often seem to have been attempted, possibly because the lay grantees either already had mansions or, if not, felt unable to embark on a building project of the scale implied.

At Netley Abbey in Hampshire (Plate 30) the nave of the church was converted into a great hall, approached across the cloister from an entrance in the vicinity of the frater. But all this has followed the abbey into ruin and there is nothing to spoil the lovely remains of the Cistercian church.

At Titchfield in Hampshire the Premonstratensian frater, which lay east and west, became the great hall of a post-Suppression mansion. The nave of the church was converted into a forebuilding to this by setting athwart it a huge turreted gatehouse which still remains when all else has gone. The grantee must have been very tower-conscious since he left the adjoining central tower of the church to keep his great gate-tower company but was forced to pull it down as its proximity made his chimneys smoke!

At Haughmond in Shropshire the great hall of the infirmary (Plate 22) was retained by the lay grantee to be his hall and the adjoining abbot's house was made into his chamber block. But all this was burnt down during the Civil War. A large mansion constructed out of the ruins of Abbotsbury Abbey in Dorset was blown up during the war.

Perhaps the most comprehensive take-over of a medieval abbey was that which may still be seen at Newstead in Nottinghamshire. The church has gone save for its south transept, incorporated into the mansion, and the fine west front with the frame of its west window looking rather forlorn beside the new domestic front based on the cellarer's range.

The cloister at Newstead is intact; the frater has become a drawing room, and the chapter house is still attached to the south transept of the church.

Another conversion of a complete claustral complex may be

found at the Augustinian nunnery of Lacock in Wiltshire. Here the church has gone save for its north wall abutting on the cloister, all of which, with its fine walling, remains. It is surrounded by the usual undercrofts and an attractive chapter house vaulted above a pair of pillars. In the storey above, the medieval apartments have been refashioned to form a post-Suppression mansion.

One of the most valuable survivals is the claustral block of the Cistercian abbey of Cleeve, popular with visitors to the coasts of Exmoor. The church has gone, but the buildings surrounding the other three sides of the cloister are intact to their roofs, the abbey having been used as a farmhouse since the Suppression. The frater is a remarkable survival, with the dorter running it close. The ground-floor chapter house (Plate 19), once clear of the east wall of the dorter, rose in height above the abbot's seat.

There are probably other houses scattered about the countryside which stand on the sites of vanished cloisters and have been built around courts which may represent these. Welbeck Abbey in Nottinghamshire contains in its cellars part of the medieval cellarer's range and even part of the west front of the abbey church.

Wilton House in Wiltshire which occupies the site of a famous Benedictine nunnery and is built round a courtyard may in fact be sited on the trace of the medieval cloister.

The finest display of monastic buildings remaining today in occupation may be seen at Forde in Dorset and comprises the north range with the frater, chapter house, abbot's hall, and part of the cloister alley.

There are probably a number of private houses today which occupy the site of one or another of the ranges of a monastic house. The western would have been the most probable choice, for here in normal circumstances would have been the lodgings for guests, or in a Benedictine abbey the abbot's house already planned and appointed to be a gentleman's residence. But anywhere south-west of the abbey church, perhaps in the great court, suitable buildings might be found for conversion.

The Carmelite friary at Aylesford in Kent has retained the whole of its outer court together with the west and south claustral ranges which were turned into a country house.

At Calder Abbey in Cumberland and Brinkburn Priory in Northumberland the present house incorporates portions of the monastic frater, while at Blanchland Abbey in the last named county the Premonstratensian guest house continues to serve travellers in the capacity of an inn. The impressive guest house of the Carthusians at Mount Grace in Yorkshire, however, has been converted into a fine country house.

A good example of the conversion of the domestic quarter of a monastic house may be seen at Notley Abbey in Buckinghamshire where the sixteenth-century abbot's lodging has been joined with the guest house and part of the cellarage to form a compact dwelling house.

The thirteenth-century abbot's house at Battle Abbey has become a girls' school.

The happy combination round its little cloister of the prior's house and infirmary hall at Much Wenlock in Shropshire has been fully described in an earlier chapter; it is possibly the most attractive of the monastic conversions.

Of Muchelney Abbey in the Somersetshire marshes near Langport only the abbot's house with his hall and chamber remain forming what was until recently a farmhouse. Adjoining the west front of the ruined church at Castle Acre in Norfolk is another attractive medieval house, this time of the Cluniac prior.

A more dramatic composition may be seen at the Augustinian priory of Lanercost in Cumberland where the first floor of the cellarer's range has been converted into a great hall with the prior's lodging at its southern end attached to it as a great chamber. Next to this is a post-Suppression tower and standing in isolation to the west is a kind of pele tower dating from monastic days and a reminder that the Border is only a few miles distant.

The curious double house of the Gilbertines at Watton in Yorkshire with its separate cloisters for canons and nuns has had its prior's house at an angle of his cloister retained to serve as a modern residence.

Many of the prior's houses in the smaller rural priories were probably taken over promptly at the time of the Suppression and put into use right away as farmhouses. The house at Shulbrede Priory in Sussex would appear to be an example.

The frater of the Premonstratensian abbey at Bradsole in Kent, standing upon its vaulted undercroft, is now a farmhouse.

Many of the monastic buildings would have been turned into barns, as was the guest hall at Ulverscroft Priory in Leicestershire. At Notley Abbey in Essex the frater was used for stabling.

An interesting aspect of the attitude towards types of building at the time of the Suppression is the obviously high regard in which the gatehouse was held. Not only was it so often retained as a gatehouse to provide a fine entrance to one's new property but in a surprising number of cases it was actually converted into a residence itself. Some of them were of course magnificent structures; that at Thornton Abbey (Plate 25) has a great hall set above its entrance passage and to live in a great castellated tower such as this must have been the next best thing to living in a castle.

The glories of Beaulieu have for the most part been swept away but its gatehouse is today designated a palace.

The great gatehouse of St. Osyth Abbey in Essex has long wings stretching away on either side of it and is in itself a fine house.

Of Butley Priory in Suffolk nothing remains but its gatehouse attractively converted, as far back as 1738, into a country house.

Among the numerous monastic gatehouses which had been preserved through their conversion into residences may be noted those of Montacute in Somerset, Cerne in Dorset; also the gatehouses of the Carthusian Charterhouses of Beauvale in Nottinghamshire and Hinton in Somerset. There are doubtless many others, some lived in, others preserved as farm buildings or simply for the dignity they may bestow upon the muddy entrance to a cow-yard. And the arches of their entrance passages are probably the most ubiquitous memorials of the age of the abbots left in this country.

This and the preceding chapters will have served to call attention to the principal monastic remains in this country. But everywhere strange relics remain: an isolated building set in a hedgerow, perhaps an undercroft used as a cowshed or a shelter from the flies for horses out at grass; or a line of broken walling, the snag of an angle, the dry course of an abbey stream. There is probably some kind of trace of three-quarters of our monasteries still visible, buried among the huddled buildings of some ancient town or the tangled brambles of a rural brake.

# 18

# The Monastic Contribution to English Architecture

When examining the surviving monuments from what might be described as the Monastic Occupation of England one must not forget those invisible legacies, the influences resulting from that long occupation. As this book is concerned with English architecture it should discuss what contribution the monastic Orders made to this.

We must credit them at the outset with two important products. The first of these is the construction of the largest buildings of their age. Admittedly these neither showed great structural inventiveness—indeed they were primitive to a degree—nor were they buildings of notable aesthetic distinctions. But they were huge, and the product of remarkable financial and structural organization.

The second and greatest gift the monks made to English architecture was the creation, a century or so later, of the loveliest buildings the world has ever seen.

The Gothic is not limited to this country. Nor do we possess the loftiest or the most elaborate examples of this medieval style. And the structural engineering of English Gothic is based upon absolute faith overcoming complete ignorance.

But English Gothic is an architectural style of unassailable integrity and purity of ordinance.

The perfection of the style in England is very possibly due to the Cistercian dislike of ornament, in which eccentricity they rivalled their great religious and military adversary, the Moslem.

The latter were not allowed the carved or painted representation of any living thing so were forced to exercise their artistic ingenuity in designing non-representational ornament.

The Cistercians went further in rejecting carved ornament of any kind whatsoever. They thus had to rely entirely upon architectural ornament for the relief of their buildings from absolute dullness.

The grim effect of the earlier 'Anglian' architecture was due to its use of the arch constructed for economy of centering upon a series of stone rings or 'orders'. Some attempt was made to soften the edges by cutting a 'roll' along the edges of each order. It was from this simple beginning that the Gothic moulding was developed, the feature which enabled the Cistercians first to lighten their arcades by introducing into their contours deep hollows between the high rolls and eventually extending the use of the principle by carrying it down into the pillars which had hitherto been either chunky Byzantine piers or equally clumsy imitation 'Romanesque' columns.

The deeply cut moulding is the soul of the Gothic as seen in the stately presbyteries of the thirteenth century.

One of the first of the great Gothic churches—not Cistercian but the creation of a bishop with strong Cistercian leanings—is Salisbury Cathedral. Apart from a lapse between the completion of the aisle vaulting and the resumption of the walling of the main span, the church is wholly Cistercian Gothic and completely unadorned by any other than architectural ornament.

One must confess that its austerity can at times be oppressive; this is, however, partly due to the smallness of the fenestration and the intensity of its glazing. And the great defect of any great church is that its principal feature, its interior arcade, is always seen seriously foreshortened, horizontally and vertically, so that no real appreciation can ever be formed of its true design.

The arcade of a Gothic church is a structural device for holding up the main walling of a church which has been widened by the addition of aisles. That is all it really is. But the master mason who built it had to design it before he cut the stone for it. His design was for one bay, this to be repeated as often as required by the length of the church.

He knew from experience that his design for the bay would never, for the reason noted above, be seen as he designed it. Nevertheless he worked upon it until he was satisfied that he could do no better, and so it was erected—to be buried in the heart of the great building and its true beauty concealed.

It was only after the destruction of the outer walls of his church to expose its arcades that this could have been seen and appreciated in its true form as the creation of a master mason of the Middle Ages who worked for the greater glory of God.

This is what we see today in the choir of Rievaulx. (Plate 10.)

Alas, such Gothic was ephemeral! The more liberal attitude of the Benedictines, the Augustinians, and eventually the relaxed Cistercians themselves, brought about the introduction of carved ornament to break into the simple lines of mouldings, structural inventiveness introduced ever more complicated vaulting systems, the precentor asked for more light and larger windows, the glazier demanded of the mason that he introduced tracery bars into the window-head. Thus the pure English Gothic joined with the developed Gothic of the Continent and thereby found itself submerged. Thereafter Gothic architecture became international and the English presentation of it different but not more distinguished than that of any other western European country.

But it had been the English architects who first introduced to this country the architecture of transcendency, in all humility, and to no lasting effect except that, albeit in ruin, we have architectural monuments unmatched in the world.

Thus we may say that the monasteries created in this country during the twelfth century the largest buildings in the world of their day and during the following century raised architectural monuments of unrivalled beauty which saw their era pass away and leave nothing but emptiness in its train.

For the Gothic has not become an historical style. It perished utterly with the Middle Ages which gave it birth, and was replaced by a style coming from overseas and owing nothing to it.

The impact of the monastic Orders upon the building trade of this country must have been tremendous. Bearing in mind that Anglo-Saxon England was a timber-building country we must

credit the monks with having introduced from the more sophisticated Continent, and developed at breakneck speed, a masonry
technique which in a few years was to help to cover the countryside with scores of huge building complexes.

The introduction of the stone vault permitted the erection of
two-storeyed buildings of architectural quality. The monks began
to convert the upper-class Englishman from sleeping on the
ground floor to a bed-chamber on the first floor, a practice which
has continued to the present time and the introduction from the
Orient of the bungalow.

This ascent from the squalor of the hall floor to the comparative
tranquillity and cleanliness of an upper chamber was an important
stage in what might be called the development of quality domestic
accommodation.

This step seems even more impressive when one realizes that
the earliest of these two-storeyed houses were not provided for a
single family but for a whole community of fifty or more people
and that while this may simply have implied in so far as the structure was concerned an increase in length, in terms of administration it introduced formidable sanitary problems. Not that one
might fear that such incidents as smells and flies would have
worried medieval men and women, but the actual discharge from
a community of several scores of persons living in a small area
would have had to be disposed of quickly.

Hence the necessity for introducing water-borne sanitation by
contriving a leat from some nearby stream and leading this under
the abbey rere-dorter, a building so sensibly designed that it could
hardly be bettered today. (Fig. 15.)

Hydraulics as represented by the levelling of a leat were of
course common knowledge to the millwrights of Anglo-Saxon
England and the use of water to flush the rere-dorter might have
seemed an obvious solution to the problem of sanitation but it is
noticeable that the idea of the communal *necessarium* seems to have
perished with the monasteries and never been transferred thence
to other large establishments such as castles and post-Suppression
mansions.

An important contribution to architecture was the monastic

'pentice' used as a means of undercover communication between buildings from which developed the cloister, the absorption of which within the building gave us the first internal corridor. The Renaissance house knew no corridors and these did not appear again until the eighteenth century.

To the monastic houses must be credited the abolition of the traditional barn-like aisled hall of the time of the Conquest which even in episcopal hands continued well into the thirteenth century, whereas the abbey fraters had rejected it as early as the eleventh. The great banqueting halls of Hampton Court and Eltham Palace are derived not from the halls of the medieval palaces and castles but by way of the abbey frater.

A type of building which was introduced by the monasteries, had its day, and was seen no more was the para-military gatehouse designed to be a magnificent entrance feature acting as advance-guard to some fine monastic façade. It seems to have been un-affected by the huge twin-towered gatehouses of the Edwardian castles, only borrowing from them the device of building a fine upper chamber or small hall over the entrance passage.

The monastic gatehouse is typical of the monastic attitude towards architecture as something to be displayed in any form whether useful or not. It may have had a hand in the development of the domestic porch. Originally this was merely designed to be a shelter for the entrance doorway of the hall, such tremendous achievements as the south porch at Malmesbury Abbey being exceptional. During the fifteenth century the porches of parish churches began to develop upper storeys and assume the propor-tions of entrance towers. Domestic halls, also, began to adopt the idea of the monumental entrance feature.

The tower-porches giving access to the houses of the abbots were raised even higher and their upper chambers—used by the way in parish church porches as muniment rooms in which docu-ments could be stored away from damp—became fine apartments lit by the tall oriel windows which the abbots seem to have adop-ted as their version of the noblemen's hall bay.

These tower porches survived the Renaissance as a popular feature of Jacobean and Elizabethan country houses, remaining so until the appeal of the Renaissance doorway with its projecting hood could no longer be ignored.

So far we have been considering the practical side of architecture and the types of building produced during the monastic era. But what of architectural design in the broad sense, the presentation of the elevation of no matter what building.

The monastic contribution to the art of composing elevational presentations is a fascinating study which belongs to the sphere of aesthetics. Nevertheless a quick glance at the elements of this art and how it was affected by planning problems may be of some interest.

Elevational design during the Middle Ages never really progressed beyond the bay, a repetition of which gave the lateral elevation of the building.

The only separately designed façade in the monastery was the west fronts of the church and chapter house, and even the latter comprised simply a doorway set between two windows.

It was the gable end of a building which gave the medieval designer trouble, for there he might have to depart from his basic practice of bay design. In the case of a two-storeyed building there was no difficulty as the abutment to the central arcade had to be indicated in the normal medieval fashion by a pilaster. This was carried up the gable and on either side of it the windows were set as in the lateral elevations. Thus a gable end two bays wide with a central pilaster became standard during the twelfth century.

In single-storeyed buildings such as parish churches one finds the central pilaster or buttress continuing in use during the thirteenth century, but in more important buildings it was omitted. Nevertheless the two-bay system remained, indicated by a pair of windows such as may be seen at Abbey Dore.

The Cistercian abbey of Croxden in Staffordshire was once famous for its magnificent *chevet* of five radiating chapels; only a fragment of one remains today. Parts of the east and south claustral ranges may be seen including the west wall of the monks' house and parts of the chapter house, warming-house, frater, and kitchen. But the most impressive fragments remaining are the west gable of the church and the south gable of its transept, the last with perhaps the finest pair of tall windows remaining amongst our abbey ruins.

The two-bay gable is an interesting example of the psychological effect of certain aspects of elevational design, for even today a gable-end containing a pair of windows always looks livelier than one with a single window, clearly due to a subconscious comparison between a human face and that of a Cyclops.

The next stage in the development of medieval gable design, however, which appears at the close of the twelfth century, was the insertion of a central window making a triplet such as one finds looking so impressive at Lanercost (Plate 13) or Frithelstock. This arrangement accepts for the first time the propriety of always having a central *opening* in a façade and never a solid wall, a discovery which eventually resulted in abandoning the bay system in the gable ends of large buildings only one storey in height. (See Plate 28 and others.)

By the close of the thirteenth century all masonry divisions had been eliminated and the group of windows replaced by one large one, a mullioned window with a traceried head.

It may be appreciated that the arrangement was not entirely a happy one, as it introduced at the gable end an aesthetic bay twice the width of the lateral ones, thus destroying the architectural rhythm as one passed round the angle of the building. This, however, gradually became remedied as the span of the arches in the main arcade became wider with the general broadening of Gothic bay design. When this widening became reflected in the bays of the aisle walling, the result more nearly approached the width of the bay at the gable end which made the rhythm more placid.

Two-storeyed buildings, however, continued to display the old two-bay elevations on their gable ends until the end of the monastic era, as at the abbot's house at Muchelney. It is for this reason that medieval domestic buildings, with or without their pilasters or buttresses, always appear so satisfying to the eye.

For one of the most soothing effects which an elevation can display is that of a steady rhythm. This was the real contribution to aesthetics of the structural bay.

The same effect could have been seen in the streets of the medieval towns with their frontages divided up into narrow plots of from sixteen to twenty feet in width. No matter how the elevational treatment of each 'bay' varied with the passing of the styles —Elizabethan, Jacobean, Stuart, Georgian, Regency, Victorian —the whole frontage remained safely gathered into a composition free from any intrusions to break its peaceful rhythm. It is not until recently that the 'layer-cake' type of elevation has intruded here and there to destroy those harmonious street frontages.

Wall decoration has been an important factor in all architectural treatments, but prior to the Middle Ages such have been mainly external. It was the elaborate elevational presentations resulting from the development of the internal structural arcade which led to the application of architectural treatment to the internal walls of buildings. The arcaded dado had been seen for centuries applied to the exteriors of churches. It now became employed internally as well. The rise of a new class of building, the monastic conference hall, led to the introduction into its interior of the arcaded glories of the church façade. By the transference of such treatments as this to an apartment of great architectural significance the first step was taken towards the introduction of architecture as interior decoration. We can see the beginnings of this at Much Wenlock chapter house and the final Gothic form in the chapter house at Thornton Abbey.

The western world at the end of the first millennium had already enjoyed a wide experience of architecture in the form of churches great and small. The employment of architecture for domestic purposes, however, was quite unknown.

The buildings comprising the abbey, although a well-planned collection of buildings, were regarded as individual compositions, gathered together for convenience but not intended to be considered as the presentation of an architectural entity.

The church always had a good west front, and very occasionally a transept front was treated with special consideration. But for the rest, especially the lateral elevation, it was merely the side of a church at which one was looking.

29. Byland

30. Netley

The first domestic façades presented to the medieval world were those of the twelfth-century Cistercian abbeys where the long elevation of the house of the lay-brothers joined with the west front of the church to produce a frontispiece of imposing length and considerable potential architectural interest.

Of these great architectural panoramas only that of Fountains remains today. (Plate 18.)

In the Benedictine abbeys, the eastern side of the *curia* or great court was formed by the western side of the cellarer's range augmented here and there by projecting wings connected with the abbot's house and lodgings for guests. The whole composition represented the front of a great house. They have all gone—but what would they have been like?

The entrance front of the ordinary large house of the period with its great hall and chamber wing would have borne no resemblance to them, having developed along an entirely different route.

The post-Suppression house does not appear to have developed so closely from its medieval—Tudor—predecessor. It would be interesting to know what effect the vanished western buildings of the Benedictine abbeys, tucked away within their great gate-houses, had upon it.

What would have been the course of England's architectural development if the abbeys had never been? The great builders of the Middle Ages were for the most part abbots—Paul de Caen at St. Albans, Samson at St. Edmundsbury, Chard at Forde, Huby at Fountains. There were no secular builders, not even the Crown built anything of note. The royal palaces were jumbles of buildings resembling a modern farm with its barn. It is true that the monasteries absorbed a quarter of the income of the whole country. But they spent it on the production of buildings of which their country may still be proud today.

There can of course be no doubt that the crafts allied to architecture—masonry and carpentry, plumbing and working in iron—must have benefited enormously from the experience gained in the abbey lodges and workshops. In even greater degree, the arts of carving in stone and wood, painting on plaster, glass and floor tiling, would have been assisted by the patronage of the abbots, without whose encouragement it is difficult to see how they could have flourished at all. Art needs an incentive and any association with worship would in the Middle Ages have supplied this in full measure. The secular aristocracy of the period would not have been disposed to provide funds to encourage the artist except in connection with heraldic or similar social displays, and in connection with the provision of personal sepulchres or chantry chapels.

The most permanent benefit contributed to this country by the monasteries was undoubtedly the reorganization of a primitive local building trade in such a fashion that it could perform marvels of constructional programmes in a country and at a period when no other organizations of any description existed. Prior to the coming of the abbeys there was nothing resembling a building firm. There were only individual tradesmen, mainly carpenters, none of them capable of erecting anything of any size.

Then, as it were overnight, we find hundreds of trained masons appearing out of nowhere and setting to work upon the erection of the building projects which ended by producing the largest buildings in the world. Such a movement could only have been the result of a training programme and this must have been initiated by the Benedictine Order.

Imagine such vast abbeys as Gloucester, Tewkesbury and Pershore rising within a few miles of each other and at approximately the same period, all in an area served by what had been a primitive timber-building society.

Consider the constructional skill developed in those early days by the organizations which built the monastic houses. Forget for a moment the splendour of the masoncraft and remember the men who were lifting the stones high in the air and setting them in arch and vault. Try to calculate the amount of scaffolding required and how this could be supported. Think of the ladders required to reach the tower-tops, the ropes needed for hauling, the creaking pulleys ... how were these made?

The tower-top finished, its crowning feature had to be considered, the soaring timber steeple. Look upwards at great beams, a foot square and sixteen feet long, swinging up into the air, half a ton at a time, to be gathered, fitted, and pegged together in the realm of the winds.

Compare these splendid achievements with the homes of the people who performed them. Only the richest among them able to find a builder to make them houses, and these but haylofts above stables.

And around the efficiently conducted activity a countryside still very primitive, with the King and his great men forever fighting each other and assaulting each others' castles. At the middle of this wonderful century came the Anarchy, when beyond the abbey precinct 'God and His Saints slept'—while still the great houses and their lovely churches rose in their scores, contemptuous of what was happening in the world about them.

Once the abbey lodges and workshops had been established and filled with trained craftsmen its building plan could have been developed at will, the abbey building organization also serving at the same time as a maintenance unit. This had the effect of establishing what was in fact a privately owned building firm. It may even have undertaken outside work for some lay noble wanting to build a house; indeed it is difficult to see how else he could have done this.

And this is where the other side of the coin begins to appear. For the countryside still remained in a primitive state, with its population living in home-made hovels, and only a few magnates living in anything approaching decent living conditions.

It is true that the tradesmen working for the monastic Orders had been recruited and trained by them, but their monopoly of practically the whole of the building industry of the country may well have been a source of discontent among the lay landowners and may partly have accounted for the gleeful sacking of the fallen abbeys at the Suppression.

For not until the national building trade had been finally liberated from its monastic servitude by the Act of 1539 could anyone begin to consider employing a professional builder to provide him with a house.

Fortunately one of the results of the Renaissance movement had been to bring to the notice of the Tudor gentleman the appreciation of aesthetic craftsmanship so that he was glad to avail himself of the skill of the abbey craftsman to fashion for him a hall screen. Thus the art-consciousness introduced by the monastic Orders did not perish entirely with them.

The same could not be said of the architecture of the medieval monks. It did indeed perish with them, overwhelmed by forces of irresistible vigour.

The monks found the modern world was marching away from the old superstitions while the architects reacted towards still older philosophies—the Humanities from which their civilization had stemmed. Smothered between the new and the very old, the Gothic vision, already obscured by twilight, faded away to rejoin the dreaming.

Three centuries later, gentlemen of the Regency began to try to recapture something of the age of the abbots. Scholarly yet romantic, already sensing something of the ugliness of the nightmare of an industrial age looking ahead, they turned towards the ruin of the Gothic for solace. Without any idea of imitation they tried to restore the daintiness of the lost style, unconcerned that the masons who had created it had long ago followed their creations into oblivion, and quite content to reproduce the feeling of the 'Gothick' in wood and plaster. Their pleasant excursions, however, were of but short duration, being thrust away once more by an even more determined movement towards Classicism, now to be regarded as suitable employment in connection with the architecture of factories and mill buildings.

Fifty years later came the saddest experiment of all when the great architects of the Victorian era, patriotic and devoted to their craft, tried to revive the glorious architecture of the abbots on a national scale. Studying, measuring, and analysing, they worked assiduously to recover the lost ordinances of the Gothic style, but never were able to recapture anything at all of the medieval spirit which had inspired those creations within a primitive country.

The architecture of the abbots returned once more into the shades where, having played its glorious part, it should henceforth be left to its dreams.

# 19

# Exploring an Abbey

For those who enjoy looking at ruins, those of the abbeys of England can provide them with spectacles of great beauty. For grandeur there cannot be many abbey ruins in Europe to compare with the splendid shell of Whitby striding high on its cliff-top. Most of the abbeys, however, especially those of the Cistercian sheep-farmers, are seen lying in sheltered valleys such as at that other dramatic Yorkshire site where the lovely arcades of Rievaulx rise from the amphitheatre of woods sweeping along the hillside above. And, rivalling Rievaulx, Fountains, the greatest ruin in England.

Another northern ruin, this time Benedictine, is that of Finchale Priory in Durham, its church rising splendidly beside the banks of the Wear and the ruin of its frater a memorable spectacle.

Returning to Yorkshire, the remains of Roche Abbey (Plate 26) are to be visited for the spectacle they present with the woodland pressing upon them in their valley. Only the huge transepts remain, of unusual interest in that the valley was dammed by Capability Brown in order that their reflection might be seen in the waters. The mark of the water level may still be seen on the ancient masonry.

The Cistercian abbey of Valle Crucis in Denbighshire is an abbey in miniature. The little cruciform church has tall triplets of lancets at either end, that to the east being reflected in a pool. The eastern range with its chapter house and the dorter over is still roofed.

Supreme among the southern Cistercian abbeys for pride of

situation is that at Tintern beside the River Wye in Monmouth-shire. (Plates 23 and 24.) The late-Gothic church stands intact save for its roofs and makes a lovely ruin of great dignity. There are many remains of the claustral buildings.

Just outside Southampton are the remains of the fine church of Netley Abbey (Plates 12 and 30), a Cistercian ruin in a setting of parkland. The arcades of the church were removed when the post-Suppression owner converted it into his great hall. The north transept was destroyed by a road contractor who then turned upon the presbytery and would have eliminated the whole church had not the tracery of the east window fallen on him and killed him!

Returning northwards into Durham to take a look at the Pre-monstratensians we can find them set in a lovely situation beside the Tees at the dramatic ruin of Eggleston Abbey of which the nave and presbytery of the church make an impressive spectacle but the transepts are almost gone. The eastern range and chapter house were converted by the post-Suppression owner into a dwelling house the ruins of which add to the interest of the site.

In Northumberland, a little farther north, on a wooded site beside the Coquet, stands the Augustinian priory of Brinkburn. (Plate 3.) Its church, though restored, is complete and presents a beautiful picture of the early Gothic, particularly charming in its presbytery. The cloister is to the south but all its buildings have disappeared except for part of the frater embedded in a modern house.

The great Augustinian abbey of Haughmond in Shropshire stands in a setting of pasture and woodland. Its church has gone, but its notable feature is the great hall of its infirmary (Plate 22) with the house of the abbot at its east end, the two having been saved at the Suppression to be converted into a house which was subsequently destroyed during the Civil War.

In the same county is another Augustinian abbey, that of Lilleshall, a really picturesque ruin well clothed with ivy and embowered amongst trees. The church remains but has lost its transepts; its presbytery is particularly impressive. Much of the frater remains.

In Sussex the Premonstratensian abbey of Bayham (Plate 31) is beautifully set and makes a perfect picture of what might be described as the natural state of a ruined abbey. The whole length of the great church remains. A portion of the south side of its nave shows fine windows and the eastern transepts suddenly rise to their full height from the ruin about them. Parts of the eastern range remain and the ruin of the frater.

The above are some of the abbeys which may be visited by those who like ruins and enjoy scenic sites.

For the amateur of architecture the churches noted in Chapter 17 as standing complete or in part can provide examples of every kind of building and all historical styles from the almost cyclopean massiveness of the St. Albans arcades to the exquisite ceilings of Sherborne or Bath.

Naves there are, as at Dunstable or Wymondham; choirs at Pershore (Plate 1), Milton or Boxgrove. (Plate 7.) Lacock can display the early perfection of its Gothic cloisters and lead to the ultimate at Gloucester. For chapter houses there are the very different examples—though both of them are Cistercian—at Buildwas and Forde.

Cistercian Rievaulx (Plates 11 and 17) and Premonstratensian Easby (Plate 16) can both produce great monastic halls, while the infirmary hall at Haughmond (Plate 22) is a spectacle not to be missed.

For the keen student of monastic planning there are many excavated sites to be examined. At Arthurian Glastonbury the sad ruins of a huge church look down upon the excavated plan of the cloister with its buildings. Nearby is Muchelney Abbey where the abbot's house stands among excavations and gazes towards the parish church which has survived where its once-mighty neighbour has been reduced to foundations.

The Cluniac priories of Thetford and Castle Acre have been thoroughly excavated so that their plans may now be studied in detail. At the latter priory, moreover, there still remains the delightful abbot's house overlooking the elaborate west front of the church.

Byland in Yorkshire (Plate 29), one of the group of great Cistercian abbeys, has kept the outer walls of a huge church with a strangely mournful looking west front retaining half a round window. The whole of the claustral buildings and those of the little cloister and kitchen court have been excavated and provide one of the most interesting of all the monastic plans.

Beside the towering transept ruin of Capability Brown's Roche (Plate 26) the plan of another Cistercian abbey has been uncovered.

Premonstratensian Easby of the great frater ruin has been excavated and its very unusual plan may now be explored. At Augustinian Kirkham in the same county of Yorkshire one can see the sad traces of its once magnificent presbytery beside which are the foundations of a large heavily buttressed chapter house. The cloister walls are standing and one can work out a great deal of the claustral plan. One of the pleasures of Kirkham is its attractive gatehouse.

In Lincolnshire one can examine the ground-trace of what was one of the largest monastic churches in the country, that of the Augustinian abbey of Thornton. The cloister and its buildings have been excavated and marked out; east of it is a splendid fragment of a fine octagonal chapter house. The site of Thornton Abbey is reached through the mightiest monastic gatehouse in all England. (Plate 25.)

The visitor to the nave of Binham Priory in Norfolk, all that is left in use today of a Benedictine house, will find beside it complicated excavations illustrating a very interesting plan of the vanished monastic buildings.

A plan is one thing. But to produce those foundations upwards with the eye of the mind, to work out whether the buildings were of one or two storeys and to cover each with a roof, is something which needs an understanding of simple building construction and some knowledge of medieval architecture.

It is for instance as well to be able to appreciate that the presence of a pillar-base in the centre of an apartment indicates that it supported a 'stone soller' and was thus two-storeyed.

When strolling through the excavations try to imagine how the buildings they represent appeared when they were standing, it is perhaps best to begin with the church. Enter this through the gap which is its west doorway set in the middle of what was an ornamental façade. Imagine the long lines of the arcades on either side leading away past the crossing towards the east window. Look up in imagination towards the windows of the clearstory—the 'over-histories' of old William of Worcester who may have preceded us just five hundred years ago at his shuffling pace of less than two feet at each step. Before you reach the crossing think of the aisle windows seen through the tall arches beside you.

Try to discover where the rood screen stood, and a bay ahead of it the entrance to the choir. If all traces of this are gone, one may guess that it was in the four bays west of the crossing.

Imagine the two rows of canopied stalls, the screens on either side leading up to the reredos with the high altar before it, and the lost panoply of tombs and chantry chapels lined beside the choir.

Pause at the crossing beneath the high lantern and glance into the tall transepts reaching away on either side. Look into their eastern aisles where the chapels used to be.

If the church should be an early one with just a short presbytery you will have nowhere else to visit, but if its eastern end had been rebuilt during the thirteenth century you may now bear left into the north aisle and walk along it until you can pass behind the high altar. Look into the eastern chapels, perhaps into a long lady chapel, then return along the south aisle into the transept just beyond which, in the aisle wall, you will find the gap indicating the processional doorway into the east walk of the cloister.

Walk to the centre of the cloister court and turn to look up at the mass of the transept with the lantern tower, crowned by its steeple, rising behind it. Look to where the façade of the chapter house stands close beside it at the centre of the north side of the cloister. Above the cloister roof will be seen the long row of small windows indicating the monks' dorter on the upper floor of their house, its roof reaching away southwards to disappear behind that of the great hall, lying alongside the cloister opposite the church. If the abbey should be Cistercian, the frater will present its gable end, probably with a large window in it, to the cloister.

Opposite the chapter house on the west side of the cloister will be a long building with small windows on its upper storey looking over the cloister roof and probably lighting guest rooms, abbot's lodgings, or, if it be Cistercian, the dorter of the lay-brothers.

Continuing our exploration of the excavations let us visit the chapter house on the east side of the cloister, passing through its fine entrance doorway flanked by two attractive windows. It will possibly be small and square and rather gloomy with only three small windows to the rear and the two good ones in the entrance front overshadowed by the cloister roof. Its low vault carried on four pillars does not help to make it seem a spacious assembly hall which is what it is intended to be. But perhaps this is its only vestibule and the chapter house itself is beyond, tall and with fine windows lighting it. It may even be polygonal with a high vault carried by a single slender pillar. All round the walls of the chapter house will be the seats of the community with that of the abbot in the centre of the wall farthest from the entrance doorway.

Leaving the chapter house and bearing left across the cloister towards the frater, we reach its fine doorway with the laver or washing place nearby. The great hall may have been raised upon an undercroft but if so you will probably find a pillar-base or two to reveal this to you. A first floor hall will need a flight of wide steps to reach it.

Within the frater imagine its ancient dignity. The fine timber roof stretching away to the upper end where the abbot sat beneath a great painted rood. The rows of tall windows down the sides. You may find traces of the reader's pulpit in the wall furthest from the cloister.

There are many other less important rooms to visit: the great kitchen with its cavernous fireplace at the lower end of the hall; the warming house with perhaps a smaller fireplace.

Walking out of the east walk of the great cloister along the slype one might come across a little cloister having the infirmary hall on the left. This might be an aisled hall several bays in length or a simple hall like the frater but lacking its imposing height. Nor need it necessarily be associated with a little cloister.

What you would certainly find to the south-east of the cloister would be the monks' rere-dorter, a tall, thin building projecting eastwards from the monks' house and possibly forming the south side of a little cloister. There will be no mistaking it, for the great drain—the 'underground passage' of legend—will be found passing under it.

In a Cistercian abbey you might well find traces of the abbot's house somewhere to the east of the slype, possibly on the east side of a little cloister.

In any other house it would certainly be worth while to go out of the west walk of the cloister through the outer parlour next the church. For there you would be in the great court of the abbey and looking back at the west front of the building under which you have passed you might see a long façade with perhaps a wing or two housing the abbot or his guests. There might be a porch tower for the abbot with perhaps an oriel window.

Outside in the great court would have been a number of structures whose foundations today would probably be too difficult to assess. Near the kitchen would be its offices—bakehouse, brewhouse—and innumerable shops for building tradesmen and the smithy. There would be guest houses and an almonry; many of these domestic buildings would be two-storeyed and the fact indicated by the remains of internal pillars.

And to the right as we leave the outer parlour we might see looming up above the precinct wall the mass of the great gatehouse of the abbey, passing through which we should arrive in the parvis of the abbey church with its west front rising on our right hand.

A once magnificent abbey represented today by a maze of foundations may not appear now as a very attractive sight. But the excavators have explored for and indicated the plan in order that you may, by comparison with the standing remains of other abbeys, attempt to construct, in the eye of the mind, the lost glories of the place.

But what of those abbeys which have neither remained in being nor been excavated and their plans recovered. This is where the amateur archaeologist can occupy himself for many days in playing the detective while he strives to unearth among the later buildings of a town or along the pastures of the countryside first where the buildings of the abbey once stood, and then how they may have appeared in the days of their pride.

The explorer of an abbey town must familiarize himself not only with the monastic plan but with the form and dimensions of each of its architectural characteristics. Any portion of medieval walling discovered—and the last chapter of this book offers some clues as to how to date walling—should be studied to try to assign it to an abbey building.

Any signs of vaulted undercrofts would of course be of the greatest value as indicating the remains of two-storeyed buildings. Within a town the major buildings such as church, chapter house, frater and perhaps monks' house would have been cleared away to provide sites for housing or commerce. There might, however, have been plenty of smaller buildings capable of being used immediately for such purposes.

There are two methods of approaching the problem of trying to restore an abbey plan on paper. One is to discover medieval buildings and try to fit them into a plan. The other is to try to work out a theoretical plan and look for buildings which might fit in.

In towns the open spaces of the *curia* and the parvis are quite likely to be still existent. The establishment of either could start off a plan.

While the cloister was most often on the sunny side of the rural abbey church, in towns it was more often on the opposite side.

The existence of a medieval parish church in an abbey town would be a useful clue as this lay on the side of the abbey, usually next to its nave, and opposite the cloister.

A factor governing the site of the cloister was the fall in the ground, for if the cloister was sited uphill of the church the great building might well act as a dam in rainy weather.

The size of the cloister of a large urban abbey might be about a hundred and fifty feet square; a smaller abbey or priory might settle for fifty feet less.

Nondescript medieval buildings would probably have been associated with the great court of the abbey west of the cloister.

A small stream left uncovered might represent the abbey stream which when it reached the claustral buildings would become the great drain.

A complete antithesis to this kind of exploration is the search for a vanished abbey on a rural site.

If portions of the buildings remain, as at Coverham in Yorkshire where part of the church is still standing, one can set to work to develop from this known point the probable sites of the rest of the abbey buildings.

A circumstance which here and there has preserved small but significant sections of monastic walling is the rural practice of constructing the lesser buildings of farmyards on the 'linhay' principle of setting posts in front of a wall and throwing a lean-to roof across onto it. For a wall can be an expensive thing to build, and the presence of some medieval wall, however decrepit, can offer the chance of running up an adequate shelter. It is surprising how many pieces of monastic walling have been preserved from destruction through this practice and how there may be found here and there in farmyards enough sections of wall for the explorer to be able to reconstruct an abbey.

Such an exploration can be a fascinating occupation. To begin with one must orientate oneself. With luck one may be able to find remains—pillar bases or walls showing traces of high vaults—which can lead one right away to the great church itself. Or there may be traces of lean-to roofing, or a processional doorway, indicating upon which side of the church the cloister lay.

The use of metrology is essential if one is to attempt to set out the bays of any building and find out where it might have ended or changed direction. The pole of sixteen feet and the 'cord' or yard of four feet will be found appearing in the plans, twenty feet or five yards being a common span in medieval times.

Buttresses indicate bays—windows of course do likewise—and angles may be detected by scars where bonding stones have been robbed; internal angles are indicated by the stones themselves rising in a vertical line.

One may find special features remaining in walling which give a clue to some particular part of the plan. A piscina—the little niche with a drain set in its sill—signifies an altar close by and gives a clue to the church. A much larger recess, often elaborately ornamented, where the monks washed their hands before meals, indicates the proximity of the frater door.

By the use of such aids the monastic plan may be built up bit by bit, filling in from one's knowledge of monastic planning lay-outs such gaps as may be left.

What is really exciting to the amateur of architectural archaeology is for him to be shown an apparently featureless pasture and asked to find an abbey under it.

When asked to excavate Sempringham, the head house of the Gilbertine Order in Lincolnshire, the writer was shown the traditional site next to the existing parish church but quickly rejected it as unsuitable for the site of an abbey.

Transferring his interest to a large field some furlongs away, he found it occupied by a curious square earthwork in no way suggestive of a monastery. When he started to dig, however, he found this to be the buried remains of a square mansion built round a courtyard during the seventeenth century. Continuing, however, he found on the very last day of the first season's excavation a squat pillar which had clearly carried a 'stone soller' . . . and the abbey was revealed.

The first thing to consider when looking for an abbey is how the land lies, as this gives one an indication as to whether one might find the cloister on the north side of the church rather than in its orthodox position. The discovery of the watercourse representing the abbey stream and the great drain is a valuable factor in helping to pin down the abbey. Bit by bit as one explores one may find here and there faint bumps in the ground representing the stumps of walls or shallow trenches whence these have been robbed away.

Gradually from that bare pasture the ancient abbey may rise, like a cathedral from the sea, the great church with its steeple, the long roof lines of dorter, frater, and western range.

Surround it with its precinct wall—with perhaps a gate or two—and who is to see that it is but a ghostly abbey which bade farewell to the monks who knew it over four centuries ago.

# 20

# The Dating of Medieval Buildings

Since the reign of James I the practice of architecture has been governed by the Three Conditions of Well Building set forth by Sir Henry Wootton and reiterated by Christopher Wren and others. The first edition of Wootton's Conditions is the necessity for providing the client with the accommodation he desires; this has largely been the Condition covered by this book.

The second Condition concerns itself with sound construction. It has been necessary to introduce into the book from time to time notes on medieval building methods for the reason that all planning is governed by the necessity of keeping the building standing and supporting its floors and roof.

The Third Condition, which both Wren, England's most famous architect, and Vitruvius, the 'Father of Architecture', place foremost in the design of buildings, is the architect's responsibility for the creation of an edifice which will delight the eye of the beholder.

The aesthetic aspect of architectural style has not been discussed in this book which has been designed to express an architect's appreciation of the problems encountered by his predecessors when building a medieval abbey and how these problems were met.

Structural design cannot, however, be ignored entirely for the reason that much of the aesthetic appearance of the building resulted from the various structural devices employed. The arcade, for instance, is purely a structural device employed for widening a building by the addition of aisles; its embellishment was the result of aesthetic enthusiasm.

Thus the elevational development of medieval architecture throughout its various periods and 'styles' is due as much as anything to the various advances in structural design, this probably aimed for the most part towards the use of less masonry or its arrangement to better purpose, to reducing internal obstructions, and to improving lighting by fuller fenestration.

In the case of the great church the aesthetic target was the achievement of the monumental element of height. By presenting the builders with ever-increasing structural problems this requirement encouraged the builders to improve their structural methods. These improvements, and the 'styles' which evolved from each major discovery, were transferred as a style to lesser buildings.

The architecture of this country was derived from what is known as Byzantine, that architecture created, in the main by Greek engineers, in the imperial city of Constantinople. It originated as a style of massive masonry piers carrying vaults and domes of the same material or of lighter brick or even pottery, but as it crossed westwards through Europe it had to abandon the use of domes for lack of structural knowledge among its builders, contenting itself with timber roofs and in the case of churches a central steeple instead of a dome.

The principal internal feature was the heavy 'ordered' arch rising above piers of massive form also divided into 'orders' to match the arches above. The surrounding portions of the original Byzantine churches were often two-storeyed which led to the arcades being in two tiers; the effect of this can be seen in the great English churches of the Benedictines such as those of Peterborough or Ely. The period might be called the pre-medieval; it is generally called 'Norman' but this would seem to be paying too much attention to the political results of the Battle of Hastings and too little credit to the native builders of this country who did not have to wait until 1066 to raise abbey churches and in any case performed the actual work.

The massive style to which we have been referring which established itself in the North, the Midlands, and East Anglia, the Anglian sphere of influence, might be accorded the same designation. For it is necessary to differentiate this from the style of the

31. Bayham

32. Bolton

great churches which began with the foundation of Gloucester Abbey, now the cathedral church, after the turn of the century. Here we find the old Byzantine piers and the two-storeyed arcade neglected and the nave arcades carried upon enormous circular pillars (Plate 2) obviously intended to be imitations of the Classical columns of the Roman basilica. This is the style more aptly called 'Romanesque', derived from Rome and developed in and around the huge abbeys of Burgundy.

The Cistercians adopted this style and used it universally in the naves of their churches (Plate 21) and during the twelfth century it took hold of the English parish churches especially in the south and west of England.

This pre-medieval period—which everyone will probably continue to call 'Norman'—is that of the greatest buildings in the twelfth-century world, the enormously long churches of the Benedictine abbeys. For the most part these were in the 'Anglian' style with the massive piers and arches and the two-tier arcades.

It was a style which used small squarish stones, not properly faced with a tool but just hacked more or less smooth with a stone-axe. Masonry was used for the principal features such as the piers and arches of arcades and the surrounds to doors and windows. The angles of buildings were strengthened by being built up with masonry 'quoins' which at the end of the twelfth century were often doubled. Any ornamental work was effected in masonry as was any area where carving or sculpture might be required. The general masonry, especially in buildings of average importance, was of rubble stone; in the lesser buildings it might be of field stone picked up off the ploughland in autumn.

But whatever material was used for walling, its quoins were always of masonry, and show by the size, the squarish form, and the rough diagonal axe-marks the date of its erection.

Pre-medieval windows are small—unglazed ones such as those of dorters very small—and round-headed.

Pre-medieval doorways are miniature versions of the 'ordered' arches in the arcades but with the difference that they are nearly always elaborately ornamented with many kinds of curiously barbaric repetitive sculpture.

Wall arcading is quite common, a popular variety being the interlacing arcade where each arch spans alternate shafts missing those of either side.

The bay arrangement of every building is indicated externally by a flat pilaster passing up the wall-face between each.

The tops of the walls are finished with a device known as a 'corbel-table' which is a projecting band of stone carried on a series of small brackets or corbels usually carved into grotesque faces. This supported the tall roof where it came out over the wall-face and produced the architectural form of the ordinary eaves.

All buildings rise above a plain plinth, a thickening of the wall at its base, a band of stone with a chamfered upper edge taking the plinth back to the wall-face above it.

The spring of an arch from its 'impost' where its curvature begins was always marked by an 'impost moulding', a projecting band of stone with its *lower* edge chamfered—in other words a reflection of the moulding to the plinth below.

Pre-medieval carving is of two kinds. By far the majority of it is of the repetitive kind and is seen round arches and up the sides of doorways. It seems to be all of a chip-carving technique, almost certainly Anglo-Saxon, though some Classical motifs such as the acanthus appear now and then, as well as the grotesques derived from Scandinavian sources and almost certainly transferred directly from the timber buildings.

The other type of pre-medieval is illustrated by the introduction of Corinthianesque caps to slim colonnettes such as may be found finishing the 'nook-shafts' at the sides of doorways. In the larger capitals crowning the circular pillars of the arcades the four angle volutes are joined by lines of scalloping seeming to suggest the acanthus leaves of the true Corinthian capital, or by bands of conical shapes derived from the Byzantine cubical capital and through it from the Doric. Small cubical capitals are also found capping the nook shafts of the Anglian style.

At the close of the twelfth century a very noticeable change comes over the architectural scene. This was partly due to the introduction of true freemasonry and the use of the wide chisel or 'bolster' struck with a mallet; this gives a smooth surface to the stone and enables each member of an architectural feature to be cut precisely to any form, or combinations of these, known to solid geometry.

The early Gothic stones are longer than their predecessors, their lengths approaching twice the height, the marks of the bolster showing as beautifully spaced lines *always vertical* on the stone.

This is the period which produced the most graceful form of the Gothic with its slender shafted pillars and its wide-span acutely pointed arches. This is the architecture of the great Benedictine presbyteries (Plate 28) the beauty of which encouraged the Cistercians to abandon their original views on austerity and build with the rest to the greater glory of God. (Plate 10.)

The style of the period is unmistakable mainly by reason of the slenderness of the supports and the general soaring effect of the arcades. (Plate 12.) The windows are still small but always have the acutely pointed heads of the early Gothic and are often grouped in pairs (Plate 20) replacing the old Byzantine *bifora* with its two lights separated by a small shaft and enclosed under a single round arch. At gable ends the grouping may be as a triplet. (Plate 11.)

Doorways have developed from the pre-medieval but now have the inevitable acutely pointed heads and while retaining the shafts embellishing the jambs have of course completely abandoned the barbaric Anglo-Saxon carved motifs.

This early-medieval period which occupied the thirteenth century is particularly notable for the elaboration of the deeply-cut mouldings which now sweep round the 'orders' of the arches and give such a strikingly beautiful character to the arcades of churches. These mouldings also appear round the heads of the doorways of the period. (Plate 13.)

Sometimes in the hollows of the mouldings you may find groups of small petals arranged in pyramids of four. This is the so-called 'dog-tooth' moulding, believed to represent a violet, and typical of the thirteenth century.

During the thirteenth century the vaulted undercrofts, so ubiquitous in the monastic buildings, abandon their old sharp-edged 'groined' vaulting for the ribbed type henceforth to be such a notable feature of the Gothic. (Plates 1 and 7.)

The medieval builders of England did not appreciate the purpose of the buttress which to them was merely a device for transferring the structural bays used in the interior of the building to its exterior as an expression of aesthetic punctuation. By the thirteenth century, however, the Continental builders seem to have understood better the principle governing abutment and were using their buttresses as splendid architectural features. In this country the corresponding development was simply the increase of the projection of the pre-medieval pilaster until this equalled its width.

What is important to the explorer of medieval buildings is the arrangement at the angle of the building. During the twelfth century a pair of pilasters were joined together to form a solid angle, but in the next century this was replaced by a pair of projecting 'buttresses', a very decorative feature but one having no structural purpose whatsoever and if anything adding unnecessary weight to the weakest point of the building.

The thirteenth century still employed the corbel-table but the grotesques disappeared and the corbels were joined together by little arches instead of flat stones.

The Corinthianesque type of cap continues to be employed during the thirteenth century but the 'bell' of the feature begins to develop sculpture, in particular a repetitive form resembling a stylized clover-leaf and possibly intended to illustrate the Trinity; antiquaries call this 'still-leaf' foliage.

But another form of cap which was coming in was a development of the impost moulding by setting a concave 'bell' below this and setting underneath the bell a narrow bull-nosed moulding derived from the Classical 'astragal' which had completed the Corinthianesque cap introduced during the previous century.

The moulded cap thereafter became standard throughout Gothic architecture, the only variations being in the ornamentation of the bell. During the thirteenth century the 'stiff-leaf' forms predominated, but with the fourteenth century beautiful naturalistic sculpture is found. In the fifteenth century this disappears and is followed by plain square *paterae* formed out of four leaves which may be intended to represent those of the oak tree.

These same carved features also appear in the wider hollows of the moulding of arches and horizontal 'string courses'. They form useful clues to dating. The uppermost moulding in horizontal combinations is always round or 'bull-nosed' during the thirteenth century. During the fourteenth it is like a rolled manuscript with the upper quadrant projecting over the lower. By the fifteenth century it had become a very large chamfer with a hollow underneath it and an astragal below that, in the fashion of a contemporary capital.

After the thirteenth century, the 'dog-tooth' type of repetitive ornament gave place to a curious little bud-like object called by antiquaries a 'ball-flower'. The wide hollows of the fifteenth century offered sites for its large square 'oak-leaf' *paterae*.

The transcendent nature of the architecture of the thirteenth century encouraged its architects to employ their best masonry even in ordinary wall-faces away from special features. The doubling of quoins at the end of the twelfth century was an indication of a general improvement in walling and soon after this the wall-faces of the finest buildings were no longer displaying rubble stone but were all being finished, inside and out, in the finest masonry.

The aspiring thirteenth century was the age of the glorious choirs, so many of which have disappeared for ever while others remain as breath-taking spectacles of ruin possibly outshining in the drama of their situation the few still in use such as at Pershore, the pillar-haunted loveliness of Abbey Dore (Plate 8), stately Milton, or the perfect choir at Boxgrove Priory. (Plate 7.) But all seems to fade before the majesty of the huge wreck at Rievaulx. (Plate 17.)

The fourteenth and fifteenth centuries covered a period during which monastic architecture made few dramatic advances comparable to those of the two preceding them. Sometimes at the end of the thirteenth century an entire church, such as that at Tintern, was rebuilt, but thereafter there were few major achievements. Exceptions are, however, the building of the great *chevet* at Vale Royal Abbey in Cheshire in 1359 and the rebuilding of the whole abbey church of Bath at the extreme end of the monastic era.

The two last centuries of monasticism were occupied by the monks in the improvement of their living conditions. The cloister in particular became a fine promenade with proper fenestration and a vaulted ceiling of architectural merit.

The most common additions to be found during this period were those connected with such domestic buildings as the abbot's house and the accommodation for guests.

The period of the High Gothic centuries is indicated by the continued use of good masonry but with the stones considerably larger, deeper in the course and often several times their length, probably the result of better arrangements for transport and for lifting to the scaffolding. As the monastic period nears its end the builders turn to ashlar, the stones no longer built into the wall but set on end as a separate facing, the edge of which shows at the angle.

The bolster is more carelessly used in dressing the faces, the strokes being untidy and always *diagonal* on the face, quite unlike the neat vertical tooling of the thirteenth century.

A study of the structure of a wall as exposed in its foundations is of help in dating it. During the eleventh and twelfth century the facing stones are small and the core of the wall was filled with pieces knocked off them. One has to remember that the twelfth century was a period at which a country with no stone-building trade to speak of was suddenly launched into a building boom of fantastic magnitude. There was probably a great deal of work which had to be done by half trained men. An immense amount had to be built, all at once, at breakneck speed, in a society still far from having any experience in organization of any sort.

Try to imagine what it must have been like during the twelfth century to set to work building a whole abbey, not forgetting its great church, while its abbot-designate and his twelve monks were hovering nearby waiting to move in!

There was no time to waste on the nice setting of the core of a wall.

But by the thirteenth century the rush had subsided and better walling could be built. And by the next century the whole of the walling, core as well, was being properly laid with large stones setting together as an entity instead of being two faces with an assortment of rubbish lying between them. It was this great improvement in technique which enabled the construction of walling with smaller supporting areas and room for the wide openings of the late-Gothic windows.

The revolutionary innovation which had changed the face of Gothic architecture had been the introduction of lead for covering roofs where hitherto wood shingles had been used. The lead mines of Derbyshire and the Mendips enabled English buildings to dispense with their fairy-tale roofs and became almost modern in the flatness of their pitch.

In order to retain the all-important element of height, the achievement of which had been the basic inspiration of the Gothic style of architecture, the walls now had to be raised to make up for the loss in dignity suffered by the lowering of the pitch of the roof.

The erection of lofty walls necessitated the provision of buttresses to stiffen them so as to allow them to be pierced by ranges of large windows of a size never before seen in architectural history. (Plate 16.)

The projecting buttress is a feature of the fourteenth and fifteenth centuries and is set *diagonally* at the angles of a building instead of in pairs as during the thirteenth century. This provides an important clue to the dating of the foundations of monastic buildings.

Once it was realized that the angle buttress served no useful purpose other than to withstand the pressure of a high vault, the diagonal 'French' form came to be exchanged for a simple arrangement, aesthetically more stable, which reverted to the pair of projections employed during the thirteenth century but with the difference that these were separated by a portion of the actual angle of the building.

The large traceried windows of the fourteenth and fifteenth centuries are familiar to us in their guises of curvilinear and rectilinear, the two forms being apparently interchangeable but the last eventually imposing its more orderly ordinance upon the dying Gothic.

We see the more graceful form at Tintern Abbey (Plate 24) and their silhouettes at stately Bolton. (Plate 32.) The ultimate perfection is illustrated at Bath Abbey—the 'Lantern of the West'.

Possibly the crowning achievement of the end of the Gothic era was the great terminal window. Their intricate network of tracery bars and mullions could never have represented a very robust form of construction and must have required a great deal of maintenance. Hence the great arched frames which are all that remain of such places as Guisborough in Yorkshire and Walsingham in Norfolk. The finest window remaining today is the east window at Gloucester, perhaps the largest window ever built in medieval days.

When trying to determine the date of a building from its foundations the plinth will probably be the only piece of moulded stonework remaining. That of the fifteenth century is unmistakable with its curious drooping 'ogee' overhanging the wallface below—a fit companion for the coarse crowning moulding of the contemporary building, so unlike the unsophisticated mouldings of the thirteenth and early fourteenth centuries. The new lead roof of the fourteenth century had no eaves but finished in a lead gutter set behind a new feature, the parapet. At first the corbel-table remained to support this, but later the corbels disappeared and only the projecting band above them was left. In the fifteenth century the parapet became battlemented like that of a castle and with the discovery of the use of the pinnacle as a topweight to buttresses this feature began to punctuate the parapet, with splendid results.

The drift away from the acutely pointed section of the old early-Gothic building had the effect of lowering the pitch of the Gothic arch to match the new internal silhouette of the building. During the fourteenth century the arches, including those of the window-heads, gradually drop away until the arch becomes four-centred, in which form it combines more easily with the panelling of joinered screenwork which has been extended in stone to be employed as wall decoration.

At the close of the monastic era the window with the flat head is appearing, probably a subtle intrusion from the Continent now being converted to the Classical forms re-appearing in the guise of the Renaissance.

The typical doorway of the fifteenth century is a combination of a low-pitched arch set within a rectangular frame. With the gradual superseding of domestic architecture over the ecclesiastical, we find the old ornamental features of sedilia and laver being neglected in favour of the oriel window for the abbot's chamber, this beginning to adopt a sedate domestic form indistinguishable from that displayed on the chamber gable of the house of the Tudor gentleman.

Which is of course as it should have been.

\* \* \*

In this modern age it might seem an idle pastime to devote any part of one's intelligence to such a futile occupation as the investigation of the relics of such a wholly archaic phase of our country's history. But the inescapable fact remains that these buildings represented practically the whole output of England's building trade during nearly five centuries. And in the course of pursuing these ephemeral extravagances their builders created an architecture of transcendent beauty equalled nowhere in the history of architecture.

It was all of course quite unnecessary.

And it was in the midst of a world of poverty, hardship, squalor and violence that the medieval builder carried on his glorious trade, almost as though in a trance.

Whence came the driving force? That there was divine inspiration there can be no doubt.

But was this entirely celestial?

Or was the spirit of the land—that deity accepted by the legionaries guarding the Wall as worthy of an altar *genio terrae Brittanicae*— about them as they worked?

\* \* \*

However exotic the whole concept of monasticism must have appeared even to the eighteenth century, and however barbaric its architecture may have appeared to the Humanist scholar—to say nothing of modern man standing upon the threshold of the Industrial Revolution—there was something about the ruined abbey dreaming in its embowered valley which was as much of England as the shadows of the trees which dappled its walls.

It was a vision of this which caused Horace Walpole to return to Twickenham and strike the first blow at that other archaic fantasy, the architecture of the Classics, brought back again vested in the sophistry of the Renaissance.

The thought which prompted him to build Strawberry Hill was undoubtedly that the Gothic—even the lath-and-plaster of its Regency revival—was indisputably English, inseparable from the English countryside, the most beautiful in the world.

'Oh the purple abbots . . .' he had mused '. . . what a spot they have chosen to slumber in!'

# Appendix

# The Apse

What are the origins of the apse and how did it come to be accepted as the architectural interpretation of reverence?

Its sudden appearance, in sophisticated—even monumental—form has never been explained. It is not found in the architecture of the ancient lands, seems to have been unknown to the great Egyptian architects, and plays no part in the Classical styles. Yet suddenly, at the close of the pagan era, it appears as the culminating feature of a great Roman temple, not long after becomes accepted as the terminal feature of the secular basilica, and finally it becomes established as the setting for the altar of the Christian church. With the barrel vault moulded to provide a semi-dome or 'conch' to serve as its covering, the complete dome soon follows and Byzantine architecture is launched upon its splendid achievements.

We can be in no doubt that the apse in architecture was intended to provide an *internal* alcove while its exterior presentation merely protruded as an ugly bulge until taken up by Gothic architects and developed into the splendour of the *chevet*.

One can regard the apse, therefore, as essentially interior architecture, first a curved back-cloth or reredos for a cult-statue and later, when the altar was brought into the building from the forecourt, an architectural setting for this. Throughout the historical development it is clear that it is the *concavity* of the apse which is its significant element.

The same applies to an arch used for spanning an opening in that it is the underside of the arch which is its functional surface, the upper edge being absorbed into the wall over.

The familiar railway arch carries the weight of the trains passing over it. Were it possible to tip the arch over so that it rested on its side, the result would be an apse. The arch, now horizontal, would be able, if required, to stand up against a horizontal thrust, such as might result from earth heaped against it.

One cannot pursue the analogy too far. If one were to employ an apse of the height to which we are accustomed as a support to a high earth bank it would quickly collapse into ruin. But a *curved* wall of moderate height—a garden wall, for example—will retain earth. The horizontal arch must however have abutment at its ends, anchors in the form of masses of masonry. Lacking such abutment the horizontal arch will collapse from either end, the falls progressing until the friction of the foundation with the ground upon which it is resting, and that of the courses of stone lying upon each other, will allow sufficient of the stonework to remain in position to form an inclined horizontal arch rising from the ground at either end and sweeping in a shallow curved silhouette to a height dependent upon the strength of the material used. The view of a canal bridge from the waterway gives one an exact picture of a horizontal arch of this description.

In the very early days of architecture the material used was earth and the summit of monumentality the burial mound. During many centuries the early builders must have discovered all that was discoverable concerning the behaviour of this material and what systems could be used for controlling it.

From beginnings as a stone cairn or earthen mound heaped over an interment to preserve it from defilement we find the simple grave developing into the family or dynastic mausoleum with subterranean chambers for a series of interments.

The chambers would have to be provided with walls and roofs. We are familiar with the remains of these as represented by great stones, standing *orthostats* and roofing slabs. It is axiomatic among students of architecture that such structures must be assigned to the trabeated style of building on the assumption that primitive man would not have attempted to raise a heavy lintel until he had first experimented with a timber beam. Thus for every stone ruin remaining today there may have been many timber prototypes that have vanished without trace (as did the splendid timber architecture of Anglo-Saxon England).

We know that the burial chambers were reached by passages like mine galleries, entered through a doorway set on the outside of the mound. This entrance doorway may well have been history's first essay in elevational architecture.

A doorway can only be set in a vertical wall. But the mound lacked this; any attempt at carving a vertical face would simply have produced a landslide and the resumption of the natural angle of the soil. The early builders were thus faced with the necessity of constructing a wall of timber or stone which would not only be able to hold up under its own weight but would in addition keep back the mound pressing against it from behind.

A stockade of timber posts would have provided an impermanent solution. If these could be replaced by large standing stones —*orthostats*—with their butts buried in the ground, the result would be a fine elevational presentation in megalithic architecture. And the discovery that stones could be leant against each other in a slight curve on the horizontal plane introduced, centuries before the elevational arch was introduced, its horizontal counterpart. In a straight line the orthostats would be able to give no support to each other, but by arranging them in a shallow curve and leaning their tops inwards so as they could rest against each other, the equivalent of a horizontal arch could be produced.

Among the great memorials of the megalithic age are the temples of Malta where an absence of soil forces the orthostats to remain standing on the surface of the rock, with each pair separated by a *parastat* set between them at right angles to support the whole construction as in the first stage of building a house of cards, and with the wide façade of the temple curving inwards to form a shallow crescent. These temples, believed to have been erected at the middle of the penultimate pagan millennium, are rather later than the structures buried within mounds, and their façades are displayed free from any earthen covering and have no supporting task to fulfil.

In the absence of timber, or of great stones suitable for use as orthostats, the entrance to the barrow would have had to be framed in ordinary moorstone. Experiments in the use of this would have eventually led to the discovery that, lacking abutment, the ends of the horizontal arch would fall away but after cautious experiment the façade could have been raised just high enough to contain the doorway—this framed of course as a *trilithon* with jambs and lintel specially procured. The upper edge of the wall would in fact form an inclined arch, its plane very close to the horizontal, and its silhouette a shallow curve similar to that of the mound behind.

Thus it may be that the first architectural elevation ever produced in stonework by primitive man was a crescent façade, rising at each end from the ground level and lifting in a shallow curve which passed above a central doorway of humble dimensions. (Fig. 31a.) Antiquaries—who are sometimes inclined to view plans as linear designs rather than as the imprints of three-dimensional structures—refer to crescent-fronted barrows as 'horned cairns'.

As time passed the ends of these façades would progressively deteriorate from either end, each fall of stones and earth adding to the abutment of the horizontal arch and helping to improve the stability of the central portion. This would have had two aesthetic results, one being the increase in apparent height of the central portion of the façade as its flanks fell away, while the accumulation of debris at either end would convert the shallow crescent into a re-entrant increasing the effect of concavity. The dummy entrances to Egyptian Fifth Dynasty *mastaba* tombs seem to suggest façades of this type.

To a people lacking any other manifestations of architecture these, to them, monumental curtains must have exerted a tremendous impact, while the recession of the central feature between its flanking salients might have invited the use of the threshold of the tomb for reverent assembly. (See Fig. 31b.)

In this recessed area before the threshold of the tomb, facing the curved façade and flanked by its lateral salients, we may perhaps detect the beginnings of that element of concavity which was to become established in architecture as the apse, a form capable of attracting, if not actually accommodating, a group of

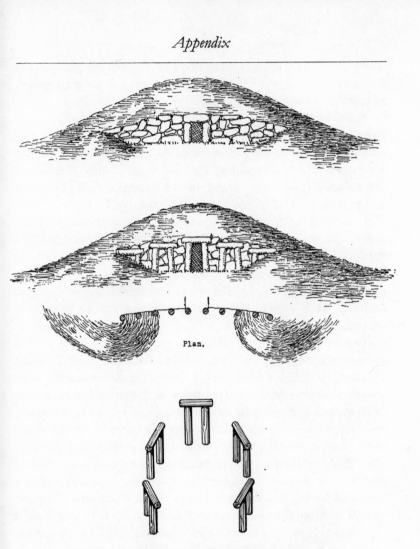

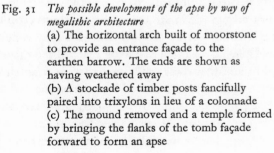

Fig. 31   *The possible development of the apse by way of megalithic architecture*
(a) The horizontal arch built of moorstone to provide an entrance façade to the earthen barrow. The ends are shown as having weathered away
(b) A stockade of timber posts fancifully paired into trixylons in lieu of a colonnade
(c) The mound removed and a temple formed by bringing the flanks of the tomb façade forward to form an apse

worshippers. Above all, we can perhaps begin to see the apse not as a mere appendage to a major building, but as an independent structure existing in its own right.

The tomb of the Sun would present a unique problem in that there would be no mound. All that would remain of the normal tomb would be its curved entrance façade, stretching in a line across the view and appearing as a meaningless wall. The loss of the mound would also entail the disappearance of its lateral wings which, by flanking the tomb façade, had created a third dimension to the front by suggesting a partly enclosed forecourt before the tomb. By having the flanks of the façade brought forward to outline this lost area the monument would have been provided with its third dimension, replacing that lost when the mound was removed. In this way some semblance of a proper building, such as an ordinary house or hut, would have been created.

The most notable example of the independent apse is seen at Stonehenge, generally accepted today as the tomb of the Sun, the Mecca of the Heliolithic Age when fearful people gathered at midwinter to see the deity sink into western skies on the shortest day of its life and to pray that it should return again to ripen their crops and bring them relief from the rigours of winter. The tomb of the Sun could have no mound other than the billowing cumulus framed in the fires of sunset, and thus the apse would stand skeletal and not as a revetment to a barrow. Its origin, however, is clearly indicated by the fact that the 'tomb entrance' represented by the central trilithon is higher than its fellows which fall away from it on either side as though following the silhouette of a mound before being beckoned inwards to enclose the apse. (Fig. 31c.)

Though megalithic in structure, the trilithons (the 'henges' or gallows which have given the temple its modern name) show that the temple may be regarded as having reached the age of trabeated architecture and that their predecessors were *trixylons* formed of timber such as may be seen carved in stone on the Etruscan tombs of the last pagan millennium (and used until recently in mine galleries). The log uprights had their tops pointed and were let into pits gouged into the lintels—an unstable form of seating which the builders of the trilithons were careful to remedy when fashioning their 'stub-tenons'.

It should be noted that the trixylon is incapable of being extended laterally to form a colonnade so that a row of them had to be substituted for the Classical feature.

The temple at Stonehenge must have been known and revered by the people of western Europe for at some period it was surrounded by a *temenos*, a sacred enclosure indicated by a peristyle. Although the workmanship of this was still megalithic, someone had come from the East to instruct the builders how to make one orthostat support the ends of two lintels so that the row of trilithons could be replaced by a continuous colonnade.

The great apse of Stonehenge, set within its temenos, survived down the centuries. As the tomb of the Sun it may have had no fellows.

By the last quarter of the pagan era the apse had still not reached architecture. The geometrical form of the *exedra* had been known to the Roman architect Vitruvius who lived a hundred years before Christ, but he makes no mention of any apse being employed as a feature of the contemporary temple.

The rate of progress from the earthen mound to the skeletal hypaethral apse of Stonehenge would have been infinitesimal.

But during the last century of the pagan era Britain was beginning to be drawn into the orbit of Roman exploration. And ten years before the birth of Christ a fully developed apse, a notable architectural feature, appears unheralded in the temple of Mars Ultor in Rome.

# Glossary

_apse:_ a semicircular alcove usually containing an altar

_arcade:_ a row of arches carried upon piers or pillars and supporting a wall over

_arcading:_ an arcade employed as decoration to a wall surface

_basilica:_ literally a royal building; the name given to the first Christian churches in Rome; a type of church having a long nave lined with arcades opening into aisles

_bay:_ the longitudinal unit in a medieval building, each bay being filled by a window and separated from its neighbour by a pillar or a pilaster; a bay of vaulting is the area enclosed by the lines joining its four supports

_bifora:_ a two-light window of primitive form having a central colonette

_boss:_ a carved stone masking the junction of vaulting ribs

_brattice:_ a partition formed of wide boards set vertically

_broach:_ the medieval term for a spire

_centering:_ the temporary timber framework upon which an arch is turned

_chamber:_ a room on an upper floor, a lodging or bedchamber

_chevet:_ the east end of a church designed as an apse surrounded by smaller ones

_choir:_ the enclosed chapel containing the seats of the monks; sometimes used to designate the whole of the eastern arm of the church

_clearstory:_ the range of small windows set above aisle roofs to light the central portion of the building

_crossing:_ the area where the four arms of the cruciform plan meet

*dorter:* the word used in the vernacular for 'dormitory'

*duplex bay:* system of bay design in which the great bays are carried upon massive piers and the intermediate ones upon pillars

*exedra:* in Classical architecture, a curved wall enclosing some feature such as a fountain

*ferramenti:* the ironwork of vertical 'stanchions' and horizontal 'saddle bars' supporting the leaded glazing of a window

*flying buttress:* an arch supporting the clearstory wall from a main buttress set in the aisle wall

*frater:* the vernacular word used to describe the great hall of the monks, a corruption of 'refectory'

*groin:* the lines where two opposing vaults intersect unsupported by vaulting ribs

*hall:* originally a spacious ground-floor apartment, later raised upon a vaulted undercroft, eventually becomes a first-floor apartment, always of importance

*hypaethral:* open to the sky

*lantern:* the low tower which carries the clearstory over the ridges of the four roofs meeting at the crossing

*laver:* the monks' washing place in the cloister

*lierne:* the short ornamental lengths of vaulting rib joining the main members

*mastaba:* a name given to a type of fifth Dynasty Egyptian tomb which may be a masonry representation of a long barrow

*misericord:* the special frater in which meat might be eaten

*moulding:* running ornament formed of continuous lines of rolls and channels

*mullion:* vertical stone bars in a window

*narthex:* the long porch crossing the west front of an early Roman or Byzantine church *nave:* the body of the church west of the crossing; the portion of this west of the monks' choir

*ogee:* the sides of an ogee arch have an S-curve bringing it to an acute point

*order:* each of the lines of stones making up an arch is called an order

*oriel:* a first-floor bay window carried upon a large stone corbel or bracket

*orthostat:* a standing stone

*parastat:* an orthostat set between two others, at right angles to them, to support them

*parlour:* a quiet room on a ground floor; an apartment in a monastery in which the rule of silence is relaxed; one of the two passages leading out of the cloister

*pier:* an isolated mass of masonry carrying an arch

*pilaster:* a small half-pier projecting from a wall usually employed for decorative or punctuation purposes

*piscina:* a niche usually on the south side of an altar having in its sill a small basin for washing sacred vessels

*presbytery:* the area between the choir stalls and the high altar; sometimes used to denote the whole of the eastern arm of a great church

*quoin:* a corner-stone

*rere-dorter:* the monastic sanitary block

*slype:* originally a sloping passage passing under a building; the inner parlour leading out of the cloister towards the infirmary and burial ground

*soller:* incorrectly spelt *solar*, a boarded floor; 'on the soller' indicates an upper storey

*trabeated:* one of the two primary styles of architecture, having a timber origin and employing beams for spanning openings whereas the arcuated style uses the arch of small stones for the same purpose

*tracery:* the interlacing of stone bars in the head of a Gothic window; the same used for wall decoration

*transept:* a structure running athwart the main building or projecting at right angles from it

*transverse arch:* an arch spanning across the main axis of a building or apartment as opposed to the arches forming a longitudinal arcade

*triforium:* incorrectly the gallery over the aisles of a great church, properly the cleaning-passage to the clearstory

*trilithon:* a pair of orthostats joined at their tops by a stone beam

*trixylon:* the timber prototype of the trilithon

*undercroft:* the ground floor beneath an important first-floor apartment

*vault:* a stone ceiling, either supporting a floor or concealing the timbering of a roof

*vaulting rib:* the slender arches upon which a 'ribbed vault' is founded are known as ribs and the vault itself carried by them is the 'web'

# Index

Milton Abbey, Dorset, 238, 241, 263, 277

misericord (flesh frater), 133

monks, clothing, 39
 daily life, 35–6
 number in monastery, 106
 sick and aged, 36–7

Mottisfont Abbey, Hants, 117, 243

Mount Grace Charterhouse, Yorks., 246

Muchelney Abbey, Som., 107, 133, 144, 177–8, 246, 255, 263

Much Wenlock Priory, Salop, 112, 120, 148, 165–6, 246, 256

narthex, 53, 59

naves, parochial, 222–3

Netley Abbey, Hants, 44, 244, 262, *plates 12 & 30*

New Foundation (cathedrals), 42

Newstead Priory, Notts., 131, 244

night stair, 105

Norwich Cathedral, 74–5, 85, 88, 143

Notley Abbey, Bucks., 246–7

nunneries, 46
 oriel window, 175–6, 190

Oxford Cathedral, 42

Pamber Priory, Hants, 241

parlour, inner, 201–2
 outer, 119, 127

parvis (Paradise), 65, 181

pentice, 139, 253

Pershore Abbey, Worcestershire, 33, 88, 90, 153, 238, 263, *plate 1*

Peterborough Cathedral, 32, 42, 73

pole (unit of measurement), 72, 269

Polsloe Priory, Devon., 145

porch-tower, 190–1, 253

portico, 58–9, 139

Premonstratensian Order, 45, 68, 88

presbytery, 80, 83, 91

processions, 97

pulpit (frater), 116–17

Quarr Abbey, Isle of Wight, 82

Ramsey Abbey, Hunts., 33–4

Reading Abbey, Berks., 150, 191

Renaissance abbeys, 227–8

Repton Abbey, Derbyshire, 233

rere-dorter, 103, 106 et seq.

retro-choir, 80

Rievaulx Abbey, Yorks., 22, 24, 44, 122, 141, 150, 161–3, 205, 250, 261, 263, 277, *plates 9, 10, 11 & 17*

Roche Abbey, Yorks., 21, 152, 261, 264, *plate 26*

Romsey Abbey, Hants, 33, 46, 53–4, 64–5, 79, 86, 144, 238–9

roofs, medieval, 135

St. Albans Abbey, Herts., 32, 37, 47, 64, 68, 74, 80, 91–2, 96, 106, 160, 172, 188–9, 214, 257, 263

St. Davids Cathedral, 81

St. Edmundsbury Abbey, Suffolk, 32, 47, 53, 68, 172, 184–6, 188, 247

St. Osyth Abbey, Essex, 189, 247

Salisbury Cathedral, 74, 76, 95, 143, 152, 284, 250

sanctuary, right of, 37

Sarum, Old, Cathedral, 66

Savigniac Order, 44

Sawley Abbey, Lancs., 207

scriptorium, 37

Selby Abbey, Yorks., 23, 84, 238

Sempringham Priory, Lincs., 46, 270

Shaftesbury Abbey, Dorset, 33, 46, 108, 242

Shap Abbey, Westmorland, 243

Sherborne Abbey, Dorset, 23, 102, 109, 120, 138, 174–5, 238–9, 263

shingles, roofing, 59, 135

Shrewsbury Abbey, Salop, 117

Shulbrede Priory, Sussex, 247

slype, 123, 159, 200

Smithfield, St. Bartholomew's Priory, 241

soller (timber floor), 99, 100, 113

spire, 56, 226

stalls, 114

Stanley St. Leonard Priory, Glos., 221, 241